WORDS BEFORE PICTURES

WORDS BEFORE PICTURES

HOW SCREENPLAYS MAKE MOVIES

SIMON PASSMORE

PALINDROME

Published by Palindrome Publishing Ltd in 2020

First published in Great Britain in 2020 by
Palindrome Publishing Ltd
Abbey House, 25 Clarendon Road, Redhill RH1 1QZ

A CIP catalogue record for for this book
is available from the British Library

ISBN 978-1-8380291-2-8

For M

CONTENTS

INTRODUCTION

Un peu de polémique ne fait pas de mal

François Truffaut

"The greatest joy that you get from screenwriting is screenwriting," according to Scott Frank (*Out of Sight, Get Shorty*). "It's not the movies that are made out of your work." Joy rarely finds its way into accounts of screenwriting and screenplays, and rarely if ever appears in academic accounts or screenwriting manuals. Yet the satisfactions offered to writers by the screenplay form is a significant factor in the large number of screenplays, many of them self-commissioned, that are written each year. This is just one aspect of the major disconnection between the practice of writing screenplays and how this is conceptualised and taught by theorists, critics and the authors of screenplay manuals. Discussion of screenplays, what they do and how they do it, usually takes place within separate silos. Industry practice, teaching (formally within taught courses and informally through screenwriting manuals) and academic screenplay studies – a relatively new field – rarely address one another. As a result, misrepresentations and mis-understandings cling on tenaciously. Why does it matter? Because these obscure the crucial and central role of screen-plays: generating films. This book tries to bring together three separate discourses that address screenplays – those of practitioners, theorists, and teachers. My aim is to coax each from its home turf and to get them talking and, perhaps more importantly, listening to one another.

Coming from a career in professional practice, as a writer and producer, I was surprised by some of the things that I heard and read when I re-entered the rarefied world of the academy. Reading some film theorists, you might think that there was no such thing as a screenplay. Yes, auteur theory is old hat, but it's still taught in some, perhaps many, schools and universities. And more current theories, in the emerging field of screenplay studies, can still insist that screenplays are not creative writing so much as industrial documents.

When once again the film industry is in turmoil, with studios sticking grimly to their bloated franchises and remakes while viewers look elsewhere for innovative and thought-provoking storytelling, it's worth considering what the consequences of undervaluing and disregarding screenplays may be.

My primary focus here is on original English-language screenplays of cinema films intended for mass audiences. The overwhelming majority of these mainstream anglophone narrative fiction films are produced from screenplays, and those screenplays are in almost all cases made of words. This might seem obvious, and yet these simple facts are routinely overlooked, sidelined, misrepresented, and disregarded.

Chapter 1 looks at the problem of defining screenplays and the debates centring on this. We lack agreement even on what a screenplay is, so I propose a working definition, then show how persistent, interacting problems in defining and historicising screenplays have impeded their study. The difficulties of distinguishing between different drafts and versions of screenplays has confused not only publishing practices but also academic arguments about screenplays. Critics' inability to agree on a definition contrasts with the practitioner discourse, where the definition of screenplays is deemed self-evident. Deep divisions continue from here to separate theory and practice. These divisions extend to other polarities within screenplay discourse, such as those between art and craft, art and science, and art and commerce. The problems of defining and historicising screenplays are exacerbated by defining and discussing them in metaphorical terms.

While definitions have been changing and contested across history, and screenplay forms and processes have also changed, one metaphor in particular has persisted, long after it became obsolete as a literal technology. **Chapter 2** analyses the ubiquitous blueprint metaphor, found within all three screenplay discourses, and the reasons for its persistence. The metaphor dates back at least to 1919, when blueprints were a current technology, and continues today, when that technology has been redundant for more than seventy years. This metaphor has misrepresented screenplays across all discourses and remains a live issue in 2020. Scholars have critiqued the metaphor, but only to reinstate it, while it continues to be invoked in screenwriting manuals and in practitioner discourse. Emphasising the industrial over the artisanal, the blueprint presents screenwriting as a mechanical, semi-skilled activity and encourages writers to think of themselves as technicians. By asserting a separation between conception and execution, it also removes writers from the creative process.

In **Chapter 3**, I look at a number of recurrent arguments that screenplays aren't writing; or, if they are, that they aren't and shouldn't be read in the same way as other kinds of more valued writing. Is it true, as many contend, that screenplays aren't read, or are read only as technical documents by a small and specialised readership? Industrial conceptions of screenplays have lowered their status as writing. Copyright laws and conflicts over ownership and authorship have encouraged studios, producers, and others to devalue screenplays as writing to their own benefit. At times screenwriters themselves have been complicit in this. Despite arguments to the contrary, cinema isn't a purely visual medium, nor are words uncinematic. The myth of the "camera-pen" has been used to undermine and obscure screenplays as writing as well as their functions in filmmaking. Writer-directors, meanwhile, routinely play down their screenplays while playing up their directing. Nevertheless, the words of screenplays persist within finished films.

Chapter 4 challenges the perception that film should be distinct from literature and literary writing. Not only is writing central to the production of all films, but the most celebrated films are predicated on writing that shares features with literary writing. Screenwriters exploit the master-scene format and the "highly-inflected screenplay" to develop distinctive writing and individual styles. Screenplays frequently employ metaphor, simile, and other devices associated with literature. Close readings of screenplays show that, far from being absent from them, their writers are also vividly present within them. Sometimes they achieve this through narrative voices that exist apart from characters, and sometimes the writers feature as characters in their own screenplays. Producers and other professionals, meanwhile, value highly a screenplay's "voice." Distinctions made between screenplays and other kinds of writing such as novels on the basis of modes of production and consumption are questionable, and this chapter questions them. The ability of screenplays to travel across media platforms demonstrates the continuities between screenplays and other kinds of writing, all of which function as components of a global entertainment industry.

While some scholars and also practitioners assert that screenplays are consumed by the process of filmmaking, **Chapter 5** shows that screenplays can and do endure in various ways. At the most literal level, screenplay words persist in films as dialogue. But they also persist within films in tone, style, and and other aspects of finished films. Nor is it the case, as frequently asserted, that screenplays can be performed only once, and are emptied or consumed by that single performance. This chapter explores related contentions that screenplays disappear before or during production, and that they're replaced by technical shooting scripts. Screenplays aren't ephemeral and don't vanish, nor do they need to be destroyed in order to make films, as some directors have insisted. On the contrary, screenplays endure even when unproduced. Claims that screenplays are incomplete and never achieve a fixed state by comparison to finished films are balanced by the fact that the same conditions apply to films themselves.

Moving beyond misrepresentations of screenplays, **Chapter 6** makes the argument for their creative agency. Their lack of completeness doesn't constitute a convincing argument against this, while their hybridity and mutability align screenplays not with completion but with process. Pulling together scholarly, pedagogic, and practitioner discourses, this final chapter draws on Aristotle's *Poetics* as a text common to all three. Aristotle's analysis of tragedy persists in screenplay discourse partly because of its attention to three perennial concerns for screenwriting: the primacy of plot, the importance of genre, and the centrality of the audience's experience. However, we can look beyond these familiar points to engage with less frequently discussed aspects of Aristotle's work, such as his insistence on working from specific practice to universal theory, and his distinction between poiesis and praxis, which offers an escape from the conception/execution dichotomy that dogs screenwriting discourses today. Another key concept from the *Poetics*, visualisation, using the "mind's eye," has widely informed screenplay practice and pedagogy. It refutes common claims that the visual enters the screenplay and film only with the advent of the camera or the director. Rather, the generative agency of screenplays stems from their feeding mind's eye visualisation into the act of writing. Accounts by practitioners show how this interaction can produce screenplays that remain separate, in the mind's eye of their writers, and also readers, from the films that may follow. This goes some way towards explaining why screenwriters, despite the hostility directed against screenplays, may still derive from them the kind of satisfaction provided by other kinds of writing, and also why their authors may be envied by other kinds of filmmakers.

Despite the pessimism of some scholars, it seems to me that screenplays are neither obsolete nor redundant, and that their continuing ability to generate and shape story and meaning remains unchanged by new media, technologies, and practices. While Robert McKee's dictum that "[a] screenplay waits for the camera" may be true, so is its reverse: the camera waits for a screenplay.

1

DEFINING AND HISTORICISING SCREENPLAYS

A screenplay is always the dream of a film.
Jean-Claude Carrière

The need to define and historicise screenplays highlights the problems of theorising screenplays, which begin with debates over their basic definition and continue with the varying and changing ways in which their history has been constructed. Nor are the definition and historicising of screenplays separate processes. They overlap and interpenetrate one another as historically changing conventions, technologies, and practices have led to different definitions of the screenplay. These different definitions of the screenplay have in turn influenced how they have been seen historically.

Defining Screenplays

A screenplay is an exploration. It's about the thing you don't know.
Charlie Kaufman

In 2020 screenplays remain, as they have been for more than a century, sites of contention between academic theorists, the authors of screenwriting manuals, and film practitioners. This contention begins with the basic question of the screenplay's definition. Practitioners and manual-writers rarely take the trouble to define screenplays at all, while for academics, screen-plays are of such uncertain nature that they debate and dispute their definitions. Often they resort to metaphors rather than accepting screenplays as objects in their own right.

As a baseline, the Oxford English Dictionary offers this definition of "screenplay": "the script from which a motion picture film is produced; formerly, the film itself." At once this draws attention to the generative role of a screenplay in bringing a film into being. It also highlights the changing and ambiguous definitions of "screenplay" from the early decades of the film industry, when the term "screen play" was applied both to the completed film and to the script that preceded it. Conflation of the screenplay with the finished film persists in critical accounts. The ambiguous and disputed status of the screenplay's role in film and relation to film has led many theorists to prefer studying screenwriting over screenplays, although the two can't be readily separated. The use of other terms such as "script" and "scenario" applied to the writing that preceded a film further draws attention to the fact that the word "screenplay" is employed to denote not a single homogeneous entity but a range of forms and formats. Nor is a screenplay the product of a simple evolutionary process of screenwriting or a static object; various forms have coexisted in film history and have been customised by their users in different ways, as scholars including Steven Price and Steven Maras have shown. While certain conventions have been within any given period of history widely adopted and led to a sense of uniformity, screenplays have continued to exhibit considerable flexibility and diversity.

The OED definition also draws attention to the porous boundaries between screenplay and film (sometimes characterised respectively as pre-text and text), between words and audiovisual objects, and between writing and filmmaking. The OED's illustrations include claims about that relationship: for example, "1977. Times Lit. Suppl. 24 June 750/3. A screenplay… is subsumed in the completed movie." Thus the notion of screenplays as ephemeral pre-texts becomes, for the OED, part of their very definition. In a similar vein, Maras locates "the difficulty of defining screenwriting as an object, and identifying an object for screenwriting" in what he nominates an "Object Problem." While screenwriting, which is a process, has less claim to object status than a screenplay, ultimately Maras denies the screenplay autonomous object status: according to him it's "not simply an autonomous work of art, but is what some theorists have dubbed an 'intermediate' work."

Price, more than Maras, is willing to see screenplays in the same way that practitioners do, as objects. In *A History of the Screenplay* he argues that the rise of the "spec script," the proliferation of recognisable screenplay templates, and the continuing popularity of the many published screenwriting manuals have together "helped to solidify the screenplay into an object with more precisely definable characteristics than at any time since the end of the silent era." Price doesn't subscribe to the OED's and Maras's view that regarding screenplays separately from their uses in filmmaking calls their very existence into question. Current formatting and template conventions, he suggests, have helped "to identify the screenplay as a particular kind of object, and as a relatively autonomous document, intended for particular kinds of reader, but removed from production." For Price, the screenplay exists – but only if it's separated from production. Neither definition allows for adequate study of the screenplay as both a written object in its own right and also an integral part of the filmmaking process.

Ted Nannicelli places these ontological concerns at the centre of his book, *A Philosophy of the Screenplay* (2013), devoting four chapters to the problem of defining the screenplay. He begins with screenplays as they're defined by those who write (and read) them:

> x is a screenplay if and only if x is a verbal object
> intended to repeat, modify, or repudiate the ways
> in which plot, characters, dialogue, shots, edits,
> sound effects, and/or other features have
> historically been suggested as constitutive
> elements by a prior screenplay(s) or screenwriting
> practice (in accordance with recognizable and live
> purposes of that practice).

Nannicelli's definition begins by accepting the screenplay as a "verbal object"; elsewhere he refers to it as an "artifact." However, it develops as a description of mainstream past practice, characterised by features that "have historically been suggested as constitutive elements," so that a screenplay is something that corresponds to what a screenplay has been in the past, allowing for the gradual changes of evolution. By contrast to Nannicelli's implication that the screenplay will continue to evolve gradually, Price, Maras, and Kathryn Millard (in *Screenwriting in a Digital Age*, 2014) all end their books by arguing that screenplays (as distinct from screenwriting) may be or become obsolescent. Such a view constitutes the most fundamental challenge to the definition of screenplays as objects that exist or will continue to exist in their own right.

To some extent the problem derives from a widespread critical wariness of the very notion that fixed definitions can be reached in any field. Yet the problems of definition seem particularly pronounced in relation to screenplays. By contrast to many other fields, where indeterminacy appeared only with poststructuralism and postmodernism, uncertainty regarding the status of screenplays can be traced back to its earliest days and most fundamental conceptions.

Price notes that "Because it is so difficult to grasp the screenplay as a text, the study of it tends towards metaphor." The tendency to define screenplays in metaphorical terms is both a consequence of the difficulties of defining them and a factor contributing to these, since it hinders definition. Indeed, Price himself doesn't offer a definition of the screenplay, taking as read the reader's understanding of his subject in both *The Screenplay: Authorship, Theory and Criticism* (2010) and *A History of the Screenplay* (2013). In this regard, he resembles the manual-readers and writers of screenplays, for whom definitions are often superfluous and unnecessary, because to them it's a self-evident fact that a screenplay is a verbal object made and produced by practitioners.

Among the screenwriting gurus Syd Field is unusual in offering a definition of screenplays. His *Screenplay: The Foundations of Screenwriting* (expanded edition, 1982) is perhaps the most ubiquitous of all screenwriting manuals, having been reprinted some 38 times in 22 languages. The opening chapter asks, "What Is a Screenplay?" His readers don't have long to wait for an answer: "A screenplay," he replies, "is a STORY TOLD WITH PICTURES." This, though, is self-evidently inaccurate. Field has described a storyboard; there are no actual pictures in a typical screenplay, which is composed entirely of words. Generations of aspiring screenwriters have nonetheless made no objection to Field's definition, accepting it as a metaphor connoting that the screenplay is a verbal construct that in some way tells a story that is emphatically visual.

Field echoes a formulation that dates back a further six decades. Epes Winthrop Sargent's *Technique of the Photoplay*, first published in 1914, is the earliest substantial screenplay writing manual that I've found (although there are earlier ones that are little more than pamphlets). Screenwriter and Hollywood historian Marc Norman refers to Sargent as "the first in the tradition of noted film instructors with no writing credits," but Sargent was the author of 144 screenplays between 1912 and 1918. In his third edition (1916), he defines the written "PHOTOPLAY" as "A story told in pictured action instead of words." His book's title suggests that the term "photoplay" didn't evolve from denoting the finished film to the screenplay over time, but that in the 1910s it already referred to both. While Sargent acknowledges the verbal nature of screenplays even while proscribing it ("instead of words"), in Field's definition words have disappeared altogether ("A screenplay is a STORY TOLD WITH PICTURES"). Screenplays, Field insists, require their writers to regard the words of which they're made not as writing, but instead as a neutral medium through which to convey pictures. This also implies a reading process in which a screenplay reader subsequently receives "PICTURES" through the screenplay's words, but in which the words themselves go unacknowledged once again.

Even those prominent manuals that have the word "screenplay" rather than "story" in their title ("story" is the key word for Robert McKee, John Truby, Christopher Booker, and others), rarely define the term. *Adventures in the Screen Trade* (1985) by William Goldman, more a writer than a guru, has, like Field's *Screenplay*, remained in print for decades. Like Field, Goldman offers his definition of screenplays in upper case (used in screenplays to "spotlight specific technical instructions"): "SCREENPLAYS ARE STRUCTURE," he trumpets. By contrast to Field's metaphorical definition, Goldman's turns to synecdoche. No one reading his own screenplay *Butch Cassidy and the Sundance Kid* would say that it consists of nothing but structure; the verbal skills that Goldman also deployed as a novelist are visible on its pages:

```
And every second, the action freezes them
in their final trip, and the scream keeps
them company, and even though the trip is
short, it still takes time for all six to
slip and stagger and crumble awkwardly to
their knees and beyond, toppling sideways
```

> and backwards and forwards, but always
> down, colliding finally with the hard
> earth, which is red now with their blood
> as it leaves the dying bodies and as the
> scream ends, the blood continues to drain
> ceaselessly into the ground--

This "action line" from *Butch Cassidy and the Sundance Kid* offers considerably more than just a narrative structure of characters engaging in a plot. The long sentence includes several rhetorical flourishes, such as the succession of clauses used to prolong the moment, metaphorical vocabulary ("crumble awkwardly to their knees"), the juxtaposition of violent death with self-consciously commonplace phrases ("keeps them company," "still takes time"), and the accumulation of verbs to accentuate the dynamic character of the action. All of these devices are at least as likely to be found in a novel (such as one of Goldman's own) as in a screenplay. Goldman' definition is no more literally true than Field's.

Other practitioners and manual writers define screenplays by analogy. When manual author Michael Hauge asserts that "Screenplays have become, for the last half of [the twentieth] century, what the Great American Novel was for the first half," the analogy is one less of writing than of what that writing represents. A number of judgments are packed into his statement. Most questionable, perhaps, is the claim to a cultural status commensurate with the novel's.

Film scholars rarely accord screenplays this kind of cultural prestige. It's more common for them to dismiss the screenplay as a minor adjunct, almost an irrelevance, to the study of film. In the ninth edition of David Bordwell's and Kristin Thompson's *Film Art: An Introduction*, a film studies textbook very widely used in university and college film courses, screenplays and screenwriting are accorded less than a page;

the chapter on sound, by contrast, is forty-three pages long. Since this book was first published in 1991, generations of film students have been encouraged to disregard screenplays.

Probably the single greatest cause of screenplays' neglect has been what might be termed the teleological fallacy: the tendency of film studies to concentrate on a finished film to the exclusion of the process that produced it. This academic discipline routinely disregards not only the screenplay but also other elements of filmmaking that aren't readily discernible in a "final" version of a film, if such a thing can even be said to exist. The physical screenplays that aren't destroyed after a film is finished often remain elusive, ephemeral, their circulation limited, their availability restricted by considerations of confidentiality and copyright, and their preservation rarely a priority. The lack of clarity as to what constitutes the definitive version of a screenplay exacerbates the problem, although, as scholars are beginning to acknowledge, this applies equally to "the" film itself. For screenplays, the difficulty of identifying a definitive version is further complicated by the multiplication of drafts and the challenge of distinguishing between them, as well as the fact that many drafts are destroyed, overwritten, or lost. Even published screenplays, often cited without reference to their provenance, might be (and often are) based not on a pre-production draft but on a post-production script. Therefore, far from being pre-shooting scripts, they also represent decisions made in production and post-production. Many such decisions owe less to aesthetic choices than to the solving of practical problems such as confused storytelling, unsatisfactory performances by actors, continuity errors, awkward framing and camera movement, and other technical considerations. Post-production scripts aren't authored in the sense that pre-production screenplays are. Usually they're created not by screenwriters, directors, or even editors, but by production personnel such as moonlighting script supervisors, and intended primarily for technical purposes such as subtitling and foreign language dubbing. Equally, post-production scripts will omit scenes, shots, and parts of shots present in the pre-production screenplay if those scenes have been cut, for whatever reason, from the finished film. Moreover, the descriptions of shots and transitions, and even of new material, are unlikely to have been written by either screenwriter or director. Legal considerations such as the risk of action for libel, defamation, or copyright infringement also affect choices about the material included in (or excluded from) the final cut and post-production script. For the reader of a published post-production script, including the scholars who study them and seek to define screenplays based on them, however, the questionable authorship of this particular version of a screenplay may not be apparent. For most literary texts the published version is generally accepted as authoritative, based as it usually is on the author's latest corrections and revisions, or on a version incorporating those of an editor yet still approved by the author. The status of published scripts can be entirely different. Where literary variants of equal authority coexist (as in, say, the 1798, 1799, 1805, and 1850 versions of William Wordsworth's poem *The Prelude*), scholars' attention will be directed to this fact. This is rarely if ever the case with the post-production script.

The practice of publishing post-production scripts as screenplays has also undermined clear definitions of screenplays. Probably it derives from presenting published screenplays as substitutes for the films themselves in the era before videocassettes, DVDs, and streamed or downloaded film files made films readily accessible. For this purpose, a post-production script would most closely resemble the film. For example, *Battleship Potemkin* (1925) has been made available to consumers in a variety of media and formats, changing with successive technologies. Occupying a prominent position in film history and academic film studies, this film has long been in demand by teachers, students, and researchers. Before the first mass-market VHS videocassette of *Battleship Potemkin* was released by Mosfilm in 1976, anyone wishing to watch the film would either have to do so in a cinema or track down a film print and a Steenbeck or Moviola. Lorrimer Publishing's 1968 English language print edition of *The Battleship Potemkin* therefore provided a version of the film to those who might find it difficult or impossible to view the film itself. This edition doesn't describe itself as the screenplay of the film. The book's title is simply that of the film, although it also includes a large number of stills from the film, which aren't identified in any way. Until the release of the VHS videocassette eight years later, the Lorrimer book was effectively the only version of the film readily available to the general public. However, when Faber and Faber issued a revised version of the Lorrimer edition in 1984 under the title *The Battleship Potemkin*, the contents page specifically identified it as "Screenplay: THE BATTLESHIP POTEMKIN." In the interim, interest in screenwriting had been stimulated by the publication of Field's *Screenplay* in 1979. The market for the 1984 English language print version had thus changed: as a version of the film, it had been superseded by VHS tapes, but the book had also acquired a new appeal and extended its potential readership, marketed as the screenplay for a film by master filmmaker Sergei Eisenstein, potentially written by him. This "screenplay," however, looks more like a post-production script, and there's no extant full version of the pre-production screenplay to confirm otherwise.

Scholars study screenplays not only as filmic pre-texts but also to understand the film. The uncertain status of the text raises the question: were the famous "montage" sequences in *Battleship Potemkin* created during post-production in the cutting room, or did they appear in the screenplay before shooting, as découpage? Bordwell explains the difference, defining "what Soviet filmmakers of the 1920s called montage" as "shot-assembling as the basic constructional activity – [what] Hollywood filmmakers called cutting or editing," in contrast to "découpage," "the parceling out of images in accordance with the script." Until the advent of digital techniques, montage called for the physical cutting and glueing of physical prints and negatives. The process of creating a découpage sequence, however, is planned in advance, and is a creative act located within the screenplay itself. Uncertainty thus permeates the status of the multiple English language print versions of *Battleship Potemkin*. In the Faber and first Lorrimer editions we have the same text presented initially as a print equivalent of a film, and subsequently as its screenplay, without any textual note to identify its provenance or status. The second Lorrimer edition, meanwhile, presents a very different written text – in effect a shot list, only 15 pages long – also as the screenplay of the same film.

As well as a lack of clarity in the way publication presents screenplays, there remains the question of which draft, whether published or not, is "the" screenplay. It's rare for any screenplay to exist as a single entity; usually there are multiple versions. Following the writer's first draft, subsequent ones will usually follow, forming parts of the development process. The last of these will be issued to cast and crew before the start of shooting, and subsequently amended during production. Finally a post-production script is created once editing is complete.

Even scholars don't always identify accurately the screenplays that they discuss. Geoff Rush and Cynthia Baughman, in their their much-cited 1997 essay, "Language as Narrative Voice: The Poetics of the Highly Inflected Screenplay," lead their argument with a quotation from "the script of *The Player* (1992)," to which they frequently return. But which draft are they referencing? Rush and Baughman build an example on the repetition of descriptive lines first as spoken dialogue, then as an action line: "He lifts her dress. She kisses him harder." In the published screenplay, however, this line appears only once, as quoted dialogue. The provenance of the lines' second instance remains obscure since Rush and Baughman, while identifying several "[u]npublished" drafts of other screenplays in their list of works cited, omit any mention of *The Player*. The screenplay's author Michael Tolkin, meanwhile, makes clear in his introduction to the published text of his screenplay that "The scripts in this book conform to the films as released," and his own view that "There is no such beast as an original version."

More recent published screenplays still frequently don't identify what they are, while those that do are more likely to circulate unofficially. In an unpublished shooting script for *Reservoir Dogs* (1992) dated "October 22, 1990" (about nine months before filming began), the first three lines of dialogue are spoken by Mr Pink, Mr Blue, and Mr Pink. In the version published by Faber, the same lines are attributed to Mr Brown, Mr Blonde, and Mr Brown, as in the completed film. However, this doesn't necessarily identify the published screenplay as a post-production script. According to *Reservoir Dogs* writer and director Quentin Tarantino, the attribution of this dialogue was one of the few elements of the film to change from first draft to final cut: "I also kept changing who said what in the opening scene. That was the thing that went through the most metamorphosis." Although the Faber edition of Tarantino's screenplay combines elements of the shooting script and the completed film, it could be one of many screenplay versions developed during production. Different versions of the screenplay, as well as published screenplay and completed film, can exist as simultaneous, parallel versions of a work in which details may change without undermining the claim of either version to be "the" *Reservoir Dogs*.

Even when pains have been taken to establish the status of a published screenplay, it isn't necessarily authoritative. One example of this is the Faber edition of Graham Greene's screenplay for *The Third Man* (1949). The status of *Battleship Potemkin* is closely associated with that of its director (also its writer or co-writer), and the attention of critics is focused on the film rather than the screenplay. The status of *The Third Man*'s screenwriter as an eminent novelist, on the other hand, is likely to have led to heightened interest in this screenplay as a piece of writing. Probably more decisive, however, was Greene's business-minded attention to contracts, since – unusually – he managed to retain publishing rights to his screenplay. The status of the screenplay remains uncertain, however. In most respects the Faber edition of this screenplay stays close to the final version of the film. Material written by Greene that was cut or changed during production or post-production is placed within square brackets, while added dialogue not written by Greene is supplied as footnotes. However, in Scene 125, for example, Calloway's lines as published by Faber differ both from those spoken by actor Trevor Howard in the film and from Howard's own hand-annotated copy of the shooting script (located in The Third Man Museum in Vienna). The published screenplay gives a speech of Calloway's as "For a good read I like a Western. Paine's lent me several of your books. 'The Lone Rider' seemed a bit drawn out." Howard's copy of the shooting script shows the same dialogue, ringed – but also a revised version of it handwritten on the back of a later page: "Paine lent me one of your books. The Lone Rider I think it was. I read a bit of it. It looked as if it was going to be pretty good" (see Figures 1 and 2 below):

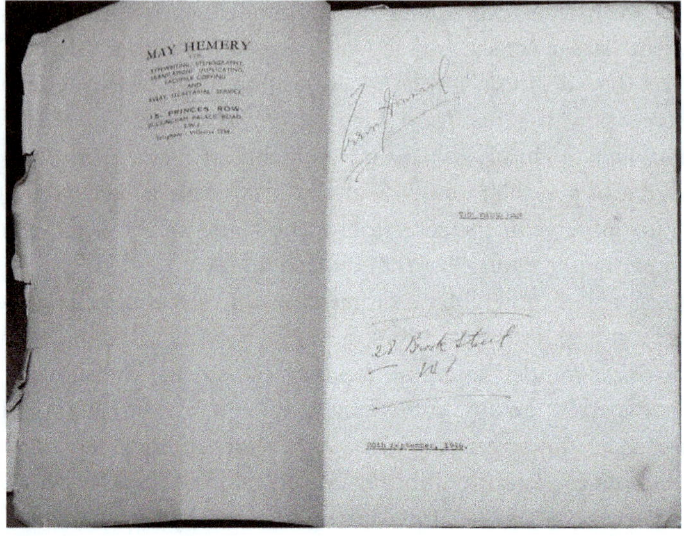

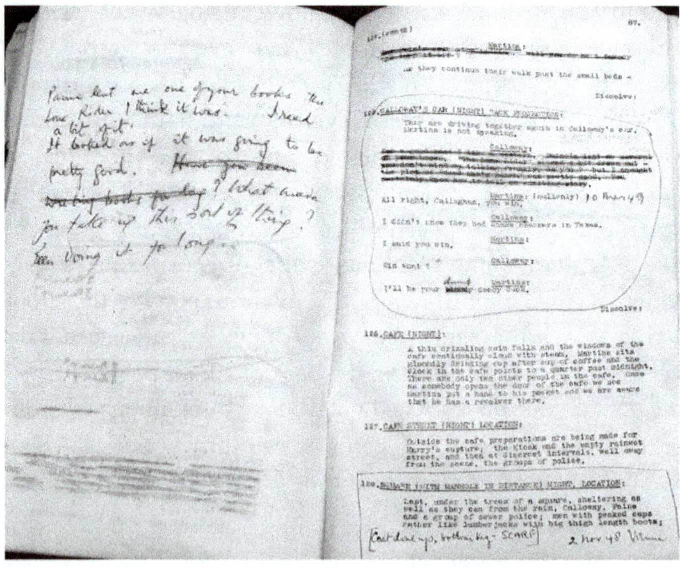

Figures 1 and 2. Trevor Howard's annotated personal copy of *The Third Man* screenplay: title page, page 87, and facing page.

In the film the same passage has become "Paine lent me one of your books. 'Oklahoma Kid' I think it was." We can surmise that, when it came to publishing the screenplay, Greene preferred his dialogue in the shooting script to both the version in Howard's script (which may or may not have been filmed) and the one which director Carol Reed included in the final cut of the film, which may have come from Howard, or Reed, or a third party. It's possible to make a case both for the film as completed by Reed and for the published screenplay as approved by Greene as the final version of the screenplay. A definitive version can't confidently be established.

Such difficulties result in part from the absence of fixed conventions about how a published screenplay is presented. Variations exist even across the output of a single publisher, while the sources of the published screenplays are rarely identified. Moreover, formatting and layout on the page, which might give a clue to provenance, are widely adapted to suit publishing rather than screenwriting practices. Published screenplays that provide no bibliographical information include Faber editions of *Naked* and other screenplays by Mike Leigh; *Avalon*, *Tin Men*, and *Diner* by Barry Levinson; *Breaking and Entering* by Anthony Minghella; *21 Grams* by Guillermo Arriaga; *The Usual Suspects* by Christopher McQuarrie; *Decalogue* by Krzysztof Kieslowski and Krzysztof Piesiewicz; and *Traffic* by Stephen Gaghan. Beyond Faber, Grove Press editions of Michael Tolkin's *Three Screenplays* (*The Player*, *The Rapture*, and *The New Age*) and Todd Haynes's *Far From Heaven*, *Safe*, and *Superstar*, Bloomsbury's edition of Jane Campion's *The Piano*, Vintage's *The Crying Game* by Neil Jordan, and Methuen's *The Long Good Friday* by Barry Keefe all fail to indicate which version of the screenplay has been published. And, while Newmarket Press's edition of *Sideways* by Alexander Payne and Jim Taylor identifies the date of the screenplay draft ("May 29, 2003"), its editions of *American Beauty* and *Adaptation* don't.

By contrast, some publications, such as Faber's of screenplays for *Seven* (1995) and *8MM* (1999) by Andrew Kevin Walker, give highly specific information:

> The draft of *Seven* featured is the third draft, dated 3 October 1994, which was fairly close to the end of the rewrite process – 85-90 per cent, says Walker – and incorporates notes from David Fincher, Brad Pitt, producer Arnold Kopelson, as well as New Line. In contrast, the draft of *8MM* presented here is, according to its author, "the absolute first draft, the warts'n'all version that went out as a spec script."

However, a "Publisher's Note" states that "the layout of the scripts in this book bears little resemblance to true screenplay format." For this one must go to the series of classic Hollywood screenplays published by the University of California Press. These are facsimiles of the shooting scripts, with dated title pages and all the original layout intact, and thus can lay claim to the level of textual authority more commonly associated with scholarly editions of literary texts.

Although Goldman's *Four Screenplays with Essays* (1997) follows book rather than screenwriting conventions, he nevertheless underlines his status as master screenwriter by providing additional information about the process of producing various versions, illustrating in the process how difficult it is to be precise about the exact status of any screenplay draft and the variability of its authorship:

> *The Princess Bride* is pretty close to the finished film. *Butch Cassidy and the Sundance Kid* has some scenes included that were shot and cut. *Marathon Man* is the second draft, the first with a director's

> input – all the stuff dealing with cities in crisis
> was a notion of the director, John Schlesinger.
> Almost none of it made the finished film. I
> included the early scenes for the Roy Scheider
> part because they are the reason he took the role.
> (…) *Misery*, for a simple story, went through a
> remarkable number of changes. (…) The version
> here is one of the fifteen revisions of the fifth
> draft.

No clear explanation of their relationship to other versions or for his selections emerges from this description of how fluid, multiple-draft screenplays become frozen into their single published forms. Goldman acknowledges, like Walker, the involvement of directors and actors. In publishing his writing, though, he reserves the right to include or exclude their contributions at will and to decide what is the definitive version of his screenplays in print, just as a director may create a director's cut that diverges significantly from an already released film. Through publishing, screenplays may return to the control of their writers after lengthy periods of enforced collaboration, and may differ from the final films.

There is, then, no widely accepted definition of screenplays within the scholarly or practitioner discourse. Indeed, any definition is contested, since this would articulate or at least imply a judgment about their nature and value, the very topics under debate. For theorist Ian Macdonald the script is a "pragmatic production tool," while for screenwriting guru John Truby it is where "story worlds" are created. As we examine more closely this range of conceptions, from useful tool to creative source, my working definition will be one that can encompass both Truby and Macdonald: a screenplay is a written verbal construct from which an audiovisual object may subsequently be made.

However, any complete definition of screenplays needs also to include a recognition of their agency in generating, rather than merely transmitting, story and meaning. French screenwriter Jean-Claude Carrière's insistence that "A screenplay is always the dream of a film" offers a definition, or description, that resists the rational and quantifiable in favour of the supra-rational and qualitative. This notion of a screenplay as a "dream" is one we'll return to in later chapters.

Historicising Screenplays

Scholars have constructed the history of screenplays as a relatively minor adjunct to an industrial process, leading to their potential obsolescence and redundancy. Practitioner literature, by contrast, rarely historicises screenplays at all, instead presenting them within a continuous present. Just as their definition, or lack of it, has made screenplays appear nebulous and impermanent, so their marginal position within film history has frequently obscured their existence. Filmmaking changed significantly through its first hundred years, largely as a consequence of its energetic adoption of new technologies and its adaptation to ever wider global markets, and these developments have tended to dominate film history. Screenplays have also evolved, but not to the same extent. For example, Francis Edward Faragoh's screenplay for *Little Caesar* (1931) isn't fundamentally dissimilar to the one by Stuart Beattie (with revisions by Frank Darabont and Michael Mann) for *Collateral* (2004). Both use similar techniques to establish their genre (crime), key props (guns, cars), and protagonists, each with his own sense of mission. Technically, however, the films are poles apart. While *Little Caesar* was shot on black and white 35mm filmstock and its soundtrack is monaural, *Collateral* employed much more advanced technology, including early adoption of digital cinematography and the Digital Intermediate (DI) post-production process, which has since become standard practice on films, rather than the old linear techniques based on film editing, splicing, and negative cutting used by *Little Caesar*. *Collateral*'s soundtrack was mixed not in single-track mono but in a digital format allowing eight-channel surround sound to be included with the 35mm release prints. Since *Collateral*'s release, the distribution of films has similarly moved from physical to digital formats, so that few continuities remain from the old Hollywood in terms of technical filmmaking processes. Faragoh would struggle to comprehend these processes, or the digital effects used to make the cast of *The Irishman* (2019) appear decades younger than their age, let alone its release not in cinemas but online by streaming platform Netflix. Nevertheless he'd recognise Steve Zaillian's screenplay for *The Irishman* as not unlike his own for *Little Caesar* – words on a page that tell a crime story, establish characters, and create the world in which these exist.

Well before the introduction of synchronised sound in 1927, growing interest in the new art of photoplay writing had stimulated the publication of many screenwriting manuals and classes. Already in 1916 Sargent warns his readers against "fake correspondence schools," noting that "the earliest one was started about 1910," and that "Most of these schools are frankly fraudulent." Manuals like Sargent's own were marketed, as were the correspondence courses, to a wide readership of aspiring screenwriters. Many of their authors were less scrupulous than Sargent himself, and closer in spirit to the "fraudulent" screenwriting schools. F. Scott Fitzgerald, by 1931 established as a Hollywood studio employee, makes his character Pat Hobby, the "scenario hack" from a series of short stories, the author of one himself. "In 1928 he and another man had concocted such a sucker-trap, *Secrets of Film Writing*. It would have made money if pictures hadn't started to talk." The notion of screenwriting manuals as sucker-traps persists to the present day, yet this stereotype warrants some reconsideration. Alongside manuals and correspondence courses there were photoplay writing programmes at American universities, including Columbia and the University of Southern California. Sargent's manual went through three editions in as many years (1913-1916), and the third is no lightweight get-rich-quick guide, but an eloquent "text book, to be studied" of nearly four hundred densely formatted pages. Sargent emphasises the serious level of commitment expected of his readers: "The writing of photoplays has ceased to be a pastime whereby the dabbler could make a few dollars. It is now a profession and must be prepared for with the same serious attention as any of the other professions." Like the vast majority of manual-writers after him, Sargent addresses his book to the aspiring, rather than established, screenwriter – a "student," a "novice writer" with ambitions to become an "artist-author."

While some scholars are eager to distinguish the modern screenplay from its antecedents, it's clear from Sargent that most, if not all, concerns of the twenty-first century manual-writer are already present in his 1916 edition. Indeed, Sargent's substantial treatise creates a template not only for "photoplays" themselves but also for its many screenwriting manual successors. As well as providing lengthy discussions of structure, technique, and the specific requirements of different genres, Sargent explains how the industry is organised, and describes the market for spec scripts. He discusses employment opportunities for screenwriters, and even prescribes what the physical appearance of a script should be, just as Field was to do six decades later. While Sargent doesn't specify the typeface (Millard and Price both identify the adoption of Courier 12-point as a key development in the standardisation of Hollywood screenplays), he does tell his readers to acquire a "typewriting machine" with a "twelve point type." Like many subsequent manuals, Sargent's book is explicit about the material requirements of professional script presentation:

> You will need a box of paper clips. Get one of the sort that will not perforate the paper nor permanently fasten it. The brass Niagara clip is about the best for this purpose... These clips are attached to the upper left hand corner of the script and but one is used.

The regard for screenplays as material objects is shared by Fitzgerald's Pat Hobby:

> At three-fifteen he returned to his office to find two copies of his script in bright new covers.

BALLET SHOES
from
René Wilcox and Pat Hobby
First Revise
It reassured him to see his name in type.

Where schools are fraudulent, guides are sucker-traps, literary stars are employed as hack writers, and there's no agreement on what a screenplay is, it's hardly surprising that the materiality of a typescript may be seen as reassuring, just as Pat's name on the title page confirms to him that he exists.

This concern with screenplays' materiality has remained remarkably consistent over the decades. A century after Sargent's book, the brand and number of clips deemed to create a professional impression have changed, but the advice remains much the same. Like Sargent, Robin Russin and William Downs induct readers of their 2012 manual, *Screenplay: Writing the Picture*, into the craft of script-binding:

> The industry standard is brass brads or Chicago
> screws only. The best brass brads are made by
> ACCO. Use their No.5 or No. 6 industrial
> heavy-duty style fasteners... Most professional
> screenwriters use only two brads per script, one in
> the top hole and one in the bottom, the middle
> hole left empty. It's just cooler that way, more Zen.

The tone has changed from the stern admonitions of Sargent to Russin and Downs's informal chat. The throwaway reference to Zen Buddhism is quashed by the suggestion that it's "cooler" to leave the middle hole empty, reducing the pseudo-mystical aspect of their instructions to the superficial level of fashion and peer approval. "[P]rofessional" and "industrial" remain the catchwords, however.

The specification of brass brads and other external elements can be seen as a response to the intractable difficulty of defining its internal ones. It supports a mechanical, structural, "nuts and bolts" approach to screenplay writing rather than a creative, imaginative one. Sargent tells his reader not only "How to Get a Plot," but also how to train his memory, to read books about railroads, construction, and surgery, and which is the best kind of notebook for a screenwriter. In 2012 Joseph McBride's advice to readers of his book *Writing in Pictures* is very similar. Like Sargent's, they should "read prodigiously," take notes, and "[k]eep scenes short," alongside more general tips: "Read Chekhov," "Get a job," and "Make your own breaks." Instruction in screenwriting manuals is frequently pitched at the most pragmatic level, far removed from the ontological challenges faced by scholars struggling to define screenplays.

Bordwell, echoing Norman's dig at Sargent, notes in *The Way Hollywood Tells It: Story and Style in Modern Movies* (2006) that one problem with manuals is that they're written not by screenwriters but by story analysts. It's a familiar accusation, but not necessarily accurate. Moreover, the fact that Aristotle was an analyst rather than a playwright hasn't devalued his views on Sophocles, nor prevented his *Poetics* from becoming the most frequently cited source across a wide range of books on screenwriting. Meanwhile Blake Snyder, author of popular manual *Save the Cat!* (2005), promotes himself as a "working professional in the entertainment industry" and asks his readers, "wouldn't it be nice if the guy writing the book on how to write a screenplay had actually sold something! *Don't you think?* And this is an area where I feel particularly qualified." Snyder writes that he has "made millions of dollars" from screenwriting. Yet Snyder's produced work – shared credits on *Blank Check* (1994) and *Stop! Or My Mom will Shoot* (1992) – appears less impressive than the sums earned from his writing. Screenwriters may not necessarily be better qualified than story analysts to offer advice on writing screenplays.

Academic examinations of screenwriting manuals frequently identify within them a mechanical and reductive, by-the-numbers approach to screenwriting. "Nothing is more central to the manuals than their structural approach to screenplays, in particular, the importance of the three-act paradigm," writes J.J. Murphy in *Me and You and* Memento *and* Fargo: *How Independent Screenplays Work* (2007). Other critiques descend into a game of counting "acts" in different ways, either to affirm or (more often) to disprove the notorious "three-act paradigm," usually traced back to Field, and to assert a different schema. The obsession with structure among both manual writers and academics obscures screenplays' immaterial elements such as their agency in generating story, meaning, and style, which are so much more difficult to define in a how-to manual or via structuralist methodologies.

Some critics accord manual writers quasi-, albeit substandard, academic status. Since McKee received the backhanded compliment of becoming a character in Charlie

Kaufman's and Spike Jonze's arch, metafilmic *Adaptation* (2002), he has replaced Field as the pre-eminent authoritarian manual author, laying down the law for neophyte screenwriters in seminars and his book *Story* (1999). Maras references McKee numerous times, connecting him (at arm's length) to scholarship by identifying his approach with New Criticism, while also noting Field's "structuralist tendencies." In both cases, the effect is to identify these manual-writers with outdated theoretical positions. However, Maras comes considerably closer than other academics to taking seriously what Bordwell refers to as "the how-to books," deconstructing their differences from theoretical writings and suggesting that "many screenwriters are already consumers of theory," while "[t]heory is embedded in many screenwriting manuals." For Price, too, McKee is a theoretically correct, "sharp and even profound story analyst," too astute to make the mistake of thinking of character as more than a "textual construct." Millard, however, sees him as a source of contagion, lamenting that "Too many story templates from the likes of Syd Field, Christopher Vogler and Robert McKee have migrated across to digital platforms, along with Final Draft and its Courier font." These templates, she suggests, reduce stylistic and thematic complexities, generate superfluous plot, and water down the distinctiveness of the original screenplay draft, just as Courier's status as the default font of computer screenwriting programmes flattens out individuality.

Conversely, screenwriting manual writers address the relationship between theory and practice in their own work. McKee cites philosophers Jean-Paul Sartre and Martin Heidegger as well as Aristotle, but only one film theorist, Christian Metz, appears in his *Story*, and then only to be castigated for his attempt "to schematize all of cinema inside 'La Gran Syntagma.'" McKee frames his critique in one of the oldest of academic antagonisms, art versus science, present in film discourse since its incipience: "[Metz's] effort to turn art to science crumbled like the Tower of Babel." The mutual exclusivity of art (here, filmmaking as practised) and science (semiology is the science of signs) is expressed in a metaphor of religious apostasy. The very idea of language as a science rather than an art is presented as blasphemous. Yet film too is scientific: cinematography, sound recording, editing, mixing, special effects, digital compositing, and many other specialisms within film production and post-production demand high levels of technical skills and scientific knowledge. Even the most artistic of cinematographers wouldn't deny that cinematography is scientific. Indeed, the practice of filmmaking seems to be one area where science and art can happily coexist. McKee's apparent antipathy towards science isn't necessarily shared by his peers. The publication in the same year, 1913, of two of the earliest screenplay manuals, entitled respectively *The Art of the Photoplay* (by Eustace Ball) and *Technique of the Photoplay* (Sargent's first edition), demonstrates that the concurrence of the artistic and scientific can be traced back for more than a century.

Even so, in this highly technological context the writer occupies an ambivalent position. Most of the people who actually make films are called "technicians," which isn't a term applied to screenwriters. The writer, with no recognised technological expertise, produces words – something which every literate person does. She lacks the formal training and demonstrable skills of a Steadicam operator, a sound recordist hunched over a mixer, or a lighting electrician striking up a high-voltage HMI lamp. To these technicians, science poses no threat. As framed by McKee, however, science does pose a threat to theories of writing as art, and even as craft. For all that manual writers and scholars may emphasise the structural emphasis of *Story*, with its insistent implication of such applied sciences as building and construction, McKee places the symbolic, abstract concerns traditionally associated with art at the centre of his book. "Artists master the form," he writes in the first paragraph of his introduction, and continues, "*Story* urges the creation of works that will excite audiences." In spite of the structural, nuts and bolts approach of most manuals, such statements preclude them from being the arid rulebooks that scholars may deem them to be.

The notion of screenwriting as a professional craft goes some way to explaining most manuals' noticeable lack of interest in theory. For manual writers, prowess in screenwriting, conceived as a craft, is acquired through practice and repetition, as a skilled artisan's is; learned on the job, not in the classroom or lecture theatre. As Dwight and Joye Swain write in *Scriptwriting: A Practical Manual* (1988), "Given enough time, enough patience, enough practice, even the most inept novice will improve. No amount of talk or theory or study can substitute for it." The manuals stress "professionalism" – like "craft," a key concept for most of them. Russin and Downs link the "correct" physical presentation of screenplays to professionalism, as do McBride and Christopher Riley, in *The Hollywood Standard* (2009). Professionalism forms part of the subtitle of Jack Epps, Jr.'s manual, *Screenwriting is Rewriting: The Art and Craft of Professional Revision* (2016); Sargent hopes that his reader "may become fully qualified to follow your profession." Field closes *Screenplay* by encouraging readers to strive for "[p]rofessional success." Writers' agent and manual author Julian Friedmann, like many others, distinguishes between the "professional writer" and the "amateur."

This links to a related and ancient opposition between art and craft. According to Field, "Writing a screenplay... is a craft that occasionally rises to the level of art." But the craft is the norm. At the end of *Screenplay* he quotes "the motto of the McDonald's Corporation," which emphasises the value of persistence over talent, genius, and education, while implicitly embracing the principles of standardisation and mass production employed by McDonald's. Similarly, "Professional writers may or may not receive critical acclaim," writes McKee, "but they're in control of the craft." Craft may be valued more highly, for itself, than the approval of outsiders.

A more central distinction between art and craft derives from the opposition of art and commerce. While practice-oriented literature may be chary of theory, it is keenly attuned to the business aspect of writing screenplays. This, too, is a concern that's as old as the screenwriting manual. "Writing the script is generally easier than selling it," Sargent notes drily in 1916. These two intertwined imperatives – write the screenplay, sell the screenplay – have kept the how-to book, along with its associated workshops and courses, buoyant for over a century. The full subtitle of Harrington Adams's 1912 book, *The Photo Play Plot: How to Write It, How to Sell It: A Complete Course in Motion Picture Play Writing with Selling Advice and an Up-to-date List of Buyers*, makes plain its engagement with the screenplay's antecedents as commercial properties. More recent titles such as Friedmann's *How to Make Money Scriptwriting* (1995) and Hauge's *Writing Screenplays that Sell* (1989) thus take their places in a long-standing tradition.

Throughout their history, screenplays have been linked to notions of easy money. Many screenplay historians refer to the "scenario fever" that stimulated the market for manuals and writing courses in waves between 1907 to 1921. Each wave is related to changing industrial practices: to how writers were employed, the growth of studios' in-house story departments, the development of copyright law, and the movement towards the standardisation of script formats. Maras draws a parallel with another powerful incitement to "get rich quick" when he suggests that "a gold-rush mentality developed in relation to the photoplay." No evidence has been put forward that a similar gold-rush mentality drew would-be directors and cameramen to the studios, since these professions required technical skills; although Hollywood exercised a comparable attraction for aspiring actors, who also needed no particular training, throughout the twentieth century and into the twenty-first. Even Sargent, stern schoolmaster though he may appear, seems to take for granted that his "students" are motivated primarily by the financial gains that they hope to make through buying and reading his book. Marketing has therefore constituted an important part of the practitioner discourse since the earliest days of screenwriting. While writing of all kinds has also been motivated by a desire to make money, the overt, unabashed, persistent concern with money is one factor in the screenplay's continuing sub-literary status. For example, Russin and Downs write:

> Perhaps the first, and in some ways hardest, truth for new screenwriters to accept is that, while some rise to the level of classics and even get published, screenplays are not intended as literature... If you want to write something intended to be read for its own literary merit, write a novel, short story or poem – even a stage play – not a screenplay.

Despite Hauge's earlier suggestion that screenplays can aspire to the same status as the "Great American Novel," literary ambition is here effectively prohibited as a motivation for screenwriting.

If a solely technical approach to screenplays leads, ultimately, to the "template" abhorred by Millard and others, a purely artistic one may lead to an individualistic self-expression, avoiding engagement with the collaborative group, the audience, the technical specifications of film production, or the business model underpinning the film industry. Screenplays can thus be seen as occupying a central space where opposing forces and theories meet and interact.

Fitzgerald's Pat Hobby may be a cynical studio hack, but the author also in one story juxtaposes him with a sensitive English playwright, who explains his newly discovered screenwriting method: "You just get behind the camera and dream." To Pat's astonishment, the novice's first screenplay is well received and rushed into production. Pat may be "a good man for structure," which suggests a manual-reader as well as a manual-writer, but the literary star focuses not on technicalities but on his imagination. This finds an echo many decades later, near the end of Norman's history of American screenwriting. He describes an experience which, he asserts, "almost all screenwriters would have sooner or later" – that of a studio executive confiding his own dream of throwing up his highly paid job "and doing what you do." Posing the question, "Why was that?", Norman's answer stands as the climax of his book: "the executives were confessing that of everybody in the business, screenwriters had the purest experience with their product. They got to see the movie first, entire, in their minds." Frank Pierson, writer of screenplays for films including *Cool Hand Luke* (1967) and *Dog Day Afternoon* (1975), agrees:

> My favorite screenplays are the ones that have never been made because they unspooled in my head exactly as I saw them, without all the compromises that have to be made in the actual making of the film, and all the accidents, because it is an accident when it all comes together.

Like the joy of screenwriting, this notion of a screenplay as the original vessel of an essential movie, pure and uncompromised, is rarely discussed by academics or film directors. Far more often, purity is ascribed to a non-verbal cinema, which screenplays are accused of contaminating, and assertions are made that filmmaking is predicated on the destruction of screenplays (see Chapter 5). Yet, despite this, Norman's anecdote resonates, at least with my own experience. It's one of the reasons, perhaps even the principal one, for my own interest in the writing of screenplays more than in the directing of them. The testimony of professional screenwriters supports this point, as shown in Chapter 6. Reconceiving screenplay theory in the light of practice will need to take this into account alongside screenplays' other, more pragmatic aspects.

The problems of defining and historicising screenplays extend to deeply divided opinions, not only about what screenplays are and how they're situated within the various discourses addressing them, but also about the terms in which they should be conceptualised and discussed. It's been noted that these frequently turn out be metaphorical. While definitions have been changing and contested across history, and screenplay forms and processes have also changed, one metaphor in particular has been insistently perpetuated, long after it has become obsolete as a technology. The next chapter explores how and why it has persisted, and still persists today.

2

SCREENPLAYS AS BLUEPRINTS

The blueprint metaphor and practitioners

The blueprint metaphor has been used to characterise screenplays throughout the history of film and underpins, often without acknowledgement, a variety of interests and agendas. It occurs across a wide range of discourses: historical, theoretical, practical, and pedagogic. While it may describe accurately some aspects of screenplays, it exaggerates, distorts, and obscures others. In particular, it has promoted the characterisation of screenplays as industrial planning documents, the conveyors of content into film rather than its source.

Just as the blueprint metaphor can support a variety of industry and cultural agendas, so too it can support differing theoretical approaches, which in most other ways are incompatible. For example, the metaphor has been engaged both to resist notions of screenplays as writing and to support Marxist industrial readings of film. In the 21st century the blueprint continues to be a popular metaphor among the authors of both technical and screenwriting manuals.

"Like the blueprint of an architect," manual author Austin Lescarboura writes in 1919, "the scenario must tell the director how to go about his work." This early appearance of the blueprint metaphor wasn't echoed in many of the earliest manuals, however. Lescarboura himself goes on to note an important sense in which it can prove misleading:

> "There is this difference, however, that... he does
> not have to follow the scenario to the letter; here
> and there, where the circumstances and his

> experience and judgment dictate, he can alter the
> action in order to produce a better picture."

Already the assumption is made that departures from the "scenario" will produce a "better" rather than a worse film.

Addressing his readership of aspiring screenwriters, Lescarboura acknowledges that a "scenario" is less prescriptive than the technical drawing prepared by an architect and passed to building contractors for execution. In 1938, in *One Act Play Magazine and Radio-drama Review*, William Kozlenko and Emerson Golden similarly draw attention to the constraints of the metaphor, even as they promote it:

> At its best, a shooting script can scarcely be easy
> reading, for it is to the director what a blueprint is
> to an architect. Between the words and the film, as
> between the ruled lines and the building, there is
> that vast change from the medium used for
> planning, to the one in which the final object is
> created.

Although their discussion notes the limitations of this conception of the screenplay, it's on the basis that this is hard to read, and that it's also difficult for the reader to extrapolate from one medium to another. In both film and building, creation is reserved for the later, production stage.

Despite reservations about it, the blueprint metaphor continued to spread and diversify. By the 1950s, it had migrated to writing manuals addressing the new medium of television; according to Robert S. Greene, behind the "extremely complicated" process of shooting in a multi-camera studio "lies a blueprint – the script." Manuals focusing on the techniques of film production continued to invoke the metaphor in the 1970s. The 1982 revised edition of Syd Field's *Screenplay* repeats and varies it. Although Field poses the question of whether a screenplay is a blueprint, he isn't consistent. Later, he nominates the sequence ("a series of scenes connected by one single idea") as "the blueprint of your screenplay." Field also extends the metaphor from practice to pedagogy, suggesting that "a model screenplay" may act as a "blueprint" for teaching purposes. In *The Scriptwriter's Handbook* of 1996, William Van Nostran similarly presents two uses of the blueprint metaphor: "[j]ust as the shooting script functions as a blueprint for the production crew, the action plan serves as a blueprint for the media writer." Van Nostran's "action plan" is thus a blueprint for a blueprint. Rachel Ballon takes the same path with her manual *Blueprint for Writing* (1994), subsequently published in a new edition as *Blueprint for Screenwriting* (2004), which proposes a blueprint to facilitate the writing of further blueprints. In 2016 Epps begins *Screenwriting is Rewriting* by insisting that "[a] screenplay is part stage play and part blueprint." According to Joseph Gillis in *The Screen Writer's Guide* (1987), "There's a good reason why scripts are often referred to as 'blueprints.' A blueprint is a program of action, a diagram of how you expect something will turn out – and that's exactly what a script is." Here the metaphor is both literalised and distorted: a blueprint is no longer a metaphor for a script, but exactly the same thing as a script (while an actual blueprint is *not* a plan of action). "Takes are assembled from dailies to create scenes, and scenes are assembled to make a show, all according to the blueprint provided by the script," according to Barbara Clark's and Susan Spohr's *Guide to Postproduction for TV and Film*, while screenwriters are identified as the providers of "the blueprint for a movie" in *FilmCraft: Screenwriting* by Tim Grierson, also published in 2013. For authors of how-to books, the metaphor offers a seemingly workmanlike and accessible conceptualisation of what might otherwise appear to be a frustratingly intangible relationship between screenplay and film.

Screenwriters themselves, with their first-hand knowledge of how screenplays come into existence, may also employ the blueprint metaphor, but tend to do so with less enthusiasm. One of the earliest screenwriters to use it in a published account is Dudley Nichols (*Bringing Up Baby, Stagecoach*), in *Twenty Best Film Plays* (1943). This was also the first publication to make a direct claim for the literary status of screenplays. Even so, in his essay, "The Writer and the Film," which forms part of the introduction to this first screenplay anthology, he argues that screenplays, unlike novels, "are not complete works in themselves, they are blueprints of projected films." Robert Alan Aurthur (*Grand Prix, All That Jazz*), writing in 1975, emphasises the lifelessness implicit in the metaphor: "At best a screenplay is a blueprint with no life of its own until it is cast with actors, moved into sets or locations, directed, visualized on film, edited and scored with sound effects and music." For Nicholas Meyer (*Sommersby, The Human Stain*) at the end of the 20th century "A screenplay is a blueprint for something – for a building that will most likely never be built."

The status of screenplays is compromised by the blueprint metaphor in other ways, chiefly through their function within a wider industrial paradigm of film making. Writing during the final period of studio-dominated production, Nichols characterises this as the age of "the Machine," in which films are "standardized products" that "come off the assembly line." The blueprint screenplay is thus associated with an industrial paradigm, in which films have become depersonalised and mass produced. Decades on, when Paul Schrader (*Taxi Driver, First Reformed*) refers to blueprints, it is with similarly negative associations to those of Nichols: "A screenwriter is not really a writer... What he does is to draft out blueprints that are executed by a team."

Other screenwriters change their views of the metaphor over time. Norman readily accepts that scripts were blueprints in 1912, but withholds the metaphor from the screenplays he himself co-wrote at the end of the century, such as *Shakespeare in Love*. William Goldman, too, modifies his position: in his introduction to the first published version of his screenplay, *Butch Cassidy and the Sundance Kid*, he affirms that "Any film is a community effort in which the screenplay is the blue-print for the actors, the director, the technicians." That was in 1969. When the same screenplay was republished with three others in 1997, the reference to blueprints had disappeared. In the later edition he protests against the conventions that contribute to the screenplay's characterisation as a uniform, industrial planning document: "The standard screenplay form is not only unreadable, it is something far worse, it is wrong. All those capital letters and numbers which stop our eye and destroy any chance at narrative flow, have nothing to do with writing... I have never used them, hate them, always will." Michael Blake (*Dances with Wolves*), interviewed by Field for *Four Screenplays* (1998), echoes Goldman. "'I try to make my screenplays readable,'" he says, and equates readability with an avoidance of the familiar metaphor: "'I never approach them as a blueprint for a movie.'"

I.A.L Diamond, who co-wrote *The Apartment* and *Some Like It Hot* with Billy Wilder, accepts the blueprint metaphor "to an extent," while protesting that "nobody goes around saying that architecture is a 'contractor's medium.'" This critique implicitly positions screenwriters alongside architects as the creative agents in film/building construction. Edward Anhalt (*Jeremiah Johnson, The Young Lions*) also endorses the metaphor ("the screenplay is essentially a blueprint"), while then extending it: "Frank Lloyd Wright also supervised the building. In other words, he was like the writer who becomes the director." This may explain why writer-director Darren Aronofsky (*Pi, Mother!*) is less dismissive of the blueprint metaphor – "the screenplay's really a blueprint." As a writer-director, Aronofsky privileges the latter role over the former: "there's barely anything in those screenplays that's in the movies, because to write everything visual that's going on in my mind... just wouldn't make a screenplay." Anthony Minghella, another writer-director (*Cold Mountain, Truly, Madly, Deeply*), also invokes without critical shading the old architectural analogy: "The screenplay, closer to an architect's drawing than it is to literature, exists as a blueprint of the film." Like Aronofsky, Minghella doesn't need to restrict his creative agency to either side of the hyphen between writer and director. Nor does Hong Kong writer-director Kar-wai Wong (*In the Mood for Love, 2046*), who said in a 2014 interview that "The script is... only the foundations. It is only a blueprint," nor writer-director John Sayles, who urges readers of his published screenplays to "Try to take them as the blueprints they are." Yet Wong equally claims literary potential, if not status, for some screenplays: "If a script is good enough, then you should be a writer, make it into a novel." Bruce Joel Rubin (*Ghost, Jacob's Ladder*) goes further, explicitly connecting his rejection of the blueprint metaphor with the screenplay's claim to literary status on its own merits, without having to be turned into a novel: "The first job of a writer is to create a literary work, not the blueprint purely for what's going to be on the screen."

Michael Mann (*Thief, Heat*), one of the relatively small group of mainstream commercial writer-directors admired as much for their screenplays as for their films, makes explicit why he and others endorse the metaphor: "I'm writing a screenplay that's a blueprint for a motion picture that I'm going to direct," he says in an interview. "The writing process is really how I prepare myself for directing." In this conception, the blueprint has changed its function from an impersonal technical drawing to become a personal document, written by someone for his own use. For many non-directing screenwriters such as Norman and Blake, however, any employment of the blueprint metaphor can be seen as an oppressive limitation on the agency of the screenplay.

The blueprint metaphor and scholars

Although the blueprint metaphor can be traced back to some of the earliest screenwriting manuals and has persisted in practitioner literature ever since, uses of the metaphor are sporadic and relatively few when the enormous number of published manuals, screenplays, and interviews with screenwriters is taken into account. For every screenwriting manual that endorses it, there are ten others that don't. Among the most popular manual authors, only Field refers to blueprints and, as has been shown, does so selectively. Others such as Robert McKee, John Truby, and Blake Snyder avoid it.

The blueprint metaphor, however, has proved central to scholarly accounts of the screenplay, particularly those adopting an historical perspective. The principal source of the industrial paradigm of filmmaking, in which the blueprint stands as emblem, is Janet Staiger's influential account of early Hollywood. In *The Classical Hollywood Cinema: Film Style and Mode of Production to 1960* published in 1985, Staiger traces the development of screenplays and their predecessors in concert with changing modes of industrial production in the United States during the first half of the twentieth century. "Besides focusing on the division of the individual work functions and the management structure and hierarchy," she writes, "I will be emphasizing the importance of the script as a blueprint for the film." As we've seen, the blueprint metaphor was current in Hollywood in 1919. Staiger, though, applies it to an even earlier period. Already in 1909, according to her account, a "standard script" had come into being during the "Director-Unit System"; during this period, "the manufacturers transformed the theatrical and vaudeville script into their working blueprint for the film." At a time of rapid technological development and innovation, words written or typed prior to filming and figured as just one component of the filmmaking process do seem to fit the metaphor's industrial connotations.

Similarly, during the next stage in Hollywood's development, the post-1914 "Central Producer System," Staiger represents the script as "a blueprint detailing the shot-by-shot breakdown of the film." Technology – the changing means of capturing, storing, and exhibiting various kinds of story material – was driving the filmmaking process, and it's consistent to characterise the written screenplay in similarly technical terms. Staiger's focus, however, isn't solely on the screenplay; she takes a much wider view of industry practice across the whole film production business. Seen in this way, the screenplay and its antecedents aren't essentially differentiated from other aspects of production, such as costume and set design, which are also parts of the industrial system. The role of screenwriters in this context was to produce "a standardized script designed to take the best advantage of its physical capacities and labor force." The screenplay is just one aspect of a larger "standardizing process" that "controlled innovation" in a system of constraints. Like her co-authors, David Bordwell and Kristin Thompson, Staiger sees the same industrial processes taking hold of the film and car manufacture industries; including, crucially, the adoption of the production line as their central paradigm. Staiger identifies this connection in writings by early filmmakers. One writer from Ince's studio in 1913 compares the production process not to a car factory, but to the car itself: "with the cogs of the big Ince machine oiled to the smallest gear and the entire plant running as smoothly as an automobile in the hands of a salesman, the picture travels from the beginning to end without delays." The mechanical analogy has no negative connotations for this writer, but is used to promote the efficiency of his studio's output by analogy to a smoothly running (and at this time new and highly desirable) machine.

While the blueprint metaphor and the notion of the screenplay as an industrial document have helped to elucidate certain aspects of filmmaking in the early and mid-twentieth century, they are less appropriate in treating later and independent films. Well before 1960 (the end of the period Staiger surveys), the Fordist production-line paradigm already appears disconnected from Hollywood practice. A more recognisable model would be one in which management provides financial structures within which creative workers (writers, directors, set designers, and others) develop and realise projects. This can accommodate a full spectrum of management styles, from the "hands-on" micro-management of, for instance, Walt Disney Pictures under Michael Eisner and Jeffrey Katzenberg (portrayed by screenwriter John Gregory Dunne in his non-fiction book *Monster*) to the relatively "hands-off" approach of MGM under Dore Schary (described by journalist Lillian Ross in her 1953 book *Picture*).

Several later scholars have critiqued the blueprint metaphor, but often only subsequently to reinstate it. One of the first to examine it in detail was Claudia Sternberg, in her 1997 book, *Written for the Screen: The American Motion-Picture Screenplay as Text*. Ultimately, though, she modifies it rather than rejecting it outright. Sternberg identifies the blueprint as the "classic metaphor used to characterize the function and significance of the screenplay." Her challenges lie not with the metaphor itself, but with promoting the interpretative functions of those "blueprint-readers" who use the screenplay for a range of different purposes, and the creative agency of those who write screenplays. On the first page of her book, she quotes Raymond Chandler's claim that "everything derives from the screenplay, and most of that which derives is an applied skill which, however adept, is artistically not in the same class with the creation of a screenplay." Thus even as Sternberg sees the screenplay as a creative, conceptual work and the filmmaking that grows out of the screenplay as interpretive, she does not reject the blueprint metaphor as metaphor. Indeed, she concludes her book with a definition of the screenplay as a "performance blueprint."

Steven Maras also objects to the metaphor, but for the quite different reason that it can "lead to an overidentification of the writer with the script." Anxious not to "minimise the creative input of other key collaborators and factors in the production process," Maras seeks to qualify the screenplay's agency. His concern is to guard against the screenplay's encroachment on the freedom of the director (and others) to depart from what the screenplay-blueprint prescribes. In so doing Maras suggests that the blueprint metaphor exaggerates, rather than understates, the screenplay's role in filmmaking:

> *On the one hand the blueprint idea allows screenwriters to gain authority and control in the filmmaking process (they're the authors of the blueprint); on the other this can misrepresent the work of reading and writing involved and lead to a particularist discourse around the script, in which the writer has a unique relationship to the blueprint to the exclusion of others.*

In his concern to avoid privileging either screenplay or writer, Maras rejects the idea that a unique relationship exists between a screenplay and the person (or persons) who wrote it. This does not describe common practice. Whatever collaborative process the screenplay may form a part of, the writing of a screenplay draft, as against earlier discussions or subsequent development, is usually done by one or at most two people.

Even in cases where multiple writers work on a script, they generally do so in a succession of separate acts of writing, as draft follows draft. It is as difficult to imagine a screenplay lacking a unique relationship with its writer as it is to conceive of a film lacking a unique relationship with its director. We can acknowledge the collaborative nature of filmmaking without denying the individual nature of the various contributions made by those who collaborate.

Despite his arguments against it, Maras too ultimately reinstates the blueprint metaphor: "I have suggested," he writes, "that three issues in particular help shape a modern or contemporary understanding of screenwriting: these include the idea of the script as blueprint." He offers three reasons for retaining it, the first being the blueprint metaphor's ability to "serve as a counterbalance to the idea that the script is an autonomous entity." His second reason is that "it goes against the visual bias of film theory and highlights the composition or design dimension of cinema." Since a blueprint is itself a visual device (in contrast to the purely verbal nature of the screenplay), it seems to emphasise rather than oppose visuality. Finally, Maras approves of the way "it highlights the industrial scale of a great deal of film production." However, in any period after that of the classical Hollywood studio, the extent to which the writing of screenplays is industrial rather than artisanal is questionable. If this is simply a question of scale, then it would apply equally to the writing and publishing of fiction, a comparison explored further in Chapter 4.

Ian Macdonald holds the blueprint metaphor at arm's length but settles on a definition of screenwriting that's analogous to it: the industrial planning document. "The screen-writer's traditional task," he writes, "is to produce industrial planning documents, the key one of which is the screenplay."

Yet in spite of retaining the blueprint, Maras also raises "the need to reconsider, on a more conceptual level, our notions of screenwriting beyond ideas of the blueprint, the screenplay and writing for the screen." Where Maras objects to the implicit privileging of the screenwriter-as-architect who draws up the master plan to be executed by technicians, Steven Price sees only the threat to the screenwriter implicit in the metaphor: "the screenwriter is, like Melville's Bartleby, essentially a drawer-up of recondite documents, rather than an artist in his or her own right." Part of what Price brings to the debate is a literary critical background that makes him equally comfortable with film writing and with other kinds of writing, and a willingness to deal with both on equal terms. "The blueprint metaphor compromises the aesthetic and thematic seriousness of the text," he argues, "because it ascribes to the screenwriter a bathetic non-imagination akin to that of the narrator of Wordsworth's ballad 'The Thorn.'" Not only is Price's simile a literary allusion; he frequently aligns the writers of screenplays with the authors of literary texts, while most scholars and manual-writers relate screenwriters instead to technicians, mechanics, and even unskilled labourers. Indeed, Epps goes so far as to liken rewriting a screenplay to "working in a construction zone... in the trenches digging away at the concrete." Price further proposes that scholars "might be interested in other potentialities within the written text (e.g. as a form of expressive literature or creative labour), and want to examine those aspects of the screenplay that exceed a purely industrial function."

Macdonald, like Price, insists that "we know better than to read [the screenplay] as merely a 'blueprint;'" but a recognition of the metaphor's limitations may not be sufficient to shift its dominance. J.J. Murphy, for instance, introduces his analysis of independent screenplays with the assertion that "As the blueprint for production and the 'selling point' of getting a project into production, the script is often the cornerstone of the filmmaking process."

Further objections to the blueprint metaphor

The blueprint metaphor dominates scholarly and academic discourses of the screenplay, and recurs in that of practitioners. Although it has been viewed with some scepticism, the case against the blueprint has not been fully made. This section presents a series of objections to it, demonstrating how the metaphor has distorted and obscured understanding of screenplays and explaining why it has nevertheless persisted across different media theories and decades.

Objection One: the blueprint is anachronistic. Price restricts the relevance of the blueprint metaphor to a narrow chronological band, "the silent continuity from 1914 to 1929," but there's more to be said about the metaphor as an anachronism. Defining the screenplay as the product of a redundant process abandoned seventy years ago taints it with the negative connotations of an obsolete technology, and reinforces notions that screenplays are a disposable and similarly obsolete aspect of filmmaking. The blueprint metaphor has become anachronistic in consequence of technological changes both in architecture and filmmaking. A nineteenth-century technique for creating copies of technical drawings using light-sensitised paper, the blueprint (originally cyanotype) was still in use in the early stages of the classical Hollywood studio period. However, as early as the 1940s blueprints were replaced by diazo prints ("whiteprints"). These were in turn succeeded by newer techniques such as computer-aided design and digital reprography. The theme of antiquated technology appears on the covers of several recently-published screenwriting manuals featuring typewriters (Field's *Screenplay*) or vintage typewriter keys (Truby's *The Anatomy of Story*) and histories of film (Donald Ogden Stewart and William Faulkner, both with typewriters, on the front and back covers of Norman's *What Happens Next*). *Story and Character: Interviews with British Screenwriters*, published in 2004, also sports an old-fashioned typewriter. In May 2020, the web page for the University of Iowa's BA in Screenwriting Arts employs similar imagery – and not just any old typewriter, but a vintage Underwood.

Other common anachronistic signifiers include clapperboards (replaced in most film practice by digital boards) and rolls of celluloid film (rarely used in an age of digital production), with or without film cans. Maras's book is adorned with a still from *Adaptation*, in which Nicolas Cage as "Charlie Kaufman" stares at the sheet of paper in his electric typewriter (a model already obsolete when the film was produced). These choices are made by book designers and marketing departments, not by film theorists, yet they illustrate the widespread association between screenplays and outdated technology, placing them in an historical past as archaic relics, while also reinforcing their location in the discarded prior stages of the film production process, a point developed further in Chapter 5. Another aspect of this appeal to archaic signifiers is the attempt to attach gravitas and cultural weight to screenplays, which by implication would otherwise lack these.

Objection Two: nostalgic uses of the anachronistic blueprint as a metaphor continue to place the screenplay in a redundant past, whether of history or filmmaking. Although actual blueprints are no longer used as industrial planning documents, they have not become totally obsolete; some are traces of an earlier industrial process, while others constitute a form of graphic fan fiction. As its primary function of conveying construction designs from architect to builders has evaporated, the blueprint has been colonised for new uses. Examples to be found online include reproductions of original blueprints for buildings that exist in reality but belong to the past, such as the Golden Gate Bridge in San Francisco, and bogus blueprints for actual objects that once existed, such as a

"Wright Brothers" aeroplane "drawn and researched by Herb Kelley." Blueprints of these kinds – the antiquated and the bogus – remove screenplays from the present, the future, and the actual. The "Wright Brothers 'Flyer'" implicitly calls into question the authority and authenticity of the Golden Gate Bridge blueprint, as the causal connection between the design and the product is broken. The fracture is taken further by examples of fantastic reverse engineering: the presentation of blueprints for structures that exist not in reality, but in imagination. The spacecraft Starship Enterprise, in actuality a combination of TV studio set and special effects model-work for the TV series *Star Trek: The Next Generation* (1987-94), has been reimagined as a blueprint in an act of graphic fan fiction, now available to buy on eBay. The blueprint's characteristic white lines and text on a blue background are here employed to lend a spurious documentary authority to something that has never existed, and never will. The blueprint is made to serve not only an industrial paradigm, but one that is unrealisable. Although it might, theoretically, be possible to construct a spaceship, the Golden Gate Bridge, or a primitive biplane from these blueprints, that is clearly not (or, in the case of the bridge, no longer) their purpose. Just as "steampunk" combines the antique and futuristic, so "blueprints" of spaceships conjoin past and future technologies in a perverse alternative present. While the blueprint metaphor promoted by Staiger may loosely fit the industrial model shared by Hollywood and American civil engineering in the 1920s, the same can't be said for the decades that followed. To claim in the 1980s that a screenplay is a blueprint, as screenwriting teacher Irwin Blacker does, or like Robin Russin and William Downs to repeat that claim in the twenty-first century, is to associate it with things that never were, and others that never could be.

Objection Three: the blueprint metaphor connotes the industrial rather than the artisanal, despite the fact that screenplays have not routinely been written in what could be described as an industrial environment since the "writers' buildings" of classical-era Hollywood studios (see Chapter 3). This emphasis on the industrial, however appropriate it may be to an analysis of the mid-twentieth-century Hollywood studio system, tends to overshadow the artisanal nature of the screenplay within the filmmaking practices that succeeded, and preceded, the classical studio period. When Staiger asserts that "the manufacturers transformed the theatrical and vaudeville script into their working blueprint for the film," the creative associations that gather around "theatrical" and to a lesser extent "vaudeville" are overshadowed, perhaps even cancelled out, by the rhetoric of industry.

It's relatively uncontentious to situate writers of screenplays as "workers" and part of the "labor force" within the classical period studio, where the notion of an assembly line can be extended to encompass screenplays written and rewritten by multiple employees at the direction of the management. "A screenwriter's output under a studio contract," notes Norman, "was 'a work for hire,' meaning piece-work, performed for a salary, the same as electricians and stage carpenters." An employee on an assembly line may take responsibility for the part she has made, but not for the finished product. Anecdotal evidence of the attitudes of contracted writers working en masse for Warner Brothers or MGM suggests that many of them regarded the screenplays on which they worked in much the same way as a worker at the Ford Motor Company might view his task on the production line. Dore Schary, a writer before he became a studio executive, told Columbia chief Harry Cohn that he would "write what I was asked to write." Schary saw himself as a worker for hire, writing to order in return for money. Employees working within an industrial conception of screenplay-writing are characterised as wage-slaves, something endorsed by the blueprint metaphor.

However, in later periods, screenplays have been written mostly by self-employed freelances, as the many screenwriting manuals make plain. When a single writer develops a story idea through multiple script drafts, often (if writing on spec) outside the confines of a formal contract, the analogy with manufacturing industries, and their division of complex tasks into repeated simple operations, becomes still less appropriate.

For the freelance screenwriters and those aspiring to join their numbers who constitute much of the readership for the manuals from the 1970s onwards, credit is often seen as being at least as important as money. As screenplay guru Truby said in a 2016 interview, "The currency in professional writing is not money, it's credits." Production line workers aren't individually credited for their output. Freelance writers building a career outside a studio system, on the contrary, need credits to establish themselves as skilled practitioners, just as artisans and craftspeople do. In this context screenplays have more in common with the products of other artisanal crafts, for instance in the plastic arts, than with those rolling off the end of a production line at the Ford Motor Company. To freelances writing screenplays, credits are essential for demonstrating competence: for example, prowess in a particular genre, such as the thriller, or in a specific subset of screenplay skills, such as dialogue. This isn't applicable to writers working on contract within the studio system, however, under which they might or might not be accorded credit, more or less at the whim of management.

Objection Four: the blueprint metaphor is mechanistic. Blueprints are sets of instructions for the construction of material objects such as bridges and houses using tools and technology. As a metaphor for screenplays, the blueprint imposes on them a limiting mechanistic conception that belies their actual function in film production. The mechanistic associations of the blueprint metaphor are evident in screenwriting manuals' obsession with structure, expressed in the same vocabulary as the heavy industry from which the blueprint derives: character is the "foundation of your screenplay," writes Field, who goes on to explain the process of "building" it. Although McKee's *Story* avoids invoking the blueprint directly, the diagrams that he marshals to make certain points are sets of instructions that mimic the precision of technical drawings. His visualisation of "The Gap in Progression" is a schematic diagram, employing graphic symbols to represent abstract screenplay elements ("Protagonist," "Object of desire") in the same way that a blueprint employs graphic symbols to represent physical ones, such as the girders and rivets of the Golden Gate Bridge. In the case of McKee's diagram, however, this precision is an illusion. Constructing a bridge is literally a mechanical process, while "constructing" a screenplay isn't. Builders construct a bridge using physical tools and materials, while a writer "constructs" a screenplay using symbolic words, some of which represent the nonliteral. In another of McKee's visualisations, "cast design" is presented as a technical diagram. Here the model is borrowed from astronomy: "Imagine a cast as a kind of solar system with the protagonist as the sun, supporting roles as planets around the sun, bit players as satellites around the planets – all held in orbit by the gravitational pull of the star at the center, each pulling at the tides of the others' natures:" As with the "Gap in Progression," McKee conceptualises relationships in physical terms, here as though a screenplay's cast members were analogous to planets orbiting the sun. He presents the psychological and symbolic as though it were reducible to the physical and concrete. McKee's employment of scientific metaphors also seems incongruous with his attack on Christian Metz's "effort to turn art to science" (see Chapter 1). He appears prepared to embrace science in support of structuralism in screenwriting manuals, but not semiotic structures in film theory. The result is to confuse rather than clarify what screenplays are and how they function.

Objection Five: by conceptualising screenplays in graphic terms, the blueprint metaphor ignores their identity as verbal texts. Words do appear in the blueprints of the Golden Gate Bridge and the Starship Enterprise, but their role is subsidiary, providing details and titles. It's the images denoted by white lines against blue backgrounds that constitute their primary component. A simple blueprint, or the overall design of a more complex one, can be taken in by someone looking at it almost instantaneously. The process of reading a screenplay, by contrast, is often compared to that of watching a film, and may take as long: hence, the "one minute to a page rule," by which widely accepted standardisations of screenplay format are supposed to produce a printed document of as many pages as there will be minutes in the completed film. Thus a screenplay functions chronologically, as a film does; like film it is a time-based medium, although much more elastic. The blueprint metaphor gives no sense of how a screenplay reader's engagement is a temporal rather than a static process. This can be illustrated by the common device (advocated in many screenwriting manuals) of withholding information to create suspense or mystery. Truby, for example, advises screenwriting tutees to "try *withholding* a lot of information," while McKee tells them that "Curiosity and Concern create three possible ways to connect the audience to the story: Mystery, Suspense, and Dramatic Irony." This withholding of information would be not only perverse for a blueprint to attempt but also impossible to achieve.

Objection Six: the blueprint metaphor encourages writers to represent themselves as technicians. By embracing the definition of the screenplay as the blueprint for a film, some screenwriting manuals of the later twentieth century make writers themselves complicit in their own de-skilling, defining themselves as technicians rather than creative authors and artistic collaborators. "A screenplay is simply a blueprint for making a film," insists Blacker. It's a modest claim for a professional screenwriter and influential teacher of screenwriting. According to Blacker's obituary in the *New York Times*, he taught from the mid-1960s until 1978 at the University of Southern California, where his students included George Lucas (*Star Wars*). Russin and Downs have a similar message for readers of their manual in 2012: "[S]creenplays are not intended as literature. They are blueprints for films." Such views ignore the fact that screenplays aren't in fact blueprints, but writing.

Objection Seven: the blueprint metaphor reinforces the notion of a separation between conception and execution. By separating conception from execution, as in Staiger's ideological framing of the Hollywood film industry, the blueprint metaphor reduces the screenplay to little more than a record of plans conceived by management. In the auteurist variant of this separation, articulated originally by François Truffaut, the screenplay is viewed as the starting block for the director's imagination. By contrast, Alfred Hitchcock, happy to be classified as an auteur by Truffaut and others, nonetheless located his authorship not in direction but in his work on the screenplay. In interviews he suggests that execution is little more than a directorial chore. Truffaut reports Hitchcock's comment that "a film is ninety-nine percent finished with the screenplay. Sometimes, I'd prefer not to have to shoot it. You conceive the film you want and after that everything goes to pieces."

The separation of conception and execution implicit in the blueprint and related industrial/mechanical metaphors can be used to support diametrically opposing views: the screenplay that contains everything, and the screenplay that offers the director carte blanche. Thus some directors invoke the blueprint metaphor in order to contest its apparent claims to control, as when John Schlesinger insists that "it's ridiculous to regard the script as the final absolute blueprint." Others, such as Nicholas Ray, invoke the same metaphor to illustrate its limitations: "even the best-written script is a blueprint for the director." In actual practice, any clear separation between conception and execution is difficult to discern. Price has shown in his study of *The Birds* that conception may have begun with (or before) the screenplay, but it continues throughout development, shooting and post-production, which most regard as stages of the film's execution.

Objection Eight: the blueprint metaphor removes the writer from the creative process. In discussing *The Birds* (1963), Hitchcock may focus on the screenplay as the conceptual be-all and end-all of the project; but in the process he erases the actual screenwriter responsible for it, Evan Hunter. Attention is directed away from Hunter, towards Hitchcock the (re-)writer and Hitchcock the director. This is possible in part because, as a technical document, the blueprint isn't acknowledged to be authored in the way that other kinds of texts are. Thus the blueprint metaphor is tainted with associations of anonymity and erasure for the writer. After all, the characteristic response to a blueprint isn't, "Who wrote this?" but, "How do we make it?". Thus by association authorship becomes an irrelevant concept, and the writer of the screenplay, as Hunter knew, is liable to disappear from view, however significant his role may be.

Objection Nine: the blueprint is overly specific. The essential function of the practical, as against the historical or fantastical, blueprint is to specify, in the sense of providing detailed technical specifications. If it were not specific, its execution would be impossible or fantastical. This isn't always the case with screenplays. In Raymond Chandler's and Billy Wilder's script for *Double Indemnity* (1944), made at the point where beyond Hollywood blueprints were being replaced by whiteprints, the level of specificity is indeed high:

```
A-11   INT. NEFF'S OFFICE - DARK

       Three desks, filing cabinets, one
       typewriter on stand, one dictaphone
       on fixed stand against wall with
       rack of records underneath,
       telephones on all three desks.
       Water cooler with inverted bottle
       and paper cup holder beside it. Two
       windows facing towards front of
       building. Venetian blinds. No
       curtains. Waste basket full, ash
       trays not emptied. The office has
       not been cleaned.

       Neff enters, switches on desk lamp.
       He looks across at dictaphone, goes
       heavily to it and lifts off the
       fabric cover. He leans down hard on
       the dictaphone stand as if feeling
       faint. He turns away from
       dictaphone, takes a few uncertain
       steps and falls heavily into a
       swivel chair. He goes far back, his
       eyes close, cold sweat shows on his
       face.
```

Here the analogy holds, at least in general terms: there is sufficient information to allow the set to be designed and propped (and the cost of that calculated), and for Neff's actions to be visualised in terms of lighting and equipment requirements, and even make-up. The Paramount Pictures style of scene numbering ("A-11") forms part of a larger industrial system designed to promote efficiency. Even so, there remains much that isn't specified by the screenplay: we don't know the make of the typewriters, nor the shape of the water cooler. What the waste basket is full of – screwed-up paper, empty whiskey bottles, copies of *Partisan Review*? – isn't specified, although this might be significant in terms of characterisation or narrative. Nor is the fact that Neff is to be played by the actor Fred MacMurray – something likely to affect many aspects of the film's execution and its subsequent reception. We aren't told how many shots there are in this part of the sequence, what sizes they will be, or how they're to be lit. We can't tell whether special equipment, such as a crane, might be required, or indeed whether the camera is moving on a dolly, or static.

This level of non-specificity wouldn't be tolerated in an actual architectural blueprint. Sheet no. 4 of Clifford C. Paine's blueprint for the "BOTTOM LATERAL SYSTEM TYPICAL CENTER SPAN PANEL" of the Golden Gate Bridge specifies not only the overall structure (the focus of most screenplay manuals) but also the material to be used ("Structural Carbon Steel"), and full details down the size of the rivets (three-eighths of an inch). Crucially, the level of specificity is sufficient for two or more different fabricators or construction managers to arrive at the same result. What the blueprint specifies isn't, of course, comprehensive. Subsidiary documents might set out secondary details, such as how the bridge is to be painted and the road surface applied. Nonetheless, no screenplay could aspire to the same level of material or spatial specificity. Indeed, screenplays aren't particularly suitable for the task of specifying, and often they appear to accord it a low priority. It could be argued that the extract from *Double Indemnity* contains enough information to qualify as an "industrial planning document." Yet the same couldn't be said of another widely admired screenplay, written three decades later:

```
FULL SCREEN PHOTOGRAPH

     grainy but unmistakably a man and woman
     making love. Photograph shakes. SOUND of
     a man MOANING in anguish. The photograph
     is dropped, REVEALING ANOTHER, MORE
     compromising one. Then another, and
     another. More moans.

                    CURLY'S VOICE
              (crying out)
           Oh, no.

INT. GITTES' OFFICE

     CURLY drops the photos on Gittes' desk.
     Curly towers over GITTES and sweats
     heavily through his workman's clothes,
     his breathing progressively more labored.
     A drop plunks on Gittes' shiny desk top.
```

The third draft of Robert Towne's screenplay *Chinatown* does provide usable and material information to its readers – but not as much as it withholds. As with the introduction of Walter Neff at the start of *Double Indemnity* two pages before the description of his office, the writer is more interested in creating a sense of mystery about the characters, one that remains present in the subsequent film.

Actual blueprints are solely concerned with the making of material, spatial objects, while writing of all kinds (including that of screenplays) conveys much more, including tone, mood, subjectivity, beliefs, ideologies, attitudes, what has passed, and what is to come. While a film may also be credited with these things, and even a building made from a blueprint may share some of them, blueprints contain substantially less rich and diverse elements. Crediting filmic effects solely to the director or to the non-verbal aspects of a film, and removing the role of writing in creating these, falsifies the actual process of film production.

The *Chinatown* screenplay exceeds the spatial and visual instructions of a blueprint. Towne's words are attuned to the nuances of storytelling and creating a fictional world. "A drop plunks on Gittes' shiny desk top," he writes, and the semi-onomatopoeic verb contributes to the evocation of the scene in the film-to-be, with its combination of visual and aural information. The action lines have a self-consciously expressive quality that doesn't evoke a blueprint. They also help set the film's tone, which includes an element of sardonic humour; "plunks" is jaunty, enjoying the inappropriateness of Curly's sweat droplet splashing onto the "shiny" desk. Beyond that, Curly's unwelcome sweat-drop joins other symbolic images indicating that he's brought the brutish physicality of the outside world into Gittes's artificial, manicured cocoon. Gittes's "white linen suit" juxtaposed with Curly's "workman's clothes," the "signed photos of several movie stars" upset by Curly's kick, the resulting "noticeable dent" in Gittes's wastebasket all indicate that Gittes will have to deal with that world no matter how hard he tries to avoid it. This theme, central to both screenplay and film, inheres in the accumulation of such small physical details. Chandler and Wilder, too, go beyond the simple provision of factual information. When they write of Neff that "cold sweat shows on his face," the cause of this (a gunshot wound) is withheld; so, alongside giving implicit instructions for the make-up department, their scene creates suspense that draws readers into its world and its story.

Ambiguity is excluded as far as possible from a blueprint, while screenplays may accentuate it for narrative effect. An apparently insignificant line of dialogue, such as the secretary's remark that "A Mrs. Mulwray is waiting" for Gittes, turns out to have a second, contradictory meaning: that this isn't *the* Mrs Mulwray, but another one, in fact a woman impersonating her – an important plot point later on.

While the blueprint is generally concerned with denoting the literal, screenplays instead seize opportunities to connote the symbolic. Applying Roland Barthes's distinction between the denotative and connotative highlights the layered meanings within screenplays and their uses of the literal, spatial, visual, and audible to convey cultural and ideological codes, thus greatly exceeding the merely denotative role of specification. In *Chinatown*, the drop of sweat is the first of many references to oppressive heat that presses the literal towards the symbolic and metaphorical. Los Angeles is trapped in a heatwave; water is scarce, and a moral drought matches the meteorological one. Water's scarce because it's being stolen and dumped to aid a political conspiracy; heat and drought threaten not just the protagonist but the entire city (and, by extension, the world). At the centre of the screenplay is the choice that Gittes must make to leave his climate-controlled life and re-engage with sweat, dirt, and blood.

Just as screenplays may do more than blueprints, so they may also do less. The one piece of specifying information that the screenplay's readers from film production departments need more than any other about *Chinatown* – that it's set not in the 1970s, when the screenplay was written, but in the 1930s – is absent from Towne's screenplay. The writer is more concerned to create a connotative layer than to specify a denotative one. Denotation, which one would expect to be the primary concern of an industrial planning document, is far from being the first priority here.

In more recent screenplays, this tendency to emphasise the connotative at the expense of the denotative expands. While the composition of a blueprint, with its lines and angles, changes little over the decades in which films are purportedly being made according to screenplay "blueprints," the symbolic language of the screenplay becomes more connotative over time and across cultures. The art department staff who would have found hard data about Walter Neff's office in *Double Indemnity*, and hints of Jake Gittes's from *Chinatown*, might struggle to extract similar information about the living room in the opening scenes of Charlie Kaufman's *Adaptation*:

```
EXT. ROCKY TERRAIN - DAY


Endless barren landscape. No sign of
life. The atmosphere is hazy,
toxic-looking. Volcanoes erupt. Meteors
bombard. Lightning strikes, concussing
murky pools of water. Silence.


INT. LARGE EMPTY LIVING ROOM - MORNING


SUBTITLE: HOLLYWOOD, CA, FOUR BILLION AND
FORTY YEARS LATER


Beamed ceilings and ostentatious
fireplace. A few birthday cards on the
mantel, two of them identical: "To Our
Dear Son on His Fortieth Birthday."
Charlie Kaufman, a fat, balding man in a
purple sweater with tags still attached,
paces the room. His incantational
voice-over carpets the scene.


                    KAUFMAN (V.O.)
          I am old. I am fat. I am bald.
          My toenails have turned
```

> strange. I am repulsive. How
> repulsive? I don't know for I
> suffer from a condition called
> Body Dysmorphic Disorder. I am
> fat, but am I as fat as I
> think? My therapist says no,
> but people lie. I believe
> others call me Fatty behind my
> back. Or Fatso. Or,
> facetiously, Slim. But I also
> believe this is simply my own
> perverted form of self-
> aggrandizement, that no one
> really talks about me at all.
> What possible interest is an
> old, bald, fat man to anyone?
> I am repulsive. I have never
> lived. I blame myself...

There's more sweat a few pages on, when "Charlie Kaufman" (the character) is given lunch by Valerie, and heat has nothing to do with it – this time it's the sweat of self-loathing and his fear of attractive women that soaks our hero from one end of the screenplay to the other. Even the living room is limited to giving glimpses into the character, its "beamed ceilings and ostentatious fireplace" indicating his grandiosity and the "few birthday cards on the mantel, two of them identical" his social isolation and identity as an identical twin. Nor is the art department being invited to create a proto-Earth – the description is part of Kaufman's ironic grandiosity rather than the production design challenge it might have been for an ambitious epic during Hollywood's first "golden age."

This isn't to suggest that most screenplays don't contain useful information for production departments. The point is rather that the notion of an industrial planning document limited to instructing production designers, costumers, and directors how to make the picture doesn't describe screenplays adequately. Although the sweat in the screenplay must be brought into existence by a make-up assistant standing by with a water spray or glycerine, its metaphorical significance is greater than its physical importance, and has increased between *Chinatown* and *Adaptation*. What these screenplays *suggest* is as least as important as what they specify.

The blueprint metaphor persists because it corresponds in several ways to how screenplays are widely perceived. However, in doing so it emphasises certain aspects while minimising others. Those it emphasises – associations with the anachronistic, redundant, industrial, pictorial, technical, denotative, objective, specific – all play down the function of writing in the screenplay. In particular the blueprint metaphor diminishes the characteristics that writing in screenplays shares with other kinds of writing. Aspects that it minimises, meanwhile, serve to remove the writer of a screenplay from the picture, or at least to demote her or him to a skilled but non-creative technician. Together these tendencies encourage both readers and writers to view screenplays as a passive form of communication rather than as active agents in the making of films.

Despite these objections, the blueprint metaphor continues to be widely used in various screenplay discourses of all kinds. Pedagogy will continue to act as a vector of its survival for as long as film studies textbooks, particularly those aimed at school students, go on referencing it. *The Writers' Store*, which claims to be "The Premier Resource For Writing And Filmmaking Tools," demonstrates its currency. "At its heart," according to this popular screenwriting website in mid-2020, "a screenplay is a blueprint for the film it will one day become." The blueprint metaphor may be dead in screenplay theory, and not workable or operative in filmmaking practice, but in screenplay discourse it refuses to lie down Despite the reservations of scholars, it keeps recurring, sometimes in strange company, as in the hybrid industrial-Romantic imagery of screenplays that are blueprints with hearts. The semantic confusion of this image corresponds to other contradictions found in screenplay discourse, on which subsequent chapters expand.

3

WRITING AND READING SCREENPLAYS

*the more cinematic a script, the less can it
claim literary status in its own right*

Andrey Tarkovsky

Even when screenplays are acknowledged – unlike blueprints – to be a kind of writing, the nature of their writing and of their reading is fiercely contested. It's time to look at some of these arguments more closely.

"Films aren't based on writing"

I write cinema.

Michael Mann

The dream of a film that owes nothing to words has haunted screenplay history and discourse from their earliest days to the present. In 1915, Vachel Lindsay characterises films as "sculpture-in-motion," "paintings-in-motion," and "architecture-in-motion," relating the new "Art of the Moving Picture" back to three emphatically non-verbal fine art forms. Nearly a century later, Steven Maras looks forward to modes of "[d]igital [s]scriptings" that eschew the verbal in favour of "computer programming, motion-capture, algorithmic decision-making, interactivity, dynamic media, and avatars." This dream does have some correlatives in actuality. During the first period of the American film industry, the stage that Janet Staiger identifies as the "'cameraman' system of production (1896-

1907)," scripts of any kind were considered unnecessary due to the simplicity of the production process, which involved only a single person. Thus the vast majority of filmmaking, in which screenplays have a significant function, is sandwiched between a remote past and an imagined future, in both of which that role is severely diminished or non-existent.

Scholars and filmmakers also argue that improvised films don't require the writing of screenplays. Yet improvisation doesn't always indicate the absence of written screenplays. It can certainly be traced back to the very earliest days of cinema, before scripting became established as the norm, and surfaces in the work of admired mid-century filmmakers, including Roberto Rossellini, as well as in the techniques of American filmmakers such as John Cassavetes, often credited as a founding father of American independent cinema. "Rossellini was opposed to scripts, to written forms of cinema, to a prewriting of cinema," writes Kathryn Millard. Yet she also acknowledges that his most admired films "such as *Shoeshine* and *Bicycle Thieves* were based on fully drafted screenplays, with [Cesare] Zavattini leading a team of writers." Indeed, Steven Price identifies Zavattini as "the brilliant writer who was as responsible as any director for the achievements of Italian neo-realism," emphasising his construction of "tight, carefully shaped stories." Rossellini himself has 46 credits as writer on IMDb, close to his 51 as director (some of which are documentaries); Zavattini, meanwhile, has 115 writing credits. Although Millard insists on Rossellini's opposition to scripts, it seems clear that he used them. For Millard, a key qualification lies in the fluidity of his screenplays ("these were fluid rather than fixed documents"); nonetheless, his improvisation was based on written screenplays.

Just as scholars have downplayed or overlooked screenplays in the work of Italian neo-realists, scholars have also obscured the role of screenplays in the films of Cassavetes.

Improvisation, for Cassavetes, was a preliminary process that grew *out* of a screenplay (which could be extremely long), rather than feeding *into* it. What actors said and did on set (as against the way they said and did them) was determined beforehand, in the screenplay. Only the first version of Cassavetes's first film, *Shadows* (1958), was made without a screenplay. Cassavetes considered this film to be a failure and remade a scripted version of the film the following year. The personal films that followed, while making the most of the actors' input during improvisation, were also based on screenplays by the writer-director. "'There aren't ten lines improvised in all of *Minnie and Moskovitz*,'" Johnny told me," reports William Froug. Cassavetes believed in "sticking to the script."

Written screenplays also play important roles in the films of improvisational British directors Ken Loach and Mike Leigh. Although sometimes bracketed together in books of film criticism, Loach's mildly propagandist social realism is distinct from the frequently satirical drama found in Leigh's films. While both employ unconventional methods in their work with screenplays, those methods differ. Loach's frequent collaborator, screenwriter Paul Laverty, explains their procedures:

> There's lots of misconceptions about how Ken works. People put him together with Mike Leigh and he's the exact opposite, there couldn't be two more different ways of working. Mike Leigh, as I understand it, meets the actors, improvises the screenplay with them. Whereas I write the screenplay, then I meet Ken and we discuss it with [script editor] Roger Smith. Then Ken never gives them the screenplay at all... But we don't incorporate what we learn from the impro-

> visations into the screenplay, the screenplay's done way before we do that.

It's clear from Laverty's account that, despite the use of improvisation, the screenplays that he writes for Loach function much as others do within the mainstream Anglo-American commercial film industry.

Leigh, also famous for employing improvisation, is nonetheless clear that he writes screenplays as well as directing films; something recognised in his five sole nominations for screenplay Academy Awards. Like Loach, he writes before shooting begins. The lengthy period of improvisation with actors is part of the development, not the production process: "I create scenes distilled from improvisations... what I do is create the dialogue, the physical action and the subtext all at the same time, as a whole." This development process is liable to take many months. Then, "once we've got the script, it's solid. We've already arrived at what we want, so there's no reason to deviate." In the cases of both Leigh and Loach, then, screenplays are written before filming and play a similar role to those of other screenplays, in spite of their improvisational methods.

Although there are instances of films produced without written screenplays that have flourished within the mainstream, closer inspection usually uncovers writing that functions in a similar way to screenplays. Richard Linklater's second feature, *Slacker* (1991), is a low-budget non-studio film that crossed over into the mainstream and found a wide audience. According to J.J. Murphy, "So convincingly does *Slacker*'s dialogue succeed in capturing the realistic sound of actual talk that many viewers mistakenly assume that it's been improvised on the spot rather than scripted." Unlike Loach and Leigh, Linklater – who enjoys comparable status to that of Cassavetes for a later generation of American independent filmmakers – did not have a written screenplay before he began shooting. However, he did have another written document, "a roughly fifteen-page treatment that contained fifty-five scenes." Following the film's eventual success, the "screenplay" was published, but, according to Murphy, "it's simply a trans-cription of what actually ended up on the screen. In other words, the script was created after the fact." *Slacker* may not have utilised a full screenplay, but nor did it realise the dream of a film without words, based as it is on a written document.

A more recent film, *Like Crazy* (2011), also went into production with a written treatment rather than a conventional screenplay. As the winner of the 2011 Grand Jury Prize Dramatic at the Sundance Film Festival, *Like Crazy* attracted considerable attention, partly for its employment of improvisation and lack of a conventional screenplay. However, director Drake Doremus explained that he "started with a very specific 50-page outline, which had scene objectives, plot, themes – everything. In fact, I think it's even more specific than a normal script because it's got back-story and things that a normal script doesn't have." Once again, this is a film based firmly on writing. Subsequent films by Doremus such as *Breathe In* (2013), *Zoe* (2018), and *Endings, Beginnings* (2019) similarly credit him not only as director but also as co-writer.

Some filmmakers argue against improvisation on the basis of the damage it can do to the words of a film. As director Sidney Lumet writes, "Words are critical. And most actors aren't writers, nor are most directors." Improvisation by non-writers can diminish the verbal facility of a film by contrast to a film based on the writing of a screenplay.

Support for the notion that screenplays aren't writing comes on occasion from the very people who've written them. Animation has been a substantial sector of the film industry from its early days, and its relationship to the written screenplay differs from that of live-action films. Animated films have lengthy production schedules within which screenplay-writing and filming often proceed in parallel. This leads some practitioners to dismiss the screenplay. Andrew Stanton, who co-wrote many of Pixar's commercial and critical hits (including *Toy Story* and *WALL-E*), said in a speech that what enabled him "to enter this craft was the realisation that screenwriting is not writing." He describes the screenplay as "not something to be held up and read as a finished piece." Instead, "It's a means of documenting cinematic storytelling." Yet it's clear that Pixar does employ written screenplays, and that these do indeed function as writing, however their writers choose to describe them. This is evident from the large number of writers accorded screenplay credits on them (see Chapter 3, section 6). Words form part of the filmmaking process, even if screenwriting and production proceed simultaneously, and words remain in the completed films in the form of dialogue – a key element in the success of *Toy Story* and its successors.

Given the overwhelming evidence to the contrary, why do scholars, directors, and even screenwriters declare screenplays and other writings that form the bases of films to be "not writing," and deny that film is based in writing? The answer lies in the commonplace fallacy that film is a visual and not a verbal medium, and that in a visual medium words are fundamentally "uncinematic."

"Film is visual not verbal and words are uncinematic"

Less extreme than the dream of a film without words, but also unsupported by evidence from actual film practice, is the argument made by some scholars and directors that film is inherently a visual and not a verbal medium. Words, this argument implies, have no place in film, nor do they constitute a solid ground for it. Adaptation scholar Thomas Leitch has described the claim that "Literary texts are verbal, films visual" as "the most enduring and pernicious" of "all the explicitly stated fallacies that have substituted for theoretical principles in adaptation study." Films, as Leitch points out, "have not been purely visual for at least seventy-five years." Besides making telling points about the "sound-driven radio aesthetics" brought into film by *Citizen Kane* as far back as 1941, Leitch observes that films' "actual signifying system... is a great deal more subtle and complex than visual iconicity." Even in the earliest period when films were silent, written words still permeated them, from the early forms of the screenplay that preceded shooting to the images of text and intertitles projected onto the screen. Subsequently, with the advent of synchronised dialogue in 1927, the role of the verbal expanded substantially. Words written in screenplays became words spoken by actors, and thus an integral part of the cinema experience for audiences and filmmakers. As Lumet points out, "Dialogue is not uncinematic. So many of the movies of the thirties and forties that we adore are constant streams of dialogue." It's also the case that dialogue might be valued more than star performers, even by as "cinematic" a director as Alfred Hitchcock. Ernest Lehman describes a discussion about the screenplay and casting of *North By Northwest* (1959): "I told Hitch, 'There's a lot of dialogue in here for [protagonist] Roger Thornhill, and with Jimmy Stewart, it'll go on forever.' He agreed with me. So I wrote this for Cary Grant, which is a big advantage." Choosing fast-talking Grant instead of the ponderous Stewart in order to avoid the need to cut Lehman's words is a clear acknowledgment of their importance.

Even so, dialogue, the principal verbal element of the screenplay to survive the transition from page to screen, is often singled out for particular disrespect. Discussing early narrative films, Price makes an evaluative distinction between action and dialogue in a way that awards higher "cinematic" status to the former. "If the AM&B scripts look like stage plays but without dialogue, *The Serenade* is a sloppily presented and exceptionally badly written draft, apparently intended for theatrical staging, dialogue-intensive and virtually unfilmable." An implicit connection is made here between "dialogue-intensive" and "virtually unfilmable," echoing the commonly held notion that dialogue is intrinsically "uncinematic." Price contrasts *The Serenade* with another proto-screenplay, "evenly divided between dialogue and stage directions," which he judges to be "a more satisfying balance between scene text and dialogue." Here Price adopts the terminology proposed by Claudia Sternberg:

> Rather than simply adapting Roman Ingarden's terms "main text" and "side text," generally used in drama theory to distinguish speech and non-speech passages (1973b [1960]: 208ff.), the less hierarchical terms dialogue text and scene text are introduced here to demarcate the dividing line between drama and screenplay.

However, despite Sternberg's concern to accord equal status to both kinds of words, Price reinstates the same hierarchy by implying that the less dialogue and the more scene text, the better. Dialogue, after all, is made of words that will remain words in the scene, a residue that resists metamorphosis by the alchemy of cinema into new visual and aural forms. Later Price praises the "prose" of another screenwriter as "remarkably lean and cinematic, with... little sign of authorial narration or comment." To be "cinematic," it appears, is to restrict words (and especially dialogue) as much as possible.

Voiceover is often considered even less acceptable than dialogue to devotees of "pure" cinema, while several screenwriting manuals forbid readers to use it. Leitch has identified a similar fallacy operating within the field of literary film adaptation: "Chatman, for instance, dismisses explicitly descriptive voiceover commentary in movies as uncinematic." Yet would anybody writing today, Leitch goes on to ask, "argue that the highly assertive and descriptive voiceover commentary by the murdered Joe Gillis in *Sunset Boulevard* (1950), a film not adapted from a literary source, was inessential to the film's effect?" Indeed, Price springs to the defence of this particular voiceover, noting that the screenplay of *Sunset Boulevard* "is a celebration of the talk and words that not only Norma, but a dominant tradition in film theory, wish to suffocate out of existence." Price supports words here, where they link with the film's themes and topics, yet elsewhere rejects them as a formal element for conveying cinematic experience.

One reason for the opprobrium that voiceover attracts is its self-conscious wordiness, the sense that it conveys of a writer knowingly verbalising, interposing his or her words and presence between a film's audience and its mise-en-scène. While in *Sunset Boulevard* the voiceover doesn't gesture to the actual screenwriter, but to a character-narrator, subsequent writers of self-reflexive screenplays such as Charlie Kaufman's *Adaptation* (2002) have extended it to assert their own writerly presence in film:

```
                    KAUFMAN (V.O.)
           I should leave here right now.
           I'll start over--
               (starts to rise)
           I need to face this project
           head on and --

                    MCKEE
           ... and God help you if you
           use voice-over in your work,
           my friends.
```

> Kaufman stops, looks up, startled. McKee
> seems to be looking directly at him.

>   MCKEE
> God fucking help you! It's
> flaccid, sloppy writing. Any
> idiot can write voice-over
> narration to explain the
> thoughts of a character. You
> must present the internal
> conflicts of your character in
> image, in symbol. Film is a
> medium of movement and image.

Kaufman has fun with the proscriptive tone common in screenwriting manuals and seminars, simultaneously employing and making fun of voiceover. He mocks himself and teases screenwriting guru Robert McKee while he's about it in a way that draws attention to the artificial, verbally constructed nature of the *Adaptation* screenplay. In *Story* the real McKee's attitude to voiceover is slightly less denunciatory. While he does warn against abusing it and "turning the cinema into what was once known as Classic Comic Books," he also praises Woody Allen for his use of "[c]ounterpoint narration," a term that seems equally applicable to Charlie Kaufman. Nonetheless, McKee acknowledges the perceived threat to cinema posed by a second level of spoken words overlaid on top of dialogue.

Other authors of screenwriting manuals warn their readers that the use of voiceover could open them to accusations of writing "uncinematic" words. "Nowadays," warn Robin Russin and William Downs in 2012, "narrative *voice-overs* (V.O.) are generally looked down on as non-cinematic," although they go on to acknowledge that "used effectively" voiceover can be a "wonderful tool." Syd Field asserts that "Voice-over is a very effective cinematic device," while Linda Seger warns that it "can easily make a story talky." Viki King explains what voiceover is, but instructs her readers that "your writing shouldn't show," discouraging anything that draws attention to words and writing, almost as though these were shameful.

The manual authors who embrace voiceover tend, like Kaufman, to value its ability to challenge surface readings and to multiply possible meanings. Voiceover, as Josh Golding puts it in *Maverick Screenwriting* (2012), undermines "the reality or truth of appearances," often using words spoken by a narrator to question other words spoken in dialogue by different characters. It is thus a common device in "puzzle films" from *Sunset Boulevard* and *Citizen Kane* to *Fight Club* (1999) and *Memento* (2000). Nevertheless, Golding, like King, warns that it "should be approached with caution." It can be dangerous for screenplays to draw attention to their own words.

Antagonism towards the verbal as the enemy of the visual isn't limited to manual authors: it has also been a persistent theme in film criticism and scholarship. Despite their importance to film, words have consistently been marginalised, obscured, ignored, and distorted in accounts that, over-whelmingly, choose to ignore their crucial role in this supposedly "visual" medium, as Kamilla Elliott has demonstrated in *Rethinking the Novel/Film Debate* (2009). "In 1998," she writes, "Bernard F. Dick put it this way: 'the script recedes into the background as it changes from a verbal to a visual text, so that by the time the film has been complete[d], the words have been translated into images.'" But, as Elliott points out, "Such a theory of filmmaking does not accord with aesthetic practice, for most screenplays consist primarily of dialogue, which transfers directly into film as words." Elliott posits this implacable antipathy towards the verbal as something so fundamental to the various theoretical positions underpinning film studies that "one could argue that the destruction and dominance of the word constitutes a principal aesthetic of film theory." Seen from this perspective "[f]ilm words" are cast "as literary, uncinematic other." Similarly, James Schamus, a practitioner-scholar who combines a background in the academy with a successful career as a Hollywood producer, has identified '"the embedding of the understanding of cinema in primarily a visual arts context" as an ongoing problem for independent cinema.

Discussing her own experience of film development, both as a writer-director and as a reader (for funding agencies) of other writers' screenplays, Millard criticises the focus in film development on the verbal. In all the deliberations about her project, *Travelling Light* (2003), "it was always invariably words on a page that were discussed, dissected and analysed, rather than images, sounds, gestures, rhythm of the cinematic qualities of the script." As she challenges the centrality of screenplays as writing to filmmaking, Millard makes the same distinction between the "cinematic qualities of the script" ("sounds, gestures, rhythm") and the implicitly uncinematic "words on a page." Accordingly, much of her book is devoted to alternative methods of screenwriting. When she challenges the "privileged position" of the "prewritten screenplay" and proposes other ways of working, it's words that she seeks to replace, suggesting that "writing is becoming more like photography" while "the digital screenwriter is a cine-composer." In common with the proponents of the blueprint metaphor, Millard metaphorises writing via static visual images. Beyond the visual/verbal dichotomy, she presses writing towards the nonverbal domain of music.

If words are being resisted as uncinematic in film, they enjoy higher status in television, resulting, in recent years, in a steady migration of film writers to the once despised medium. In *Difficult Men* (2013), an account of recent American TV drama series, Brett Martin points to defections by directors who have in their time been icons of "New Hollywood" and "independent" cinema:

> There might have been no more emblematic moment than when Martin Scorsese, hero of the seventies New Cinema, signed on to be an executive producer of *Boardwalk Empire* and to direct its pilot... Steven Soderbergh, a Scorsese of the indie film movement, was right behind [him]. After directing thirty-three movies, large and small, he told the Associated Press, he was giving up and switching to television.

These filmmakers, whose cinematic credentials are uncontested, and others like them, have in part chosen television alongside or even over cinema itself due to the greater opportunities it offers for complex, word-driven storytelling. "'American movie audiences now just don't seem to be very interested in any kind of ambiguity or any kind of real complexity of character or narrative,'" according to Soderbergh. "'I think those qualities are now being seen on television and that people who want to see stories that have those kind of qualities are watching television.'" His sentiments are echoed by story guru John Truby: "the best writing, the best stories in the world are on TV right now. TV is the most powerful writing medium in the world right now, and nothing else is even close." Soderbergh sees an attractive opportunity for people like him: "Directing does seem like the one area where television hasn't reached its full potential yet. The acting is great, the writing is great."

Television, in sharp contrast to film, is acknowledged to be a writer's medium rather than a director's one. In this new "Golden Age" of television drama, those responsible are, as in the previous ones, writers. Marc Norman, writing of the first "Golden Age" of television in the 1950s, quotes Gore Vidal: "We were the auteurs... Millions of people switched on to see our plays, not the actors, and never the directors." Vince Gilligan, creator of *Breaking Bad* (2008-13), explains that "'Historically, this [TV] has been a medium in which you say more than you show. You just didn't have the budgets and scheduling largesse that movies had, so you had to have two people in a room, talking it through.'" The implication is that if television could afford to be less wordy and more visual, it would be. And indeed, as television budgets and ambitions have increased, shows such as *Breaking Bad* have shown themselves eager to embrace the same hierarchy that privileges the visual over the verbal. As Martin notes:

> *Breaking Bad* is by far the most visually stylized show of the Third Golden Age. It employs and empties the entire filmic bag of tricks – from high-speed time-lapse montages to wide-open landscapes that are more John Ford than anything a revisionist [TV] western like *Deadwood* could ever allow itself.

In this writer-driven medium, Gilligan isn't just the creator of *Breaking Bad*. He was also its showrunner, a role combining the responsibilities of chief writer with those of executive producer and often, as here, lead director. The spread of the showrunner role is perhaps the best index of the writer's higher status in TV drama. It places her or (more often) him at the very centre of the enterprise. As showrunner, Gilligan directed the pilot of *Breaking Bad* and several other episodes, as well as choosing the other writers, producers, and directors. Indeed, the reduced status of the director in this "writers' medium" underlines the sense of frustration with film expressed by Soderbergh. According to *Mad Men* showrunner Matthew Wiener, "the director means *nothing*" in television. Even allowing for the gleeful overstatement of a showrunner, it's clear that ultimate authority on these projects rests not with directors but with writers. Sought-after directors such as Soderbergh who have moved from film to television must see powerful incentives that outweigh directors' loss of status and control, and these incentives cluster around the written screenplay.

Along with bigger budgets and more creative autonomy, those writing the screenplays that underpin television's third "Golden Age" may aspire to the same "cinematic" qualities that the medium has until recently been denied. When Froug, himself a television producer, interviewed twelve screenwriters in 1972, he argued that only economic pressures led them to work also in television. (This was a time of severe recession in the Hollywood film industry.) His first question to David Giler is, "Did you start as a screenwriter, or did you work your way 'up' through television?" Giler replies that his father, Bernie, a television writer, "presented the fine art of writing for TV as a trade – rather like plumbing. As something which, once learned, I could always have to fall back on if I failed at everything else." In the twenty-first century television's status has risen considerably, and with this change has come a shift in attention from the verbal to the visual. Martin notes of *Breaking Bad* that "the show is obsessed with the concrete and literal. The camera lingers with intense curiosity on significant objects – a broken pair of glasses, a box cutter, the missing eye of a stuffed animal – and on processes, How Things Work." This is a commitment to visual storytelling, to those values that have traditionally been associated with cinema rather than with television – showing, not telling. This commitment, however, is already present in the writing, in the words on the page of the screenplay:

Midway through season three, Gilligan said, [writer] Peter Gould had come up to him,

> beaming. "Look at my script that we're about to start shooting," Gould said. "I've counted and there's five uninterrupted pages where not a word of dialogue is spoken!"
>
> "I was so proud of him," Gilligan said. "I was like, 'Yeah, man, that's something to be excited about! That excites me, too!'"

For Gilligan and *Breaking Bad* this "cinematic" approach was a conscious strategy, played out not on set, but in the writers' room, and on the written pages of screenplay after screenplay. The show's visual aspects aren't viewed as being in competition with the verbal; instead, writers celebrate their ability to bring the visual into being through the verbal. At the same time, however, cinema's long-standing aversion to "uncinematic" dialogue is once again endorsed.

Alan Ball, writer of the original screenplay *American Beauty* (1999), as well as many television episodes, says, "when I'm writing for the medium of film, which is a visual medium, I write visually." Worded thus, Ball accepts the visuality of film without denying the verbal nature of his own screenplay. "I see the shots," he says; "I put them on paper." Words both create the objective visuality of the film *American Beauty* subsequently realised by the material processes of production, and also describe the subjective visuality of the writer's imagination, as "shots" that can't yet be seen in actuality but can be verbalised "on paper." For writers such as Ball (also showrunner of the television series *True Blood* from 2008 to 2012) and Gilligan, who began his career as a movie screenwriter, television offers the appeal of continuous creative control all the way from the writing to the close of production. This not only extends across an enormous story architecture (62 episodes in the case of *Breaking Bad*), but also dictates the kind of visual imagery in which *Breaking Bad* abounds – the teddy bear's eye that represents a mid-air collision between two passenger planes, the recreational vehicle repurposed as a mobile methamphetamine lab. Here, as throughout film and television, words remain as dialogue and as various kinds of on-screen text. And where the words don't remain as words, instead generating characters and action, the verbal isn't opposed to the visual, but instead provides a basis for it.

Words are particularly foregrounded in literary film adaptations: three of the most financially successful film franchises of recent decades, the James Bond, Harry Potter, and J.R.R. Tolkien movies, all began as sequences of novels, with the novels acknowledged as sources for the films. Even so, these literary-based, big-budget spectaculars are rarely, if ever, deemed "uncinematic," since visuals dominate this particular manifestation of the cinema of multiple attractions. While the Bond movies have strayed far from the books by Ian Fleming, the Potter ones, by contrast, have prioritised fidelity to J.K. Rowling's novels, since these have a wider readership than any other recent works of fiction. Similarly, after unsuccessful earlier attempts at film adaptation, the *Lord of the Rings* trilogy (2001-3) and *The Hobbit* (2012-4) also follow their source novels closely to appease the fan cult that has grown up around the books, to the extent of retaining lengthy digressions that might otherwise have been excised. As a result, the intricate fantasy world of Hogwarts School represented in eight films owes its visual manifestation, right down to tiny details, to the seven novels by Rowling, reworded in the screenplays written by Steve Kloves. The even more elaborate Middle Earth of the *Lord of the Rings* films, with its hobbits, orcs, and elves remains another fundamentally visual construct adhering faithfully to Tolkien's verbal representations of it. A professional philologist, Tolkien constructed entire languages complete with grammars for his imaginary characters, placing words at the centre of his project, and elements of these have been carried over into the screenplays. Thus the screenplays include not only the spoken English words common to most Anglo-American films, but also others constructed from Tolkien's "Elvish," as spoken by Galadriel, an "Elvish" character:

```
BLACK SCREEN


SUPER: New Line Cinema Presents


SUPER: A Wingnut Films Production


BLACK CONTINUES: ... ELVISH SINGING ... A
WOMAN'S VOICE IS whispering, tinged with
SADNESS and REGRET:
                    GALADRIEL (V.O.)
              (Elvish: subtitled)
          "I amar prestar aen: han
          mathon ne nen, han mathon ne
          chae ... a han noston ned
          wilith."
              (English:)
          The world is changed: I feel
          it in the water, I feel it in
          the earth, I smell it in the
          air ... Much that once was is
          lost, for none now live who
          remember it.
```

The grandiose and spectacular *Lord of the Rings* trilogy begins not with images – the screen is black – but with words, first as text on screen, and then spoken words, not English but in the invented language of "Elvish." Subtitling these in English doubles the effect: English words seen on screen and "Elvish" words heard simultaneously. Both "Elvish" and English remain in the film, highlighting the centrality of words to the creation of "Middle Earth." Even such spectacularly visual films as this owe their visuality to words.

"Screenplays should be read as industrial documents"

While the blueprint metaphor is the most pervasive expression of the way that screenplays are framed by the industrial paradigm, it's by no means the only one. As Chapter 2 shows, the blueprint metaphor renders screenplays, scripts, scenarios, and treatments more as visual than as verbal objects; blueprints themselves emphasise the visual, as two-dimensional drawings of three-dimensional buildings or artefacts, with words minimised. In actuality, screenplays are verbal constructs containing visual elements working to construct hybrid visual-audio-verbal objects, the films-to-be. The industrial paradigm also addressed in Chapter 2 supports a mechanistic, materialist view of screenplays so that even Ian Macdonald, who rejects the blueprint metaphor, describes the screenplay as "a pragmatic production tool."

As a result of these paradigms, practitioners and scholars have viewed screenplays and other film writing analogues as primarily denotative from the earliest days of film to the present. In Epes Winthrop Sargent's 1916 screenwriting manual, each "scene" (i.e. shot) of the "photoplay" (screenplay) is described both in terms of its story content and, at times, its size. Even more akin to a blueprint is Sargent's own photoplay, *The Narrow Paths of Fate*. This consists of a short synopsis and cast list, a single page "scene plot" listing the sets and interiors, and an eight-page "script" or "plot of action." The "script" is constructed so as to represent the structure of what will later be the completed film, including cuts, so that the "scenes" (shots) are assembled into a continuous narrative, much like a building completed from a blueprint. This script tells the cameraman and/or director what he needs to shoot, including what shot sizes to use, and the "cutter" (or film editor) how to join the shots together once they have been developed and printed. Such denotative functions sit comfortably within the conception of the screenplay (or its precursor) as an industrial planning document, in spite of the occasional fine arts metaphor within the screenplay.

Two decades later, during the classical Hollywood studio period, the studios' employment practices had strengthened the industrial paradigm. While scripts such as *The Narrow Paths of Fate* had been written by freelances, mainstream films in the 1930s were the product of salaried employees, whose working conditions mirrored those in other forms of factory-type labour. Studios hired large numbers of screenwriters, and (despite higher rates of pay) writing practices reflected those of industrial mass production, rather than the self-directed work of an artist or craftsman. Billy Wilder, best known today as the director of notable Hollywood films including *Double Indemnity* (1944), *Sunset Boulevard* (1950), and *Some Like It Hot* (1959) began and continued his career as a screenwriter, and recalled how "at Paramount, the studio had a swarm of writers under contract – a hundred and four!" While "swarm" may suggest the organic image of a hive rather than the mechanistic production line, bees, each with its rank and function, working ceaselessly, don't differ markedly from factory workers. Writers employed by studios were also treated much like factory workers: "It was all very tightly controlled. We even worked on Saturdays from nine until noon... When the unions negotiated the workweek back to five days, the executives ran around screaming the studio was going to go broke." There's nothing to differentiate the writing of screenplays under this system from the construction of sets and props, the technicalities of filming, and all the other activities of a labour force that clocked on and off at prescribed times. Such similarities contributed further to the industrial paradigm of screenwriting.

Another factor supporting the industrial conception of screenplays during the earlier decades of the twentieth century was the way that management assigned several writers to the same project, leading to the simultaneous writing of parallel screenplay versions by different authors. It was Irving Thalberg at MGM "who took [Thomas] Ince's system and divided the labor of screenwriting even more," according to Tom Stempel, and "instituted the practice of having several writers or even teams of writers at work on the same script without, supposedly, the other writers knowing it." The result, according to screenwriter Ring Lardner, Jr. (*M*A*S*H*, *The Cincinnati Kid*), was that "people within the industry and without said you couldn't really tell who had written what." As well as obscuring individual authorship of screenplays, these practices also downgraded the notion of originality in screenplays by the multiplication of different versions. If one version of a screenplay failed to satisfy the head of production, he could opt to pursue another being written in a different office. Additionally, they undermined the notion that great writing was enduring: large numbers of screenplay drafts created by a workforce of studio hacks inevitably proved redundant when concurrent versions were chosen instead for production.

In another parallel with manufacturing industries, and in stark contrast to aesthetic theories of fine writing, output was measured by quantity rather than quality. "All the writers were required to hand in eleven pages every Thursday," Wilder recalled. "Why on Thursday? Who knows? Why eleven pages? Who knows? Over a thousand pages a week were being written." Of these thousand pages, only a small fraction would find their way onto a set: "Most of the writing just gathered dust."

Hollywood studios in the classical period effectively invented an industrialised form of fictive writing, the mass production of screenplays. In a sociological study from the period drawing on first-hand research, including hundreds of questionnaires filled in by practitioners, screenwriter Leo Rosten finds that "Hollywood's writers are employees, units in a vast and complex manufacturing process." Ongoing work was signalled by the noise of type hammers striking paper. Jack Warner was rumoured to prowl the corridors listening for the reassuring sound of continuous typing. Conditions in Hollywood contrasted sharply with those associated with the writing of literary works. This production of screenplays mirrors the production of typescripts in a typing pool, another invention of the period that applied the same principle of mass production to the mechanical reproduction, rather than production, of words. The difficulty of distinguishing typing (reproduced writing) from initial writing, when the two activities look and sound the same, helped further to undermine screenplays' claim to creative agency.

For many scholars, these industrial associations lower screenplays' status as writing. Price makes "prevailing relationships between screen writing and film industries" central to his *History of the Screenplay*, insisting that "Any commentary on screenwriting is bound to observe that it is tied to a particular industry in a way that the novel, poem or even theatrical play is not" (a view challenged in Chapter 4). He also asserts that "These industrial contexts impose some limitations on the properties of the text." His focus is, like Staiger's, on "Hollywood as an industrial system" and Price insists that "all subsequent studies of screenplay history need to take account of Staiger's work as a starting point." Macdonald, while acknowledging that a screenplay may also be "written (and read) as a piece of art," foregrounds its function as "the central planning document around which a screenwork is costed and produced." Staiger's work is cited also by Maras, Millard, and Ted Nannicelli. Thus, even in the 2010s, the industrial paradigm remains for scholars the governing – and constraining – conceptualisation of what screenplays are.

As this paradigm extends beyond the classical Hollywood studio period, however, it becomes increasingly problematic. Scholars such as Macdonald and Price, who question and ultimately banish the blueprint metaphor, nevertheless carry forward industrial concepts related to it. The "shooting script," characterised as a version or successor of the screenplay employed during production, is presented as an even more denotative form of screenplay, encoding a set of instructions for the director and other readers. Such a view continues to place scripts and screenplays in the domain of conception and film production in the domain of execution.

However, even during the classical studio period, some screenplays were extending their role beyond simply denoting how a film should be made in a practical sense. Already by 1941, when John Gassner and Dudley Nichols published the first anthology of screenplays (see Chapter 2, section 1), numbered shots had been largely replaced by written descriptions, which nonetheless connoted clearly to production personnel what shots were required, as in the screenplay of *Stagecoach* (1939):

```
The main titles and the following
foreword are superimposed over
magnificent action shots of furiously
riding Apaches, to give an impression of
the savagery and desperation that set the
Apaches apart... sweeping past the camera
in various directions — groups of two and
three riding straight past the camera.
```

As well as specifying shots – the screenplay's official denotative role – this extract operates connotatively, as Sargent's script *The*

Narrow Paths of Fate does not. The screenplay of *Stagecoach* engages here not only with technical information unique to film but also with the mythology of the Old West. The screenwriter is more than a technician writing an industrial document; complex and even contradictory attitudes towards the various characters are present within this screenplay. The Apaches exhibit "savagery" and "desperation," but are also depicted more sympathetically as resisting "the white invader." They embrace "death rather than submit to the white man's will." The banker Gatewood, who makes a speech asserting that "what's good business for the banks is good for the country," is later exposed as a liar and a thief, in an implicit critique of capitalism; Nichols himself was a union organiser. His character Ringo, an unfairly convicted fugitive from justice, escapes at the end to a "new life" with the spirited heroine Dallas "over the Border." The film's happy ending thus depends on principal characters abandoning oppressive American territory for the perceived freedom of Mexico. Sargent's script tells the director what to photograph, and how. Nichols's sets out what to shoot (Apaches on horseback), how (a series of medium and medium-wide shots), but also *why* (to capture both the threat and the freedom that the Apache riders represent). Sargent's script also contains ideology: the "pretty, willful and weak" Ruth, who elopes from her husband with a succession of men, is eventually killed by one of them, while the hero Jack is reconciled with his best friend Jim. Sargent's happy ending thus celebrates male friendship triumphing over female willfulness and weakness. However, the social conventions to which Sargent's characters conform are treated by him neutrally, while Nichols challenges ideas likely to be accepted by his readers and audiences, that Mexicans and Apaches are inferior to Americans, just as women in *The Narrow Paths of Fate* are represented as inferior to men. Nichols hints but does not specify that Dallas is a frontier-town prostitute, comparable in some respects to Sargent's Ruth. But he presents her escape from the harsh social conditions and moral intransigence of the Old West as positive, and makes his happy ending her getaway with jailbird Ringo. Ideological values are connoted but sublimated in Sargent's script. In Nichols's, however, they're didactically written, showing his consciousness of the screenplay's capacity for complexity and the layering of representation. Reading Nichols's screenplay simply as an industrial document, rather than as writing, will thus fail to capture all that it's doing.

"The camera does the writing, not the screenplay"

Some theorists and practitioners have argued that filmmakers should write with light (a literal translation of "photography"), using the camera as a "pen," and so attempt to banish actual writing and thus screenplays from film altogether. Early expressions of these ideas are found in Soviet film theory, in particular that of Dziga Vertov, director of *Man with a Movie Camera* (1929). The opening cards of this film draw attention to the absence of a screenplay ("without intertitles… without a script"), and some critics and scholars have nominated this "pure cinema." Vertov himself wrote that the film was "'written' directly in sequences and shots."

However, making a documentary (such as *Man with a Movie Camera*) without a screenplay is common practice. The notion of writing a fiction film directly with the camera is much more radical. French director Alexandre Astruc proposed in 1948 that cinema was becoming a "language," defined as "a form in which and by which an artist can express his thoughts, however abstract they may be, or translate his obsessions exactly as he does in the contemporary essay or novel." Astruc goes on to formulate an influential new metaphor: "I would like to call this new age of cinema the age of *caméra-stylo* [camera-pen]." Directly and indirectly, Astruc and the *caméra-stylo* have continued to exert a negative influence on the status of the screenplay as valued writing, particularly in their appeal to collapse the separate roles of writer and director into one. Furthermore, the idea of the *caméra-stylo* tempts directors to defer resolving the challenges of writing until the shooting stage. This is a danger of which prominent director Alexander Mackendrick (*Whiskey Galore, The Sweet Smell of Success*), in his role as film school tutor, warns:

> The overwhelming temptation of many students when faced with problems of dramatic construction in the scripting stage is to dodge the real challenges by fantasising about the much more pleasurable (and indeed easier) problems involved in actually shooting the film.

Astruc's manifesto can be seen as encouraging just such dodging of the "real challenges."

Another temptation offered directors by the *caméra-stylo* metaphor is the chimera of total creative control. This, were it possible, could free the director from any sense of being a glorified technician realising someone else's screenplay and a mere part of a collaborative creative team. Instead the director would become (in Astruc's words) "an artist" expressing individual, independent thoughts. "Direction," according to Astruc, "is no longer a means of illustrating or presenting a scene, but a true act of writing. The film-maker/author writes with his camera as a writer writes with his pen."

However, Astruc's maxim obscures rather than clarifies the role of the screenplay within this conception of filmmaking and attribution of its authorship. He insists that "the scriptwriter directs his own scripts," which isn't the same as proposing that the director writes his own scripts. When the writer of the screenplay goes on to direct it, the screenplay remains as the first stage of his or her twofold process of authorship. Conversely, when a director writes his own screenplay, he usually privileges the directing stage, and may perceive the screenplay as no more than a chore to be completed before the "more pleasurable" process of filming can begin, as Mackendrick's comment indicates.

Astruc's article is known best as one of the earliest manifestos of the writer-director, but it also contains other ideas, less frequently cited but even more radically hostile to the writing of screenplays. He states his desire to make room for "a different and individual kind of film-making": in particular, a direct and unmediated cinema of ideas. "[I]t will soon be possible," he predicts, "to write ideas directly on film." Identifying the "fundamental problem of the cinema" as "how to express thought," Astruc asserts that "a Descartes of today would already have shut himself up in his bedroom with a 16mm camera and some film, and would be writing his philosophy on film." A bold claim in 1948, it became even more fantastical in the succeeding decades, as cinema turned increasingly to the realist mainstream. Yet in our own century, when making personal videos in bedrooms and posting them on YouTube has become commonplace, and a philosopher such as Slavoj Žižek is as likely to make a film as write a book to communicate his ideas, Astruc's claim now appears realisable. In Astruc's own time, however, examples were hard to find, and he points to *L'Espoir* (1945) by writer-director (formerly novelist) André Malraux as a film "in which, perhaps for the first time ever, film language is the exact equivalent of literary language." Astruc provides no support for this assertion that the sounds and images of Malraux's film are the "exact equivalent" of the written language he employed in his novels, and indeed it seems impossible that any actual sounds and images could be the exact equivalent of writing. Nor has *L'Espoir* become a touchstone of "pure" cinema.

Despite the limitations of Astruc's argument, "Du stylo à la caméra et de la caméra au stylo" has endured in other ways. One vector of its influence has been the writings of Astruc's contemporary André Bazin, the mentor of Truffaut, who returns to the question of film language a decade later in his essay, "L'Évolution du langage." Bazin writes, "aujourd'hui enfin, on peut dire que le metteur en scène *écrit* directement en cinéma" ("today one can finally say that the director *writes* in film"). Adopted with enthusiasm by some film scholars, Bazin's observations, like those of Astruc, are based on viewings of completed films. Therefore they are subject to the teleological oversight common throughout film studies that causes the screenplay to disappear.

Even as Astruc devalues screenwriting with the *caméra-stylo* metaphor, he doesn't do so in order to vaunt the visual over the verbal. "This metaphor has a very precise sense. By it I mean that the cinema will gradually break free from the tyranny of what is visual, from the image for its own sake, from the immediate and concrete demands of the narrative, to become a means of writing just as flexible and subtle as written language" (32). Rather than promoting the visual through subjugating the written screenplay to it, then, Astruc sees the visual as something that holds cinema back, when it is mere spectacle or placed solely in the service of telling the story. Readers of his essay (which, after all, he chose to write, rather than make as a film) have tended to emphasise only one half of his metaphor – the camera, and not the pen. What Astruc advocates appears to be a much more radical reconception of filmmaking than merely combining writer and director in a single "author." He argues not for rejecting writing but for extending it, beyond the screenplay and into the shooting process itself, so that film is to emulate writing and do what writing does. Elliott, however, has argued that this is part of a familiar two-stage process of overthrow and usurpation in debates over hybrid media: film emulates literature and language by borrowing its rhetoric, then exiles actual literature and language from film by robbing it of its own rhetoric and figuring it as a blueprint or in terms of other nonlinguistic or nonliterary media. Thus, despite Astruc's reservations about the visual, there's no evidence that he's ultimately concerned to reinstate the verbal.

"The authorship of auteur directors is more important than their authorship as writers"

Following Astruc's promotion of the *caméra-stylo*, Truffaut's even more influential polemic, "Une certaine tendance du cinéma français," focuses attention on the director as auteur. Here, too, emulation becomes overthrow in taking the language of authorship away from the writer. However, just as Truffaut underplays the writer-director's role as writer, so too critics tend to overlook the fact that auteurs are also writers. Truffaut's essay was written to challenge the novel-based "Tradition de la Qualité" that dominated French cinema in the 1950s, and to propose a kind of filmmaking different from literary adaptation. When Truffaut uses the word *"auteurs"* (italics in original) he does so in the traditional sense of "authors" who write films: Jean Renoir, Jacques Tati, Robert Bresson, and the others that he cites are distinguished both as "cinéastes français" ("French filmmakers") and as *"auteurs* qui écrivent souvent leur dialogue et quelqu'uns inventent eux-mêmes les histoires qu'ils mettent en scène" ("*authors* who often write their dialogue and some of whom even devise the stories that they direct"). Auteurs are thus by definition writer-directors, in contrast to the other kind of director Truffaut discusses, "le monsieur qui met des cadrages là-dessus" ("the gentleman who lines up the shots"). It's thus writing, and not directing, that distinguishes the two groups from one another. The directors whom Truffaut denigrates for making "screenwriters' films" ("Des films de scénaristes") aren't writer-directors as Renoir, Tati, and Bresson are. Jean Delannoy, Claude Autant-Lara, and Yves Allégret do have some writing credits, but only on a fraction of their output as directors, and usually shared and/or for only a single aspect of the screenplay, such as "adaptation" or dialogue. So Truffaut sets two kinds of writing and directing in contest with one another: authors who write original screenplays, and then direct them (Renoir, Bresson, Tati), and adaptors who collaborate in transferring a novel to the screen.

Moreover, when he wrote these words, Truffaut was himself not a director but a writer, contributing film criticism to the periodical *Cahiers du cinéma*, under Bazin's editorship. Truffaut wrote and directed his first film, the short *Une visite* (1955), the year after "Une certaine tendance" was published in *Cahiers*. Bazin, too, was a writer, one who never directed a film. Jean-Luc Godard, another key figure in auteur theory, also published articles in *Cahiers* for three years before venturing into directing with *Une femme coquette* (1955), itself not an original but a pseudonymous adaptation of a Maupassant story (and so related to the "Tradition de la Qualité" mocked by Truffaut). Auteurism begins in writing, with the publication of articles written by writers who only subsequently become writer-directors, just as written screenplays precede the directing of films. Like Astruc, who fantasised about a camera-pen but instead used words to write his polemic, Truffaut, Bazin, and Godard were all writers before they were anything else: the words came before the pictures. Much later, in 2014, Godard made a short film (*Khan Khanne*) explaining to Gilles Jacob why he wouldn't be attending the 67th Cannes Film festival, but – as with Vertov's *Man With a Movie Camera* and Žižek's filmed polemics – this was non-fiction, to which the camera-pen may be better suited.

Godard's first feature film, *À bout de souffle* (1960), was hailed as the realisation of Astruc's *caméra-stylo*, and indeed Godard didn't work from a conventional screenplay. However, the text from which the actors improvised was nevertheless verbal and written, and thus writing formed the basis of his direction in spite of its unconventional format. The film's star, Jean-Paul Belmondo, recounts in a 1961 interview how he was given only a three-page outline (written by Truffaut) before shooting began. Subsequently, writer-director Godard wrote each day's scenes on set, while the actors drank coffee, and these script pages then formed the basis of improvisations by the actors. Moreover, Godard had previously written much of a conventional screenplay, but chose not to use it – at least, not directly. The filmmaking process thus remained one based on writing and, in his career to date, Godard has accumulated 97 screenwriting credits, accounting for the majority of the 128 films he has directed. He also continues to publish not only books of film theory and criticism, but also screenplays. Truffaut, meanwhile, wrote even more films than he directed: 36 and 28 credits respectively. The filmmaking practices of both Truffaut and Godard thus privilege rather than reject writing.

Indeed, the argument that auteur theory is more rooted in writing than in directing can be extended further, beyond France. Even Andrew Sarris, the American critic who popularised auteur theory and insisted on the pre-eminence of the director in the US, was himself a writer who never made a film. Stempel connects the uptake of auteur theory by academics to the growth of film studies as an academic discipline:

> Sarris and others established the auteur theory in
> America just as film studies were getting estab-

lished in American universities. The auteur approach helped persuade nonfilm academics that film study was a respectable line of work and therefore film departments and courses could be considered legitimate academic endeavors.

Thus auteur theory can be seen as the invention of writers, enthusiastically adopted by readers (and also viewers), but less closely connected with directors, directing, and filmmaking practice. It has been used to legitimate film as a serious academic subject by analogy to philosophical, critical, aesthetic, and literary writing. Screenwriter I.A.L. Diamond notes that the American directors admired as auteurs by French critics "deal mainly in violence," which is non-verbal. He suggests that "Naturally the French critics overstress the visual elements, because they don't dig English dialogue." Those elements of a film most evidently dependent on writing, such as dialogue, prove more problematic than visual ones when it comes to crossing linguistic frontiers – something recognised by the global dubbing and subtitling of English language films outside anglophone territories.

Additionally, even the writer-directors placed on pedestals by auteur theory may emphasise the importance of their screenplays over their directing work. In the series of interviews with Orson Welles conducted by Peter Bogdanovich across several decades, the older writer-director fences with his acolyte's repeated attempts to validate Welles (and, by extension, himself) as an auteur. Bogdanovich is anxious to base these claims not in Welles's writing, but in his directing. Accepting the desirability of the writer-director role, Welles then places the emphasis (to Bogdanovich's dismay) on the first, not the second, part of the hyphenated title:

> OW: What have you got now – another quote to qualify?
>
> PB: [reading]: "Writers should have the first and last word in moviemaking, the only better alternative being the writer-director, with stress on the first word."
>
> OW: I'll stick with that. Just plain directing is the world's easiest job.
>
> PB: You'd better qualify that one!
>
> OW: Peter, there isn't another trade in the world where a man can blithely go on for thirty years with no one ever finding out that he's incompetent. Give him a good script, a good cast, and a good cutter – or just one of those elements – all he has to say is "Action" and "Cut", and the movie makes itself…. I mean it, Peter. Movie directing is a perfect refuge for the mediocre.

Thus, far from valorising directing as the supreme art of filmmaking, Welles instead promotes writing above it.

Industry reasons for the devaluation of screenplays as writing

> [W]hen a writer works for a studio, he becomes an employee engaged in the manufacture of an extremely expensive commodity.
>
> Leo Rosten

Scholars and practitioners have often colluded in the fallacy that screenplays aren't writing like other writing, and as such shouldn't be read in the same way. Their reasons for doing so span a range of entrenched prejudices and concealed agendas.

Studios exhibit the clearest motivation for denying screenplays' claim to be regarded and read like other writing.

The greater the agency attributed to screenplays, the greater the power of their writers; the power of studios is thus reduced in proportion. Early in the twentieth century, the Hollywood studios took control of screenplays through their use of copyright legislation, making screenplays their property rather than the writers', and have clung to it ever since. Power and control are enshrined in the studios' arrogation of authorial rights. Norman documents how writers were contracted from the earliest days of the film industry through the use of a key phrase – "'the studio, hereinafter referred to as the author'" – not present in the contracts of other employees. While there's no record of when this expression was first used, Norman notes that "it probably goes back to the 1910s, perhaps even the Gene Gauntier days" – the 1900s. The reason that Sargent chose to include his script *The Narrow Paths of Fate* in his 1916 screenwriting manual may well have been that, since it was unproduced, it remained his own property, unlike most of his output. In 1972, screenwriter Fay Kanin, then president of the Screen Branch of the Writers Guild of America, West (WGAW), said, "I have never been able to sign my name to the contract that one signs in Hollywood, which says that the studio is the author of your screenplay, without feeling angry and humiliated." A more comprehensive version of the same clause still exists today and forms part of the standard writer's contract template used in the United States. In the current Writers Theatrical Short-Form Contract agreed between the WGA and the Alliance of Motion Picture and Television Producers (representing the major studios as well as mini-majors and production companies) it appears thus:

> Writer acknowledges that all results, product and proceeds of Writer's services (including all original ideas in connection therewith) are being specially ordered by Producer for use as part of a

> Motion Picture and shall be considered a "work made for hire" for Producer as specially commissioned for use as a part of a motion picture in accordance with Sections 101 and 201 of Title 17 of the U.S. Copyright Act. Therefore, Producer shall be the author and copyright owner thereof for all purposes throughout the universe without limitation of any kind or nature. In consideration of the monies paid to Lender hereunder, Producer shall solely and exclusively own throughout the universe in perpetuity all rights of every kind and nature whether now or hereafter known or created in and in connection with such results, product and proceeds, in whatever stage of completion as may exist from time to time...

The writers' union offers no protection or redress for this transfer of ownership – ownership elsewhere accorded to and retained by literary authors, playwrights, reviewers, critics, and scholars. Any screenwriter who enters into a union contract (as is used at all studios) automatically surrenders not only the copyright in her or his screenplay to the "Producer" (that is, studio or production company), but also the very notion of authorship. Although the contract is regularly renegotiated, and indeed was amended as recently as May 2017, this central clause is never up for discussion, let alone renegotiation.

Similar terms apply to screenplays in the UK, with the additional requirement for writers to sign a "moral rights" waiver that nullifies the otherwise inalienable moral rights of authors within the European Union, one of which is to be identified as the author of a written work. (The waiver may become redundant as the UK leaves the EU.) The motive is clear: legal authorship of screenplays allows producers much more freedom in the financing and commercial exploitation of films than would otherwise be the case, and so studios and other production entities will resist fiercely any attempts to wrest this away. The more that screenplays are perceived and discussed as an inferior, unauthored, commercial form fundamentally unlike other kinds of creative writing, the easier it is for studios to defend an alienation of moral human rights that might otherwise appear unreasonable and inequitable.

Writers have long been suspected of being too attached to their words and reluctant to cut or change them, irregardless of the commercial consequences. This led to further erosion of their authorship. Based on his primary research, Rosten notes in 1941 that "Most directors think that writers 'fall in love' with their characters and situations." The producer, meanwhile, asks of the screenplay "Will it make money?" and does not trust the writer to share his priorities. F. Scott Fitzgerald was promised sole authorship of the screenplay adapting best-selling novel *Three Comrades* (1938) for MGM, but producer (and former screenwriter) Joseph Mankiewicz brought in studio hack E.E. Paramore. Fitzgerald declined to co-write, but Mankiewicz insisted. Then, when actress Margaret Sullavan complained about the dialogue of her character Pat, Mankiewicz rewrote the screenplay himself. Fitzgerald responded in a letter, "I gave you a drawing and you simply took a box of chalk. Pat has now become a sentimental girl from Brooklyn." As Rosten wrote a few years later, "[t]he clash between creative desires and movie costs arises a hundred times a week," because "[t]he very purpose of Hollywood's producers is opposed to the basic motivation of writers." The job of producers within the studio system was to make movies that reaped profits by their broad appeal to a mass market. If Fitzgerald were acknowledged as the author of *Three Comrades* in the way that he had been of his novel *Tender is the Night* three years previously, then Mankiewicz wouldn't have been able to rewrite him against

Fitzgerald's will, in the belief that his own version would prove more commercial.

The principle that producers must not only own the screenplays of their projects but also deny authorship to writers became more difficult to enforce after the classical Hollywood studio period. Indeed, even during that period, major independent producers such as David O. Selznick began to negotiate the authorship of screenplays somewhat differently. Well before the "package-unit system" became the production norm after 1955, Anglo-Hungarian producer Alexander Korda assembled the "package" for *The Third Man* and in 1948 approached Hollywood producer Selznick for co-funding. *The Third Man* was subject to the same market forces and dependent on appealing to the same audience as *Three Comrades* or other studio product, and Korda was as much bound by commercial considerations as Mankiewicz had been ten years earlier. One of Korda's principal motives for developing a film that could be shot on location in Vienna was entirely commercial: to use funds frozen in Austria by strict postwar currency controls. Unlike Mankiewicz and MGM, neither Korda nor Selznick had a roomful of writers under contract, so the "package-unit" arrangement gave the screenplay a different status. It became an "element," part of the project's commercial appeal. Thus when Korda went shopping for an original screenplay he sought one from a high-profile writer with an international literary reputation. At this point in his career Graham Greene had published twelve novels, several of which had been filmed. Like Fitzgerald, Greene was an established literary author; unlike Fitzgerald's career, though, Greene's was in the ascendant. However, no Hollywood studio would have been likely to hire him. In 1938 the English magazine *Night and Day* had been forced to close after Twentieth Century Fox successfully sued it and Greene over his film review of *Wee Willie Winkie* (1937), in which he accused the studio of "procuring" Shirley Temple for "immoral purposes." Greene was thus the opposite of a "studio hack." He had every reason to stress his literary credentials and his independence from Hollywood custom and practice. In the wrangling with Selznick that continued throughout development, filming, and post-production, it was Greene's literary status (together with director Carol Reed's help) that enabled Greene to assert his authorship, and thus retain creative control over the screenplay. When *The Third Man* was released in Britain, Greene's status as a literary heavyweight empowered him to insist on the opening of the film he wanted: the dispassionate, cynical voice-over (spoken by Reed himself) used to set the scene in Vienna. For the theatrical release in the United States, where Greene's literary authorship was trumped by Selznick's authority as co-producer, a different version of the voice-over was used (spoken by Joseph Cotten), which instead aligns the audience with the naive protagonist, Holly Martins.

Unlike Fitzgerald, Greene was able on this independent production to assert his authorship of the *Third Man* screenplay from the outset by advancing his literary credentials. He undertook the preliminary work in a specifically literary manner that underlined his claim not only to authorship but also to ownership. He negotiated a concession from Korda, one rarely achieved by screenwriters, of retaining the copyright in his own screenplay. Andrew Sinclair's introduction to the Faber edition of *The Third Man* notes that Greene "has wisely retained all literary rights in the property (a rare and usually impossible thing to do)." Indeed, it would be extremely difficult for the authors of most screenplays to win acceptance of the notion that "literary rights" in a screenplay even exist. Greene's writing of *The Third Man* then proceeded in a way that drew attention to his authorship. Insisting that "Even a film depends on more than plot, on a certain measure of characterization, on mood and atmosphere," Greene wrote that "these seem to me almost impossible to capture for the first time in the dull shorthand of a script." Instead, he opted to write *The Third Man* first of all in the form of a "story." The previous year, 1947, Greene had published the collection *Nineteen Stories*, so this was a specifically literary form in which he had an established public profile. Furthermore, by Greene's own account even his very first idea, from which *The Third Man* would grow, was set down not as notes, but in a fully formed passage of prose:

> I had paid my last farewell to Harry a week ago, when his coffin was lowered into the frozen February ground, so that it was with incredulity that I saw him pass by, without a sign of recognition, among the host of strangers in the Strand.

Greene referred to this as "an opening paragraph," confirming that he approached his screenplay commission from a literary starting point. In a letter he described how he believed "I've got a *book* coming." While Mankiewicz rewrote Fitzgerald's screenplay for *Three Comrades* as part of his role as studio producer, Korda as an independent producer had no incentive to diminish Greene's authorship of *The Third Man*, or to play down his literary reputation. On the contrary, both Korda and Greene could enhance their project's appeal by playing it up instead.

Greene was thus not only secure in his literary authorship, as Fitzgerald was, but also successfully asserted his authorship of the *Third Man* screenplay. In addition he was able to insist on sharing control of it through his retention of "all literary rights." From this unusually privileged position Greene is happy to credit the director for his contribution: "Carol Reed and I worked closely together." At the same time Greene maintains his own authorial authority, even over the portions of the published screenplay that were cut from the film: "The reader will notice many differences between the story and the film, and he should not imagine these changes were forced on an unwilling author: as likely as not they were suggested by the author." In so doing, he asserts a status not available to most screenwriters in this period. He may work closely with the director, but it's he, the screenwriter, who remains "the [sole] author" – not only of the screenplay, and of the story on which it is based, but also of "changes" preceding and during production. Greene, like Fitzgerald, may be a novelist eager to earn money writing for the movies. Unlike Fitzgerald, however, he hasn't been compelled to relinquish his sense of creative agency and authorial ownership.

As author and co-owner of the *Third Man* screenplay, which began as a written paragraph and was developed as a short story, Greene continued to assert continuities between the screenplay and his literary output. While Fitzgerald complained that his drawing had been replaced by chalk marks, Greene's screenplay continues to share characteristics with his fiction. One might expect Greene's screenplay dialogue to resemble closely the dialogue in one of his novels or stories. However, this applies not only to dialogue but also in places to the action lines:

```
ANNA moves from the bed. Twice she puts
out her hand and touches the wall. She
comes to the dressing table. In the
mirror is stuck a snapshot. It is of
herself, laughing into the camera. Above
it she sees her face in the mirror with
tousled hair and hopeless eyes.
Automatically she puts her hand down to
the right hand drawer. She does not have
to look. She opens the drawer and pulls
```

> out a comb. Still only half-conscious of
> what she is doing, she raises it to her
> head and is just going to use the comb
> when her eye falls on something in the
> drawer belonging to HARRY. She drops the
> comb, slams the drawer to, and puts her
> hand over her face.

This functions as action does in any screenplay, providing information for director, actor, and various technical departments: production design, costume, props, make-up and hair, camera. But the words chosen, and the manner in which they're deployed, share much with other writing by Greene:

> Anne Crowder walked up and down the small room in her heavy tweed coat; she didn't want to waste a shilling on the gas meter, because she wouldn't get her shilling's worth before morning. She told herself, I'm lucky to have got that job. I'm glad to be going off to work again, but she wasn't convinced. It was eight now; they would have four hours together till midnight.

Anna from *The Third Man* and Anne from *A Gun for Sale* (1936) may be separated by thirteen years and nearly a thousand miles, but they belong to the same world – "Greeneland." There are distinctions to be made: the screenplay employs the present tense, the novel exploits the opportunity to tell us what Anne is thinking. Nevertheless, put the stage directions from *The Third Man* into the past tense and the stylistic distinction all but evaporates. Despite attacks by producers on writers' authorship and ownership of screenplays, here Greene demonstrates the continuity between his literary writing and screenplay, and the potential for other screenplays to do the same.

Although the package system made screenplays and their writers more visible, a pattern of serial rewriting frequently erases the screenplays of first and subsequent writers. *The Third Man* remains a highly unusual example where authorship and (partial) ownership of a screenplay belong to its writer. As the package-unit system expanded to become the Hollywood norm, screenplays achieved and retained a higher profile than within the classical studio system. However, for the vast majority of writers, copyright and ownership proved as elusive as before. The duplication of writing by multiple writers working simultaneously, as in the studios' factory writing system, was replaced by a model of serial writing, in which individual writers rarely see a project through from start to finish and a succession of writers replacing their predecessors has become standard practice. Screenwriter John August (*Big Fish, The Corpse Bride*) notes that he "worked on *Blue Streak, Jurassic Park III, Minority Report, The Rundown*, and other movies as the second, third or eighth writer."

Many contributions, especially the later interventions by "script doctors" who are highly paid to rewrite projects about to enter production, remain anonymous due to strict WGA rules about credit. According to film researcher Stephen Follows, on average the screenplays of live action films between 1994 and 2013 have 3.5 credited writers. However, Follows points out that "[a]nimated films are not covered by the WGA agreement with the studios and thereby reveal what writing credits for all films might look if they were unregulated." Not only was the average number of writers on the screenplays of animated films much higher at 7.4, but some animated films employed very many more writers: 31 worked on *Mulan* (1998), 29 on *The Lion King* (1994), 28 on *Pocahontas* (1995), and 24 on *The Hunchback of Notre Dame* (1996). In such a situation authorship for most writers may remain very nearly as elusive as copyright.

Even in cases where writers aren't replaced, their ownership and authorship of screenplays are further compromised by demands for them to rewrite their own screenplays. The screenplay frequently becomes the focus of a power struggle and competition for creative authority. This is often expressed through requiring the current writer to rewrite according to notes from producers, executive, actors, and – most of all – directors. Many directors insist on their right to modify and on occasions rewrite the screenplay. This might become problematic if a screenplay were to enjoy the same status as, say, a theatre play. Here the playwright has the right of refusal over changes – a right enshrined in contracts between members of the Dramatists Guild of America or the Writers Guild of Great Britain and theatre producers. Books that promise to initiate aspiring screenwriters into how things work in the film industry stress the inevitability of rewrites, with or without the writer's agreement. Thus Lew Hunter tells his readers that "A script that does not go through the rewriting mill is rarer than sandstorms around the timberline of Mount Everest."

Other authors of screenplay manuals similarly underline the inevitability of rewriting that often erases the original screenplay. Indeed, for some screenwriting manuals, rewriting is everything. The very title of Jack Epps, Jr's manual, *Screenwriting is Rewriting: The Art and Craft of Professional Revision* (2016) suggests that the writing of a screenplay is no more than a brief prelude to an open-ended process of rewriting in which even a single, unreplaced screenwriter may erase much or all of her own screenplay. Another manual author, Linda Seger, similarly endorses rewriting in *Making a Good Script Great* (1987), but in her Epilogue connects rewriting with defence of the screenplay: "I hope this book has given you more control over the rewriting process. And by understanding the issues that need to be addressed in rewriting, you will be in a better position to protect your work." The implication is that rewriting will be forced on the screenplay in any case, and the screenwriter needs tools with which to compete for control and defend the screenplay from excessive interference. If the screenwriter doesn't collude in changing her original draft it will be changed anyway, and she may be powerless to "protect" it. Film scholarship often draws attention to directorial and cinematographic erosions of the screenplay, but doesn't scrutinise in the same way changes to screenplays (however unwelcome) made by other writers, and indeed by the original writers.

Often in the rewriting process screenplays' status as authored texts in their own right is diminished. Writers are caught in a triple bind. If they agree with the proposed changes, they should have thought of them by themselves, and have thus demonstrated their need of "input" from collaborators. If they disagree but have to make the changes anyway, they appear weak and even ineffectual. If they refuse, they're replaced, and other writers make the changes in their place. One strategy for screenwriters wishing to avoid this triple bind is to include surplus dialogue, scenes, and even characters in their screenplays simply so that they can later be removed as part of a process of negotiation between writer and producer, director, or executive. Don Roos (*The Opposite of Sex, Bounce*) explains how he wrote material that he considered crass, but which executives demanded, since he knew that it would be cut at a later stage. "We had a scene where the Ben Affleck character says, 'I want to tell her. I should have been on the plane, and I really love her, and she's really special to me.' It's not in the movie. I never expected it to be." Sometimes screenwriters may suspect that changes are demanded for no good reason, other than to demonstrate the power of a director, producer, actor, or other collaborator. "Many scripts get worse and worse in the rewrite process... The solution might seem to be 'Don't rewrite!' It is, unfortunately, not an alternative," according to Seger. "Some requirements may go beyond subjective opinion and have strong, Aristotelian validity," Hunter writes. "Other requirements may be invalid, unnecessary." Irregardless, "you *have* to deal with any and all such requests." This, he and other manual authors such as Epps and Seger insist, is what it means to be a professional screenwriter. The notion is questionable. A distinguishing feature of those screenplays that do retain a sense of their own authority (such as *The Third Man*) may be the writer's ability to accept notes without conceding ownership or surrendering authorial status, as Greene does, instead assuming authorship and ownership of any rewriting, by himself or anyone else. His experience shows that it's possible to rewrite without surrendering authorship and ownership, while that of many other screenwriters underlines the difficulty of achieving this.

As a screenplay journeys through development towards production it becomes increasingly difficult for its writer to retain ownership and control, and more likely that the original screenplay will be overwritten and even erased. The first draft spec screenplay is the form most closely associated with the ownership and rights of a single, independent author – the only one that truly "belongs to the writer," in William Goldman's words. After that not only ownership but creative control is commonly shared, as the screenplay becomes an "open text" and invites (or tolerates) collaboration, and not necessarily for the better. David Mamet drives the point home: "My experience as a screenwriter is this: a script usually gets worse from the first draft on." Kaufman's breakthrough screenplay, *Being John Malkovich*, was written on spec and sent out as a writing sample. His plan was to "use it to get work." At that stage in his career Kaufman was a TV writer who wanted to break into movies, yet his screenplay doesn't foreground commercially appealing elements. It calls for a "60 foot puppet" of canonical poet Emily Dickinson and the participation of a single, nominated actor who was to be teased mercilessly and made to appear ridiculous. "I wasn't really expecting it to get made," Kaufman has said. What this spec screenplay did was showcase Kaufman's extraordinary ability to fuse his own bold variation on generic Hollywood storytelling with his individual imagination, and with his interest in questions (such as identity, perception, the theory of knowledge) that go unexplored in most studio output. Moreover, it's extremely unlikely that anyone – producer, development executive, or director – would have commissioned this screenplay, and relatively few uncommissioned, spec scripts are subsequently produced. Since the release of *Being John Malkovich* (1999), Kaufman has become as important a Hollywood "name" as the directors who have made films from his screenplays, Spike Jonze and Michel Gondry. Norman observes that "*Malkovich* fans perceived the picture was the product of its screenwriter," and were "standing in line outside theaters – and continuing to stand in line, as other Kaufman scripts were released – because of who'd written the movie." Some drafts of his screenplays have been turned into films, but others still circulate in their original form. While legally these may be owned and "authored" by the producers of the films, most readers will identify Kaufman himself as their author and owner. The experience of Kaufman and Greene proves that some screenplays are able to resist erasure by rewriting. Ultimately this aspect of their persistence is a question of authorship and ownership. Writers who are able successfully to assert these, such as Greene and Kaufman, are able to ensure the persistence of their screenplays while many others like Fitzgerald are not.

Not only studios but also individual producers have had a similar interest in arguing that screenplays are industrial, barely human forms of writing. Irving Thalberg is credited by Norman with the invention of the producer by appointing production lieutenants at MGM in the mid-1920s. As a studio chief's underlings, producers shared the interests of the studios that employed them. Later, towards the end of the classical studio period, some of the more ambitious producers, such as Selznick, struck out and set up on their own. Without the backing of studios, these independent producers needed full control of the screenplays that they bought or commissioned even more than the Hollywood majors. Responsible for arranging the financing of each production, independent producers had no incentive to improve the contractual terms for the writing of screenplays.

These unfavourable contracts appear harsher still when you recall that many producers working within the studio system had been writers themselves. Rosten notes in 1941 that "36.1 percent of Hollywood's producers... have worked as writers." They knew the conditions of writing for the studios from both sides of the negotiating table, yet showed little sympathy towards the writers that they hired. Rosten detects a muffled class war between studio-period writers and producers, which played into producers' reluctance to value the writing of screenplays more highly. He notes that "[t]he percentage of movie writers holding college degrees (48.6) is much higher than... producers (13.8)," and describes the "rage" felt by a writer told ungrammatically by a producer that "'the dialogue don't add up, and the characters ain't refined.'" Rosten suggests that

> The fact that words are used to exercise authority
> intensifies the writer's antagonism. For the writer
> is an expert in words and feels superior to his
> superiors when words are used. The writer often
> complains about the producer's decisions when
> he really is contemptuous of the producer's
> vocabulary.

The relationship between producers and writers that Rosten depicts is one of mutual mistrust and scorn, with the result that the screenplays that formed the focus of their spiky relationship were further devalued.

Directors, while also studio employees working to the instructions of management, similarly lacked any motive to raise the status of screenplays. They too were often locked in power struggles with writers over control of the screenplay. Acknowledging screenplays as writing would strengthen the writers' hand in script discussions, and so weaken their own, and they furthermore resented the writers' inability or unwillingness to deliver what they wanted. Drawing on his own experience and research, Rosten observes that "few directors and writers can work together amicably." He reports that "[m]any directors... think that writers are given too much praise for the screenplay." Directors with this attitude towards the screenplay are unlikely to promote it as respected, creative writing. The power of directors increased greatly with the collapse of the studio system in the 1960s, in which the spread of auteur theory played a part. Their struggle with writers for creative control ended in a clear victory for the directors, and still today there's little incentive for them to relinquish any of that power by applauding screenplays. It's commonplace for a writer to be replaced on a project, even one originated by that writer, at the whim of a director.

Beyond the power struggles of studios, producers, and directors with screenwriters, screenwriting has become so devalued that writers frequently assign screenplays lower status than other kinds of writing done by themselves and by others. Their reasons for doing so vary. Perhaps the easiest group to understand are the "factory writers" of Hollywood's classical studio period, working within a system predicated on the mass production of screenplays (see Chapter 3, section 3). As Norman expresses it, "A Hollywood writer's creations no more belonged to him or her than the Renaissance set standing on Stage 10 belonged to the men who hammered it together." Like the factory worker on an assembly line, the writer of screenplays within the studio system was in essence a labourer working on an enterprise belonging to someone or something else. Besides issues of ownership, there was the question of integrity. When a screenplay combined bits and pieces from different writers and drafts, it was unlikely to be identified as the work of any single individual. Rosten goes further, to argue that work by an individual would be unlikely to succeed:

> Many writers in Hollywood (to say nothing of producers and directors) would agree with the statement that there are just not enough writers in the movie colony who can turn out a complete, competent screenplay single-handed.

It's hard to say whether this perception is due to the limited abilities of the writers or to a mode of practice that forced writers, however unwillingly, to collaborate with others who might be indifferent to or in conflict with their ideas.

The disconnection made by the factory writing system resulted in screenplays being frequently spurned by their authors (or co-authors). Theatre scholar Gassner, who sought to give the screenplay literary status (see Chapter 2, section 1), observed in 1943 that screenwriters "have indulged in self-depreciation until their sincerity has been put under suspicion." Writers expressed their frustration at the loss of control over their work by disparaging their own screenplays. "I never knew when I was writing a movie," Ben Hecht said, "whether my heroine would end up being called Joe or Mabel or whether the locale would be Peking o[r] Akron."

The metaphors by which they deprecate their own work are as telling as the blueprint and factory metaphors used by film historians and critics. Herman Mankiewicz (*Citizen Kane*) referred to his own screenplays as "'shit,' or 'vomit.'" Metaphors of bodily waste and purgation displace the traditional imagery of writerly creativity, such as childbirth and the growth of natural organisms. Mankiewicz's writing is expressed as something natural but not artistic, a source of shame rather than pride. It's insistently physical but embodies no life, and can't lay claim to the spirituality of literature. Nor can it be admired, or even allowed to remain in sight. Instead its offensiveness makes it a source of embarrassment, and it must be urgently cleared away since it offends not only the writer but also all those around him. Shame is apparent also in one of Hecht's rhymes from the same period, which ends poignantly "'Why do you make me write like that?'"

Compelled to give up authorship and ownership of screenplays, screenwriters accept in their place money and credits, reinforcing the mythical divide between great writing free from mercenary interests and hack writing concerned only with them. Some writers in Hollywood found it easier to accept the lowly status of their writing than others, adopting a hard-boiled approach to screenwriting as primarily a commercial transaction; in particular, former journalists such as Mankiewicz. "It is significant," writes Rosten, "that the writers who find it easiest to adjust to Hollywood are... newspaper-men, advertising writers, publicists." Many of the early screenwriters, including Hecht, Wilder, Mankiewicz, and others going all the way back to Sargent in the 1910s, came from journalism. They must have felt at home in Hollywood, as the writers' buildings on studio lots in some ways resembled newspaper offices. *The Front Page* (1931), set in a newsroom, was written by two former journalists, Hecht and Charles MacArthur, and reflects journalism as a group activity, like factory writing, rather than the solitary occupation of a play or novel author. Journalists worked to the instructions of sub-editors and editors, just as studio writers worked to those of producers and heads of production. Journalists' words would be rewritten by both editors and other journalists. The style of writing was formulaic, and new recruits would learn how to write like those already established in the newsroom. Like a studio screenplay, a newspaper article was liable to be an amalgam of many writers' contributions, whether acknowledged as such or not. Journalists were often paid by the word, as screenwriters might be by the page, and both received weekly wages. Article bylines, like screenplay credits, were negotiable. Script pages were viewed in the studios as being no less ephemeral than daily newspapers. Thus journalist-screenwriters may have encouraged themselves, and each other, to view screenplays in the same way that others viewed journalism, as a lower class of writing. Both were known as "hacks." The term was current for journalists by 1831, already with a strongly pejorative sense; the OED defines a hack as "a person who hires himself or herself out to do any kind of literary work; (hence) a writer producing dull, unoriginal work, esp. to order." Nunnally Johnson (*The Grapes of Wrath*, *The Three Faces of Eve*) was a successful columnist on New York newspapers before becoming a studio screenwriter in 1932. He traces the disparagement of screenplays back to journalists reviewing films in newspapers: "suddenly these reporters were getting $350 or $500 a week out in Hollywood. And I think that was one of the reasons why the newspaper reviewers celebrated the director. Not the writer. I think it was jealousy." Hack journalists, called upon to judge the work of ex-journalist screenwriting hacks, were pre-disposed to an unflattering opinion of their former colleagues' writing. Johnson himself was always in high demand. "I've done closer to 150 screenplays," he told Froug. Yet his modesty about his own screenplays is typical of the ex-journalists: "I may not have been good, but I was reliable." He takes pride less in the quality of his screenplays, emphasising that "It's not easy to get a good script," than in his reliability – much as a working journalist might.

Novelist-screenwriters, even more than journalist-screenwriters, are liable to dismiss their own screenwriting. Novelist-screenwriters have been a persistent feature of Hollywood from the second decade of the twentieth century, when Samuel Goldwyn's "Eminent Authors" initiative among others brought Eastern novelists out to the studios in 1919. Goldwyn also approached English literary stars, including W. Somerset Maugham and Arnold Bennett, who wrote an original screenplay for the 1919 film *Battling Jane*. Elinor Glyn, a popular English novelist, arrived two years later and pursued a successful parallel career writing screenplays in the 1920s and 1930s. Hecht was similarly active in both forms from the 1920s. It wasn't long before other literary novelists were also developing careers as screenwriters: F. Scott Fitzgerald in the late 1920s, William Faulkner, Aldous Huxley, and others early in the 1930s. At the same time, the tone of the widely cited telegram sent by Mankiewicz in Hollywood to Hecht in New York that began Hecht's film career – "MILLIONS ARE TO BE GRABBED OUT HERE" – supports the idea that Hecht's motivation for writing screenplays, and perhaps Mankiewicz's too, was primarily financial. Whatever Hecht's literary aspirations were, Mankiewicz here appeals to the "gold-rush mentality" noted by Maras (see Chapter 1, section 2). Many novelist-screenwriters seem to have worked at their screenplay assignments as well as they could, and although the Hollywood experience was often a frustrating one, they utilised its financial support to underpin their literary careers and, in some cases, also provide story material for it. Norman convincingly challenges the popular myth of Fitzgerald as a fey novelist unwilling to graft at screenplays. In a letter to producer Joseph Mankiewicz, Fitzgerald refers to his "months of work" on the screenplay of *Three Comrades*. He was fascinated by Hollywood, as evidenced by his unfinished novel *The Last Tycoon*, and appeared anxious to succeed as a screenwriter.

However, some novelist-screenwriters were concerned that Hollywood might taint more than their literary reputations, and adopted a strategy of disowning their Hollywood writing while drawing attention to their literary output. As well as being established as a widely admired novelist when he was commissioned by Korda to write the screenplay for *The Third Man*, Greene also had prior experience of writing "scenarios" for *The Green Cockatoo* (1937) and *21 Days Together* (1940). These he regarded as "prentice scripts," suggesting an artisanal context for his early screenplays. "My first script," Greene writes of *21 Days*, "was a terrible affair," while writing *The Green Cockatoo* was the result of pitching an idea to Korda "on the spur of the moment" and accepting the commission "[b]ecause I was very short of money." The result, says Greene, was "the worst and least successful of Korda's productions," which he dismisses wholesale as "so many undistinguished and positively bad films." Greene later singles out his screenplay of his own novel *Brighton Rock* as one of the few that he's "ready to defend." He deplores "what can happen on the floor to your words, your continuity, your idea, the extra dialogue inserted during production," and rejects even the principle of employment: "a writer should not be employed by anyone but himself." Enthusiastic about movies, Greene nevertheless viewed screenwriting with deep suspicion: "If you are using words in one craft, it is impossible not to corrupt them by employing them in another medium under direction." Screenwriting is "the side of my association with the films that I most regret," Greene continues, "and would like most to avoid in future if taxation allows me to." Only financial necessity justifies the novelist compromising his words and independence by writing screenplays.

Already when he came to write *The Third Man* Greene was differentiating screenplays unfavourably from novel writing ("the dull shorthand of a script"). With its suggestion of journalism (journalists being the main users of shorthand), this is writing as a means of recording spoken words of others, rather than the creation of original writing (journalists don't write their articles in shorthand.) Greene was himself employed in journalism at the start of his career, as a sub-editor on *The Times*. There his job was to reduce other journalists' writing not merely to "the shortest number of words, but the shortest number of letters." Greene's shorthand metaphor contrasts the bare-bones minimalism of screenplay writing with the richer creative possibilities of prose fiction. Thus Greene devalues both his screenwriting and journalistic writing by comparison to his literary writing. Exercising a high degree of control over the copyright for his novels, stories, and "entertainments" (popular fiction such as *A Gun for Sale* and *Stamboul Train*), Greene included these in his Collected Works, while excluding much of his journalism and all his screenplays. Of the screenplays, only *The Third Man* was subsequently published. Although Greene preferred *The Fallen Idol* (1948), based on his short story "The Basement Room," to the film *The Third Man*, he didn't sanction publication of the *Fallen Idol* screenplay, because the underlying story "unlike *The Third Man* was not written for the films," and, he continues, "That is only one of many reasons why I prefer it." Years later, he explained that preference more fully: "it was more, I felt, a writer's film, and *The Third Man* more a director's film." The film's writerly qualities might appear to justify publication of the screenplay, but despite the large amount of his work now in print beyond the Collected Works, from novels to letters and journalism, Greene's screenplay for *The Fallen Idol* remains unpublished. In this way it doesn't threaten to encroach on the source story "The Basement Room," acknowledged by Greene as literary in a way that the story *The Third Man* isn't. Screenplays are the result of employment accepted to pay tax demands, while stories such as "The Basement Room" are the product of a lifetime dedicated to literary creation. Greene remarks that "In Italy I wrote the treatment of *The Third Man*, but more importantly for the future I found the small house in Anacapri where all my later books were to be at least part written." For Greene the physical space in which literary work may be undertaken is more important than the actual writing of a film treatment.

Screenplays and their status as writing receive scant attention in most novels by screenwriters, and when they do appear, they're often similarly disparaged. Robert Towne remembers that, when he started writing screenplays,

> It was aesthetically slumming; pandering for big bucks. Screenwriting was that thing that Nathanael West and Dorothy Parker and Fitzgerald and those people did between their serious work to make some money, and tried not to do it too long in order not to become hopelessly compromised.

If screenwriting was seen to compromise writers of talent, screenwriters were represented as writers without talent in the first place in the fiction of novelist-screenwriters. In *The Last Tycoon*, his only novel set in Hollywood, F. Scott Fitzgerald is more interested in capturing the charisma of studio head Thalberg (fictionalised as "Monroe Stahr") than in depicting screenwriters and screenplays. When Fitzgerald does make the writing of screenplays his subject, in the *Pat Hobby Stories*, the portrait isn't a flattering one. Pat the studio hack "was a writer but he had never written much, nor even read all the 'originals' he worked from, because it made his head bang to read much." He's neither a writer nor a reader, and certainly not an artist. "This was no art, as he often said – this was an industry." Pat's primary concern is to secure cash for his next drink, and the screenplays on which he works sporadically are no more to him than a form of currency. Budd Schulberg's portrait of a shameless screenwriter on the make in his novel *What Makes Sammy Run?* (1941) refers to "ditch-digging work" on a story with "the makings of a fair C picture." In *Karoo* (1998), the novel about a script doctor by screenwriter Steve Tesich (*Breaking Away, The World According to Garp*), the protagonist describes his work in dismissive terms: "I rewrite screenplays written by men and women who don't have any talent either." In Karoo's experience, good screenplays are rare. "Most of the time... I work on screenplays that are so bad I could have written them myself." Not all screenplays are flawed; occasionally Karoo is given one to fix "that doesn't need any fixing. It's fine as it is. All it really needs is to be made properly into a film." This happens, though, "very rarely." The irony, of course, is that Tesich's own novel is highly accomplished, just as his screenplays are.

Larry McMurtry, with credits including *The Last Picture Show* (1971), adapted from his own novel, and *Brokeback Mountain* (2005), also disparages his screenwriting. "I will always be grateful to Hollywood for... well... it's essentially financed my fiction, my rare book business, and, to a huge degree, my adult life," he writes. His screenplays have disappeared, subsumed within "Hollywood," while what remains visible are his novels and his rare books, with their perceived higher value. McMurtry echoes Greene, with his tax bills and writing retreat in Anacapri. While acknowledging his screenplays' monetary value, McMurtry reveals (or pretends) indifference to their value as writing: "Unless there's something singular about the producers or actors involved, I quickly forget what I may have just written." This and similar statements demonstrate how writers themselves often buy into the notion of the disposable screenplay, not enduring in itself, a forgettable form not even worth remembering alongside the same writer's novels.

Even those who write only screenplays, and not other forms with higher status, may devalue their own screenwriting by comparison to literary writing. "I'm very clear about my talent," says Bruce Joel Rubin (*Ghost*, *Jacob's Ladder*). "We're not talking great literature here. My hope is to be a good popular entertainer." Nicholas Meyer goes further: "I think it helps to be illiterate as a screenwriter." According to screenwriter and former WGA president Frank Pierson, "They've accepted the idea of being third-class citizens'" in the Hollywood microcosm. Their willingness to accept the general low opinion of screenplays as writing reflects this.

For all his defence of screenwriters and their mistreatment by the film industry, sociologist-screenwriter Rosten himself devalues screenplays by comparison to literary writing. "The movie writer does not need to know how to write," he suggests; "[H]e does need a talent for plot contrivance and a sense of colloquial dialogue. This has been true of movies since the beginning." It's an observation that matches those of the screenwriting manual writers. McKee, for example, insists that "Story talent is primary, literary talent secondary," but he goes on to insist that literary talent is nonetheless "essential."

Scholars, meanwhile, have their own motives for arguing against screenplays as writing and in favour of them as technical documents. Emphasising the discontinuities between screenplays and other writing helps to assert the film scholar's authority in this field, and to resist territorial encroachments from other, literature-based disciplines that seek to colonise it. Meanwhile in university media and communications departments the screenplay as writing is often barely discernible among the many research areas and approaches of these broad fields.

Finally, the reading of screenplays has itself proved problematic. Some novelist-screenwriters have gone beyond disparaging screenplays by comparison to other writing to argue that screenplays aren't even writing that's meant to be read. Like many others already a successful novelist when he started work on his first screenplay, John Gregory Dunne told an interviewer: "There's no such thing as a great screenplay. Because they are not meant to be read. There are just great movies." "The screenwriter's problem," he asserts, "is that he is neither a writer, in the sense that a script is not meant to be read but seen and its quality only then judged, nor is he a filmmaker, in the sense that he is not in control of the finished product." But the screenplay *is* meant to be read, though not necessarily by the film's audience. Numerous people read screenplays on the way to making films, and their readings have a significant impact on these subsequent films.

Even when screenplays are acknowledged as writing to be read, however, there's a widely held view among screenwriters that the executives who do read their screenplays are incompetent. "[M]ost studio people do not know how to read a screenplay," Walter Brown Newman (*Ace in the Hole, Cat Ballou*) said in 1972. Stempel makes the same point, attributing United Artists' *Heaven's Gate* (1980) fiasco to the fact that UA executives "simply did not know how to read a screenplay." According to writer-director John Sayles, "most people can't read. They can't tell a good script from a bad script." Nor is it only studios and their development staff in whom writers have little confidence. Diamond, quoting Wilder, says that "The trouble with most directors is not that they can't write, but that they can't read." Sometimes even screenwriters struggle with reading. William Bowers admits "I hate reading a screenplay. To me it's the dullest thing in the world." Reading is usually understood as a fundamental and continuous process within a literate professional community, and yet here it's pictured by screenwriters, who are highly dependent on the reading skills of others, as dysfunctional. Inadequate reading threatens to undervalue screenplays, particularly in those areas where they're operating connotatively rather than denotatively.

The difficulties of reading screenplays extend to production personnel. Stirling Silliphant gives a dramatic account of one such person struggling with his screenplay:

> Now the production guy looking at this says, "What is this, what the hell, how do I break this down?" He says, "The dawn has brought no relief from the night? What's that?" I say, "You don't break it down. You know it's dawn and you know it's hot and therefore the character has got to be sweating, because he's also running down a dusty mountain, right?" So the guy says, "EXTERIOR MOUNTAIN – DAY." I say, "No, you see the difference is that my thing conveys a mood, your thing is something else." "Yeah, but we got to have our thing to budget." And I say, "But it's all there. You have to read it, though. Read it and then you underline it so you can break it down.

Many screenplay readers will have similarly specific, but different, uses for the screenplay, and there is potential conflict between them. As French screenwriter Jean-Claude Carrière writes in *The Secret Language of Film*:

> Of all writing, a screenplay is the one doomed to the smallest readership: at most, a hundred people. And each of those readers will consult it for his own particular, professional ends. Actors will often see in it only their own part (what is known as the "selfish reading"). Producers and distributors will look only for signs of its potential success. The production manager will count the number of extras, of night shoots. The sound engineer will be hearing the film as he turns the

pages, while the head cameraman will be seeing the lighting, and so on. A whole series of special readings.

Readings of the kind given by Silliphant's "production guy" are focused on information in ways that the reading of a novel rarely is – although stage plays are frequently read in both ways. Carrière doesn't mention directors or development executives – those whose reading ability is questioned by screenwriters. Their readings are likely to take account both of information and of other aspects common to literary writing, such as genre, story structure, thematic content, and verbal style. For all these readers, as for a "production guy," any reading of a screenplay is likely to focus on certain attributes relevant to that specific reader's concerns. Thus the readership of screenplays isn't only tiny, compared to most other forms of writing, but also fragmented.

The reading of screenplays often takes place within a context that's challenging or manifestly hostile. Their writing is "a bastard art, in a sense, in that no one reads what you write, except people who are going to destroy it," according to screenwriter Giler. Whether it's the "production guy" impatient to "break down" the screenplay into information, the development executive who wants to identify the story "beats" and underlying structure prescribed by screenwriting convention, the producer who asks "Will it make money?" or the actor "only concerned with the appearance he wants to create before his fans," all the principal screenplay readers demand that it satisfies their own particular needs. This readership is highly atypical and unusually willing to insist that the writing must be changed to meet their requirements. As a novelist and non-fiction author, as well as a screenwriter, Meyer asks for his screenplays to receive the same kind of reading that his books do: "I write for people who read, whether it's a movie or anything else." Yet screenplays are unlikely to be received in the same disinterested manner. Those who do read screenplays in the same way as novels are more likely to be situated outside the small circle of industry readers: fans, aspiring screenwriters, and some scholars.

Both scholars and practitioners, then, make a wide range of challenges to screenplays as writing. They contest that films aren't based on writing, that words in films are inherently uncinematic, and that when screenplay words are acknowledged, they should be read in a different and narrower way than other kinds of writing. Some seek to displace screenplays altogether by writing with a camera-pen, while privileging the directing of auteurs over their writing. We've seen that the motivation for these challenges frequently derives from struggles for authorship, ownership, and control. Writers themselves have colluded in the disparagement of screenplays for a variety of reasons including the favouring of their literary work over their screenwriting. The next chapter explores the ways in which, despite this, screenplays do indeed function like other writing, as texts to be read.

4

SCREENPLAY STYLE AND VOICE

If it's not quite 'Art' and it's not quite 'Entertainment,' it's here on my desk.

David Mamet

Chapter 3 challenges the widespread view that screenplays aren't writing at all but industrial documents in which writing is disregarded and at best irrelevant, at worst detrimental to film production. This chapter and the next question the perception that film should be seen as distinct from literature and literary writing. The point here is not to claim literary status for screenplays, but to demonstrate that screenplays frequently function in a comparable way to other writing that isn't subjected to the same strictures.

Not only is writing central to the production of all films, but the most celebrated films are predicated on writing that shares features with literary writing. Far from being bound by normative format rules, writers have exploited opportunities offered by master-scene format and the "highly-inflected screenplay" to develop screenplays' capability for creating distinctive writing and individual styles. What's more, writers aren't absent from their work (as the writer of an industrial document may well be), but are often are vividly present within it in various ways. These range from narrative voices that exist apart from characters to writers becoming characters in their own screenplays. Despite what some have affirmed, screenplays frequently employ metaphor, simile, and other devices associated with literature, while producers and other professionals recognise the value of a screenplay's "voice." The chapter questions distinctions made between screenplays and other kinds of writing on the basis of writers' identities, and on modes of production and consumption. It suggests that novels are no more separable from the publishing industry than screenplays are from the film industry. Finally, the ability of screenplays to travel across media platforms can be seen to accentuate these continuities between screenplays and other kinds of writing – all of which function as components of a global entertainment industry.

"Screenplays aren't distinctive in ways that resemble literature"

Ever since the earliest claims were made for screenplays to be considered as literature, these have been contested by both scholars and practitioners. The anthology *Twenty Best Film Plays* (see Chapter 2, section 1), published in 1943, may be the first publication to stake a literary claim. Of its two editors, one, Dudley Nichols, was a screenplay practitioner and the other, John Gassner, a critic and historian of theatre plays. Their respective introductory essays contradict one another. Gassner the critic uses "The Screenplay as Literature" to make an unequivocal case for recognising the screenplay's literary status. He compares screenplays to theatre plays, the novel, and "the spare modern kind of poetry written by Robert Frost, and by T.S. Eliot and Archibald McLeish in their later phases," arguing strenuously for the status of the "film play" to be upgraded on the basis of this relationship. However, in his companion essay, "The Writer and the Film," Nichols the screenwriter is more circumspect. He invokes the blueprint metaphor and insists that "it is difficult for the screenplay to be enjoyed as a literary form in itself" because "it is not and never can be a finished product." In the absence of a final version, Nichols emphasises process and invokes the idea of "a series of creations" through which a film travels before acquiring its final shape as a completed film. The screenplay is thus one stage, although a crucial one, in this series. As such, it's writing – even literature – but also differs from published literary works.

The only other substantial intervention is Douglas Winston's 1973 book, *The Screenplay as Literature*. Here, too, the claim is complicated by differences between literary writing and film creation. After this, Steven Maras notes that "the 'screenplay as literature' problem has taken different paths. The issue of literature and film relations has been expanded hugely and taken up in academic circles, initially via adaptation theory," while more recently, "efforts to re-evaluate the screenplay as a form in its own right have emerged... some of these efforts drawing on contemporary textual theory."

Steven Price, like Maras, sidelines the literary question on the basis of "the post-1968 critical reorientation away from notions of the literary work and towards an idea of the 'text,'" which removes the evaluative aspect of literature as high art and views all texts, aesthetically valorised or not, as potential objects of study. The "unfinished" nature of a screenplay has ceased to distinguish it from literary works when viewed from a postmodern perspective that characterises all texts as essentially unstable and questions whether any version can be considered final.

However, the question of screenplays' literary status has persisted within screenwriting manuals. Just as these have frequently adopted the blueprint metaphor, so too they have tended to follow Nichols, the practitioner, rather than Gassner, the scholar, in their views of screenplays' literary status. "[S]creenplays are not intended as literature," according to manual authors Robin Russin and William Downs, and are "not read as literary material." To Michael Hauge, "literature" is "a good source of material" that can be adapted into a screenplay, rather than something screenwriters write. Joseph McBride, another blueprint enthusiast, not only states emphatically that "screenwriting is not literature," but also asserts that "it's not writing in the sense of a novelist's work in creating an entire, self-sufficient world on paper, or even a playwright's work in creating a dramatic world that can be appreciated without necessarily seeing it staged and performed." Robert McKee deflects the question onto the screenwriter, who needs both "story talent," which is "rare," and "literary talent," which is "common," thereby devaluing the literature that was in 1943 seen to lend higher status to screenwriting.

Even practitioners mostly agree that screenplays aren't literary. Screenwriter and sociologist Leo Rosten insists that "The Hollywood writer is not writing prose or producing literature," while screenwriter Chris Weitz (*Cinderella*, *The Golden Compass*) says, "I don't think it's literature, really – rarely and unintentionally does it achieve that status." Director Nicholas Ray states flatly that "the theatre is literary; film is not." As with filmic hostility to words in film more generally, there's widespread suspicion of anything in the screenplay that might be considered "literary," which is often used to imply inappropriate stylistic flourishes, as McKee indicates:

> Pity the poor screenwriter, for he cannot be a poet.
> He cannot use metaphor and simile, assonance
> and alliteration, rhythm and rhyme, synecdoche
> and metonymy, hyperbole and meiosis, the grand
> tropes. Instead, his work must contain all the
> substance of literature but not be literary.

For McKee, the "substance" of literature that belongs in a screenplay distills down to "story." In spite of claims that screenplays are literature, these claims have been partial, qualified, denied, and, even when conceded, deemed inappropriate, pretentious, and limited across a range of discourses and decades.

Screenplays share the characteristics of literary writing

While more recent screenwriting manuals agree that screenplays are fundamentally unliterary or avoid the debate altogether, in one of the earliest manuals, Epes Winthrop Sargent argues the opposite. He writes:

> Today, as in the past, literary skill is not required in expressing the story in words, but almost weekly the demand increases for scripts with ideas of a higher degree of literary merit... Literary skill and judgment most assuredly are required of the author in plotting his story as well as in originating ideas, but literary expression can be shown only in the leaders.

There's a clear sense here that "literary skill" has an important role to play in the earliest forms of the screenplay, although "literary expression" must be confined to literal words in the film's intertitles ("leaders"). Sargent locates "[l]iterary skill and judgment" not only in the mechanical "plotting" of the story, as McKee would later do, but also in the conceptual work of the screenplay, where it is essential for "originating ideas" (see Chapter 6).

Moreover, despite McBride's assertion that screenplays don't create worlds in the ways that novels and stage plays do, authors of recent screenwriting manuals take a contrasting view. John Truby writes: "you can tell a story without adding the texture of the story world. But it's a big loss." His examples range from canonical literature (James Joyce's *Ulysses*; Charles Dickens's *A Christmas Carol*) to popular fiction (the Harry Potter books) and stage plays (*Copenhagen* by Michael Frayn), as well as more recent screenplays (*Four Weddings and a Funeral*) and those from the classical studio period (*It's a Wonderful Life;*

Citizen Kane). Truby makes no distinction between the literary and the non-literary in their creation of "story worlds" demonstrating instead how all share common features.

William Froug's interviews with screenwriters find variable views regarding the literariness of screenplays, but no one who denies that screenplays are writing. While screenwriter David Giler suggests that a screenplay "is like any other kind of writing in that it basically involves words... literary style," Froug recounts that his interview with screenwriter Nunnally Johnson took place in Johnson's "elegantly furnished living room," in which the two "were surrounded by leather-bound volumes of his screenplays." Having his screenplays bound like antique editions of classic literature, Johnson makes an implicit and indirect claim for his screenplays to be considered literature's equal. Similarly, screenwriter Fay Kanin insists that "it's as honorable to write a good original screenplay as to write an original play for the theater." Here original screenplays are elevated not only by comparison to original stage plays, but also by differentiation from other, unoriginal screenplays. Occupying a middle ground between these poles, screenwriter Bruce Joel Rubin, while modest about his own talents, nevertheless proposes that "The first job of a writer is to create a literary work, not the blueprint purely for what's going to be on the screen." The resultant screenplay may not be "great literature," but it remains a "literary work" all the same, functioning in a comparable way to more obviously "honorable" stage plays.

Claudia Sternberg points out that the practice of regarding theatre plays as literature is a relatively recent development dating from the Romantic period, and that, prior to this, plays were "used as working scripts read by professionals." From this historical perspective, it may be no more than a question of time before screenplays are accorded similar status. Barbara Korte and Ralf Schneider discuss historical practices in which some writers write and publish both stage plays and screenplays, arguing that their screenplays must be therefore considered equally "literary."

In "The Appreciation of the Screenplay as Literature" Ted Nannicelli concludes his overview of the debate by claiming: "Many, if not most, screenplays can plausibly be identified as literary works even without assuming any specific definition or characterization of literature... Thus the vexed question – 'what is literature?' – need not be answered for us to plausibly identify screenplays as literary works." In effect Nannicelli abandons the debate over what formal or narratological features define literature as literature or screenplays as screenplays, as well as distinctions made between ordinary writing and literary writing. He concludes that screenplays are literary works because they "easily meet the conditions for literary status" specified by the "various prominent definitions of literature" reviewed within Nannicelli's book. Meanwhile arguments will continue to be made for and against the screenplay as literature across scholarship, pedagogy, and practice, serving a variety of agendas, from screenwriters' self-promotion (and self-deprecation) to film's battle to be deemed an art in its own right, to the financial imperative driving the sale of screenwriting manuals to as many readers as possible.

Lastly, there's the evidence of literary writers themselves. Novelists have employed screenplay form within their work, or written entire books as "screenplays" that are published as literature and never enter the arena of filmmaking. William Burroughs, who experimented widely with literary form, wrote *The Last Words of Dutch Schultz* (1969) entirely as a screenplay; it's subtitled *A Fiction in the Form of a Film Script*, and adopts an archaic, studio-period format that matches the 1930s period of its subject matter, with each page divided into action and sound columns, and interspersed with still photographs. There's no evidence that Burroughs ever intended his screenplay to be produced rather than read alongside his other fiction works. A contemporary review in *Publishers Weekly* calls this "Burroughs' most accessible, tightly knit work of fiction... it's almost as if this is the form that Burroughs has always needed," making it clear that the book was not perceived by literary critics in the 1960s as separate from the body of the author's oeuvre. Other literary authors who've written wholly or partly in screenplay form include the novelists Adam Thorpe (*Ulverton*, 1992), Carol Shields (*Mary Swann*, 1993), Anthony Burgess (*Mozart and the Wolf Gang*, 1991), and John Collier (*Milton's Paradise Lost: Screenplay for Cinema of the Mind*, 1973). Writers such as Tony Harrison, meanwhile, have also explored in depth the textual affinities existing between screenplays and poetry; Harrison's *Collected Film Poetry* (2007) runs to some 480 pages.

"Screenplays are unliterary because they're bound by normative format rules"

Screenwriting manuals, like script formatting textbooks and software, have helped to promote a technical uniformity of formatting that has become part of the debate over whether screenplays should be considered literature. A recurrent criticism of screenplays, made to support assertions of their unliterariness, draws attention to their lack of variety, and to the repeated use of standardised formatting, such as scene headings: INT. ROOM – DAY.

The diversity of formats that characterised the screenplay and its variants in the first half of the twentieth century subsequently shrank to a single norm – the master-scene screenplay. According to Janet Staiger, "The form that eventually became standard (the master-scene) was a combination of theatrical and pre-sound film scripts, a variant of the continuity synopsis used in the 1920s." This format avoids overt technical specifications and especially shot-by-shot segmentation. Instead it offers an overview of the action, with a dramatic construction that seeks to engage the reader, just as the implicit film-to-be will seek to engage the viewer:

```
INT. OFFICES - THE NEXT MORNING


Kiko, the one Young Female Intern, PULLS
A HUGE DOLLY stacked with reams of
printer paper down a row of cubicles.
She's delivering the paper to each desk.
Guys in the office scoot past her as she
lugs the dolly forward, Ben arrives to
help, pushing the dolly for her.


                    BEN (cont'd)
          I'll push, you deliver.
                    KIKO
          Thank you!!!
```

Nancy Meyers's screenplay for *The Intern* (2014) keeps description to a minimum. The only information it provides about a new character introduced in this scene is that she's "the one Young Female Intern." The screenplay informs the reader approximately how old Kiko is, but not what she looks like or how she's dressed. The slug line identifies the set simply as "OFFICES." Since these have previously been established as "[a] former factory retrofitted as an enormous bullpen. It's a football field of cubicles buzzing like a trading floor" (1), the reader can't tell where in this area the size of a "football field" the action takes place. Nor is who the "[g]uys" are and why they "scoot past" explained. The writing here is about essentials – what McKee would call "story": the interaction between protagonist Ben and minor character Kiko, with just enough information to make this comprehensible. The streamlined format accentuates forward movement, the rapid progression of story events, hustling the reader from one incident to the next. There's nothing about camera movement, shot sizes, or other technical information to impede this flow. Nevertheless, the screenplay foregrounds writing that will be part of the final film, in that the interaction between characters unfolds primarily through dialogue.

Although scholars often credit screenwriting manuals with the widespread adoption of master-scene format, its development owes more to practising screenwriters. While Price considers that "the current understanding of the screenplay as a document with very precise formal requirements derives not from industrial practice but from the effect of screenwriting manuals, beginning with those written in the late 1970s," a standardised format had already emerged within the industry before then. When Froug interviews twelve screenwriters for his 1972 book, *The Screenwriter Looks at the Screenwriter*, he asks several whether they "write only master scenes" or "include shots and angles." While this suggests that master-scene format could not yet be taken for granted, the screenplay pages that he includes (one for each writer) demonstrate that not only do all twelve indeed employ the master-scene format, but also that these are formally similar. Froug's interviewees form part of mainstream Hollywood industry practice, and the majority of them (Johnson, Kanin, William Bowers, Walter Brown Newman, Ring Lardner, Jr., I.A.L. Diamond, Edward Anhalt, Stirling Silliphant) began their careers well within the classical studio period. Nonetheless, the screenplay pages that Froug reproduces, which date from the beginning of the 1970s, exhibit consistent master-scene form. Newman also refers to seeing the same format across a range of other writers' output, read by him as part of his duties at the Writers Guild of America: "The screenplays that have come across my desk in arbitration proceedings do tend more and more to be written in master scenes." Writing in camera angles and shots is, he says, "out of date." It's clear, then, that widespread adoption of the master-scene format in Hollywood had already taken place years before the first edition of Syd Field's *Screenplay* was published in 1979, and derived from screenwriters themselves.

Since then, both screenwriting manuals and scholars have invoked industry practice to validate the dominance of the master scene. "ONLY WRITE IN MASTER SCENES," instructs manual author Lew Hunter. Field concurs: "[a] scene is written in *master shot*" describing his illustrative example as "the proper, contemporary, and professional screenplay form." Other screenwriting guides agree with Field in nominating this "proper" format (for example, Russin and Downs and Hauge). Scholars who read screenwriting manuals as evidence of industry practice grant them authority. For instance, Price quotes Christopher Riley's screenplay formatting manual: "too many writers who think they're turning in professionally formatted scripts are in fact often turning in scripts that brand them as amateurs. ... The fact is that a standard format exists today in Hollywood." On the grounds that Riley's book accurately reflects current industrial practice, Price endorses this view, while deprecating its didacticism: "Although this is highly prescriptive, it is also essentially correct."

However, the detailed instructions of *The Hollywood Standard* target aspiring screenwriters rather than describing the best screenplays produced by working professionals. Four of the five screenplays nominated for best original screenplay for the 88th Academy Awards disobey Riley's prescriptions in many ways. *Inside Out* plays by the Riley rule book but, *Spotlight*, the Oscar winner, uses bold, forbidden by Riley ("**Don't use bold or italics**;" bold in original), in its opening lines:

<u>1 INT. POLICE STATION, BOSTON – NIGHT, 1976</u>

A quiet, cold winter night. An OLDER COP emerges from an INTERVIEW ROOM, walks down a long hall.

Boston, MA – December, 1976

The scene heading ("slug line") is emboldened and also underlined. If the indented words identifying the period and location of the scene are intended to be a "superimposition" that will appear on screen, they should instead, according to Riley, be introduced by "SUPERIMPOSE:" at the left-hand margin, in capitals but not in bold, and enclosed in quotation marks. *Bridge of Spies*, by Matt Charman, Ethan Coen, and Joel Coen, also begins in bold type and furthermore ignores Riley's instruction to "The first time a speaking character appears on screen, capitalize that character's name." Abel and the Agent, the first two speaking characters to appear in this screenplay, go uncapitalised, as do others when they're introduced. Similarly, even though Riley indicates that "CUT TO" should be "tabbed far to the right side of the page," the opening scene of *Ex Machina*, by British writer-director Alex Garland, aligns transitions at the left-hand margin and also uses bold type:

CUT TO –
– EXTREME CLOSE UP of a pinhole web-cam lens in CALEB'S monitor.

CUT TO –
the POV of the web-cam.

The screenplay uses prohibited italics on the next page ("Then mouths the word: *Fuck.*"). On its first page, *Straight Outta Compton* falls foul of Riley's rule against capitalising props when "Eazy unscrews a CERWIN-VEGA sub-woofer. Grabs a bulging BROWN BAG out of the speaker." These may seem nitpicking examples, but it's precisely this level of nitpicking detail that *The Hollywood Standard* polices and which aspiring screenwriters are instructed to follow religiously. Clearly there's more flexibility in the "professional" format than either Riley or Price acknowledges.

Distinctive screenplay style, voice and authorial self-reflexivity

Beyond those questioning the freedom to embolden, italicise, and indent at will, there are more significant critiques of screenplay uniformity. Master-scene screenplays often appear generic and lacking in individuality. McKee caricatures the typical master-scene screenplay in the hands of an unskilled writer:

```
EXT. HOUSE — DAY


Description, description, description.
Characters A and B enter.


                CHARACTER A
        Dialogue, dialogue, dialogue.


                CHARACTER B
        Dialogue, dialogue, dialogue.


Description, description, description,
description, description.
```

Parodied in this way, the master-scene format emerges as a restrictive template to be filled with predictable dialogue and description. However, in "Language as Narrative Voice: The Poetics of the Highly Inflected Screenplay," Jeff Rush and Cynthia Baughman argue that "pure story form itself is limited," in opposition to story-driven screenwriting manuals such as McKee's. They go on to analyse how "inferential or evocative language functions to determine meaning and focus" in a range of films from the 1980s and 1990s, pointing out that "perspectives" such as "those of commentary, of irony, or of close-in lyrical experience" must be expressed in other ways. One way that screenplays achieve this is by creating a tension between the "dramatic mode" (described action) and "narrative mode" (how the reader is positioned by the screenplay in relation to this). Thus in the opening of *Blue Velvet* (1986) the dramatic mode informs the reader that small-town life is idyllic, while the narrative mode alerts her to the unreliability of this view. The result is a "shifting of tone" that "breaks down the clear separation between character and narrator," something that more basic manuals work so hard to distinguish, as they do the standard "elements" of the screenplay.

In some cases, characters' dialogue, "parentheticals" describing how they speak, and descriptions of their actions may belong to a separate narrator (who is frequently identified with the screenwriter). They may, alternatively, belong to another character or to another, unidentified narrator. "The lack of a tag," according to Rush and Baughman, "causes the narrator's and the characters' voices to bleed into one another, to contest one another, to become polyvocal." This technique greatly extends the connotative and tonal capabilities of the screenplay.

However, Rush and Baughman limit their examples to a relatively small, if high-profile, subsection of the film industry, the crossover area between studio and independent cinema. These are films produced on smaller budgets that anticipate smaller audiences, though sometimes with A-list talent: *The Player* (1992), *After Hours* (1985), *Blue Velvet* (1986), *Heathers* (1988), and *My Own Private Idaho* (1991). Implicit in their essay is the idea that the "highly inflected screenplay" is limited to this somewhat rarefied domain favouring "stories whose focus is on the tension between events and their telling."

The principle of the highly inflected screenplay can, however, be extended more widely to include screenplays for mainstream commercial films, as well as farther back in time to classical cinema. While most of Graham Greene's screenplay for the 1949 film, *The Third Man*, remains within the confines of objective, uninflected storytelling, its opening sequence offers an early and mainstream example of inflection. Commentary and irony are created by the juxtaposition of shots with anonymous voice-over:

```
Of course, a situation like that does
tend to amateurs — Shot of a body
floating in an icy river — but you know
they can't stay the course like a
professional.
```

This breezy euphemism for murder cannot confidently be attributed to the "narrator" of the screenplay, or to writer Greene, or to any character in the story. The unidentified speaker continues casually, "I was going to tell you about Holly Martins from America – he came all the way here to visit a friend of his... The name was Lime, Harry Lime." Although absent from the version of Greene's screenplay used during production, and probably written by Greene in collaboration with director Carol Reed during post-production (see Chapter 3, section 6), these comments match the "polyvocalism" of his novels and short stories, showing Greene to be an early adopter of the highly inflected screenplay.

Inflection can be found in many later screenplays, including some that lay claim to being "uninflected." David Mamet insists that the job of writer and director is "simply to *tell* the story" through "the juxtaposition of uninflected images," claiming Eisenstein as his authority: "Mr Eisenstein tells us that the best image is an uninflected image… otherwise you have not got dramatic action, you have narration." Yet telling the story in cuts, "a juxtaposition of images that are basically uninflected," doesn't remove inflection from Mamet's screenplays any more than from his stage plays. Mamet may banish a narrating writerly presence from his action lines, but it still finds its way into the dialogue text instead, as in this example:

MARTY

Look: okay. Okay. Look: look
you're driving, countryside,
so on, you picked her up, she
was hitch...

WALT

No, hey, hey...al, she hid in
the back of the car! Happens
all the...

Marty and Walt in *State and Main* talk much as Aaronow and Moss do in *Glengarry Glen Ross* (both the stage play and, here, the virtually identical screenplay):

AARONOW

You need money? Is that the...

MOSS

Hey, hey, let's just keep it
simple, what I need is not
the...what do you need...?

All four talk like other Mamet characters, using the broken lines, ellipses, rhythms, emphases, and repetitions that are hallmarks of Mamet's dialogue. The screenplays' master-scene format doesn't shut out Mamet's distinctive style.

The capacity of the screenplay to employ "evocative language" that "functions as an expression of narrative voice" has continued to travel beyond the arthouse in the twenty-first century. Of the 88th Academy Awards nominees, *Straight Outta Compton* immediately lays claim to this type of agency, as action lines read like dialogue:

```
EAZY vibes with it. Can't fuckin' help
it. Shit is dope. Finally, once THE BEAT
IS FULLY REALIZED, Dre CUES him --
```

It's not clear who's speaking these lines that describe Dr Dre at work in Lonzo's studio, implying a writerly narrator or even the presence of the writers themselves. They narrate omnisciently, as a novelist might, giving their readers access to the inside of Eazy's head, which the camera can't penetrate. Here and throughout the screenplay the vocabulary of the action lines, regardless of who's in the scene, maintain the same hip-hop rhythms and vocabulary as the principal characters' dialogue. Two pages later Eazy is again described – this time, objectively:

```
Eazy emerges from a RUN-DOWN HOUSE, jogs
across the street to his BUCKET, climbs
inside, opens his STASH SPOT, stuffs a
large WAD of CASH inside. A hustler is
always hustlin --
```

It's impossible to determine who reflects that "A hustler is always hustlin." "Bucket," meanwhile, is a slang term for a car;

positioning the reader within the hip-hop world of its characters and story is what this writing sets out to achieve. As Rush and Baughman wrote of Gus Van Sant's screenplay, *My Own Private Idaho*, the feeling here is "experiential rather than dramatic."

Over time, developments within master-scene screenplays have drawn attention to the position of the writer and enabled other kinds of distinctive writing that also appear in other kinds of literature. For Rush and Baughman, "Reading a screenplay is like any other interpretative reading, a matter of both looking through language to see what is represented and looking at language to understand how it reflects back on the writer." By contrast, screenplays have been seen in the past to erase the writer: Sargent's technique in *The Narrow Paths of Fate* of 1916, for example, is self-effacing. However, by 1939, Nichols is more assertive in his screenplay, *Stagecoach*, expressing cultural views and personal attitudes such as those about the "savagery and desperation" of the Apaches and "picturesque" Mexicans, as seen in Chapter 3, section 3.

By 1987, the opening scene of *Lethal Weapon* – a commercial film written by Shane Black – has gone much further, to insist as much on the storyteller as on the story itself. From the first scene heading, in which the location (Los Angeles) is rendered archly as the "CITY OF ANGELS," the screenplay places its writer-narrator within the world he's creating:

```
CAMERA CONTINUES TO MOVE IN THROUGH
billowing curtains, INTO the inner
sanctum of a penthouse apartment, and
here, boys and girls, is where we lose
our breath, because --

spread-eagled on a sumptuous designer
sofa lies the single most beautiful GIRL
in the city.
```

Addressing its readers in the diction of a children's storyteller ("boys and girls"), Black – like Kaufman – makes himself visible within his screenplay, using direct address to establish his presence and assert his authority. In the following scene, as Riggs the protagonist takes on a group of knife-wielding punks, the narrator ironises his thriller tropes by interjecting narratorial comments:

```
Riggs, completely heedless, once again
attends to the dog:

                    RIGGS
        What's that ... ? The one ...
        in the middle... 'is a stupid
        fat duck'... What ... ?
            (listens again)
        Oh ... Oh! A 'stupid fat
        fuck!' Right.

He looks up, shakes his head.

                    RIGGS
        Boy, this dog is pissed.

The one in the middle grabs Riggs by the
collar.

Hoists him to his feet. Gulp.
```

Having inserted his extraneous comments, and after a build-up lasting three and a half pages, Black then denies his reader the anticipated pay-off. Instead of the expected blow-by-blow account of this one-against-four fight, Black dismisses the entire sequence:

    And then Punk #1 springs...

    Big mistake.

    Needless to say, mincemeat is made of the
    four meddlesome dog-torturers.

By saying that the outcome of the fight is "needless to say," Black simultaneously asserts his authorship and discounts it. Emphasising that this is only a story that he's telling, he again affirms that everything is under his control, because he's the one telling everything. Yet he's equally happy to share his omniscient authority as he reaches the screenplay's big "reveal":

    Riggs, meanwhile, looking around
    frantically, he's trying to find the guy
    with the gun who is, of course, himself.

The throwaway aside, "of course," creates a sense of knowing collusion between reader and screenwriter.

In 2002 Charlie Kaufman takes this collusion to new heights, while giving an extreme demonstration of writerly visibility. He draws attention to his presence in the screenplay of *Adaptation* by dramatising himself as a character, redoubled by the addition of a twin brother, alter-ego "Donald Kaufman," who's also a writer. Protagonist Charlie Kaufman's two voices, exterior and interior, also bear an alter-ego relation to each other. Twinned and split, Kaufman thus redoubles his presence as writer and narrator in the film. Kaufman exploits these possibilities to establish himself not only as a character in the screenplay, but also as the film's protagonist:

    Kaufman, wearing his purple sweater sans
    tags, sits with Valerie, an attractive

```
     woman in wire-rim glasses. They pick at

     salads. Kaufman steals glances at her

     lips, her hair, her breasts.


     She looks up at him. He blanches, looks

     away.
                    KAUFMAN (V.O.)
          I'm old. I'm bald. I'm

          repulsive.
                    VALERIE
          We think you're just great.
                    KAUFMAN
               (with studied modesty)
          Oh, thank you.
```

The *Adaptation* screenplay isn't only writing that insists on the act of reading, but is also writing in which the writer himself asserts his presence, objectifying himself within the reading experience. He nudges the reader with the knowing irony of "sans," which echoes Shakespeare's melancholy Jacques from *As You Like It* ("Sans teeth, eyes, sans taste, sans everything"). The writer of *Adaptation* has read Shakespeare, and expects his reader also to have read Shakespeare, and to register the quotation. The reference to "studied modesty" asks the reader to reflect on the ironic gulf stretching between what the words say and the display of supercharged egotism to which they relate. In McKee's story seminar, which Kaufman parodies in his screenplay (see Chapter 3, section 2), the screenwriting guru tells his students to "get out of the way of the story," but Kaufman the writer and Kaufman the character resolutely refuse to do so in the *Adaptation* screenplay and film.

Along with the increased visibility in screenplays of the writer, individual style – the "writer's voice," distinct from the story she tells and the characters she describes – has increasingly become one of their most highly prized elements. This aligns some screenplays with other kinds of personal as opposed to formulaic or factory writing. Like the highly inflected screenplay, the distinctive voices of screenwriters within their screenplays become more prominent after the classical Hollywood studio period. Nichols criticises the production line approach to filmmaking in his 1943 essay because it "tends to destroy that individuality of style which is the mark of any superior work of art." Since then, the "distinctive voice" has become shorthand for this "individuality of style."

In the "package-unit system" that succeeded the classical studio period, the screenplay became a much more important element of the package of commercial elements assembled by a producer (see Chapter 3, section 6). It was therefore in the interests of both producer and writer for screenwriters to develop a recognisable style which would make their screenplays stand out from the crowd. The rise of the "new Hollywood" in the 1960s encouraged this trend as independent filmmakers aligned themselves with groundbreaking films such as *Bonnie and Clyde* (1967) in opposition to the more generic output of the studios. *Bonnie and Clyde*'s first-time screenwriters, Robert Benton and David Newman, taught themselves to write by reading François Truffaut and rewatching Alfred Hitchcock films. Their screenplay might be the first in that period of rapid change within the film industry to showcase a distinctive (if uneven) writerly voice: a messy hybrid of prim narration, colloquial Texan dialogue, and lengthy parentheticals. It combines denotative shot instructions – "The camera pulls back and over the car" – with psychological editorialising: "The weapon has an immediate effect on her. She touches it in a manner almost sexual, full of repressed excitement." The self-reflexive awareness visible in other films, which would later become so prominent in the work of writers such as Quentin Tarantino, is already present here. A near-miss on the road is described as "almost Mack Sennett stuff, but not quite that much". Here, the writers don't describe the event itself but substitute a personal memory of seeing an old comedic film that they want this scene to resemble, with modifications dictated by them. More than such details it's the writers' attitudes – to crime (portraying it as fun), to sexuality (linking it with other kinds of excitement, such as violence), and to filmmaking itself (their obsession with the French New Wave) – that mark this as the kind of writing that, half a century later, would be sought by film production organisations. However, while their *Bonnie and Clyde* screenplay might have a distinctive voice, this didn't extend to the same writers' work on other projects such as *Oh! Calcutta!* (1972) and *Superman* (1978).

By contrast, other writers in this period fuse story choice, tone, format, attitude, and writing style into a "voice" that can be traced across different screenplays. These tend to be writer-directors, such as John Cassavetes, while William Goldman is a pre-eminent example of a screenwriter who isn't a director, yet has a distinctive "voice" already recognisable in the 1960s. Others achieve distinctiveness later: Woody Allen and David Lynch in the 1970s, the Coen brothers in the 1980s, Tarantino and Wes Anderson in the 1990s, Kaufman and Christopher Nolan at the end of the twentieth century. Their prominence in the industry in terms of awards and reviews corresponds to the distinctiveness of their voices.

So high is the value placed on a distinctive "voice" being discernible in the screenplay that it's become part of the rhetoric employed by organisations that recruit new writers of screenplays. BBC Films, the BBC's feature film division, highlighted this aspect of its productions on its public website in 2015 (subsequently merged into the BBC's corporate website):

> What unites *Billy Elliot, Truly Madly Deeply, Philomena, In the Loop, Dirty Pretty Things, Mrs Brown, Fish Tank, An Education, My Summer of Love, Iris, Made in Dagenham*, to name but a few, is that they were all made by BBC Films, they each offer a unique perspective on British life and they each come from a distinctive voice.

Here the "voices" of films in the BBC Films catalogue are invoked, rather than the familiar privileging of the visual over the verbal, often encapsulated in the phrase "director's vision." Ranging across more than three decades (from 1990 to 2013), these eleven films were selected from a total output of 274 to represent BBC Films to the public. The singular case – these films each derive from "a distinctive voice" – might suggest that all are the work of writer-directors. However, this is true of only three: Anthony Minghella's *Truly Madly Deeply* (1990), Pawel Pawlikowski's *My Summer of Love* (2004), based on the novel by Helen Cross, and Andrea Arnold's *Fish Tank* (2009). On another two, *Iris* (2001) and *In The Loop* (2009), the directors were also co-writers. The remaining six, more than half of the BBC Films selection, are collaborations between writers who write and directors who direct. Whose, then, is the "distinctive voice" of these films? In many cases, perhaps most or even all, it is that of the writer. However, the BBC's slightly odd rhetoric – "they each come from a distinctive voice" – suggests that in some way each project, as against the screenplay or director's work, generates that highly valued voice.

Film4, the BBC's main rival for film projects within the UK, similarly highlighted in the same year that the company was "particularly interested in distinctive voices." Although Film4 projects tend to be more director-driven than those of BBC Films, a note on the commissioning web page in 2020, addressed to producers, continues to advise them that "[a]gents, similarly to production companies, will be looking for a new and distinctive voice to come through in someone's writing." Here "voice" isn't a metaphor for film visuals but instead is directly tied to the writing and speaking of words. Film4 seeks distinctive voices first of all in writing; long before a director gets the opportunity to showcase their "vision" by directing a project in production, that project must first be developed as a screenplay. Any decision on whether or not to commission that screenplay will be based substantially on assessments by producers, executives, and agents of the writer's ability to offer the "distinctive voice" that they seek. BBC Films and Film4 thus direct their search for distinctive voices in the first place to screenplays. This implicitly recognises the truth of the old industry wisdom that the script is everything. Distinctiveness is crucial since any film must stand out in a crowded marketplace; the screenplay is recognised by BBC Films and Film4 as the locus of that distinctiveness.

Nor is it only BBC Films and Film4 that encourage writers to create screenplays showcasing distinctive voices. Ian Macdonald's research into professional script readers in the UK shows that they similarly "describe seeking an original voice." The same emphasis can be found in Hollywood, where McKee insists that "[g]reat screenwriters are distinguished by a personal storytelling style;" "unique" and "original" are his watchwords. "If you show a brilliant, original script to agents," he tells readers of *Story*, "they'll fight for the right to represent you."

The rhetoric of distinctive voice isn't limited to screenwriting. One of the largest of the London talent agencies, Curtis Brown, addresses very similar language to aspiring novelists. Agents Felicity Blunt and Jonny Geller are looking for "a distinctive voice," while their colleagues seek "confident writing voices" (Gordon Wise), and "a voice that will stand out" (Sheila Crowley). The search for distinctiveness is a commercial imperative, not medium-specific, nor a public relations bromide. The desired qualities are the same ones sought by BBC Films, Film4, Hollywood studios, and independent production companies. Truby reinforces the importance of both "voice" and originality: "It is essential that, whatever medium you work in, you create your original story world and your original voice."

This focus on a distinctive voice as the most highly valued element of a screenplay may be relatively recent in film practitioner discourse, but it has roots in Romanticism that persist in modernism, just as the conception behind it, that individuality is to be prized, is a form of modernism that persists in postmodernism. A "mistake writers make is not being true to their own voice," says screenwriter Scott Frank, endorsing a Romantic conception of voice as representative of individual personality. Buck Henry (*The Graduate, Catch 22*) comments on the clashing voices of screenwriter and novelist as a major problem of adapting novels to screenplays: "your voice and his voice interfere with each other." When novelist and screenwriter are the same individual the clash can be replaced by reinforcement. Bruce Robinson (*The Killing Fields, Withnail and I*) recounts that when he first wrote *Withnail and I*, as a novel, he was speaking with his "own voice" and that, having discovered that voice, he wanted to ensure it also informed the screenplay. The voice telling the story was as important to him as the story: "That was what I wanted to say and how I wanted to say it." Nor was this confined to dialogue: "If the script is a comedy I want you to be laughing through the stage directions as well."

Some screenwriters consider that a writer's voice can prove a negative factor in screenplays when it overrides the distinctiveness of characters. Rubin notes that "Most films in Hollywood... have one voice – the writer's." For example, in *Juno* (2007) by Diablo Cody (*Young Adult, Tully*), a single voice dominates both description and dialogue:

                    JUNO
          I think the last one was
          defective. The plus sign
          looked more like a division
          sign.

Rollo regards her with intense
skepticism.

                    JUNO
          I remain unconvinced.

Rollo pulls the bathroom key out of
reach.

                    ROLLO
          This is your third test today,
          Mama Bear. Your eggo is
          preggo, no doubt bout it!

An eavesdropping TOUGH GIRL wearing an
oversized jacket and lots of makeup gapes
at Juno from the beauty aisle.

                    TOUGH GIRL
          Three times? Oh girl, you are
          way pregnant. It's easy to
          tell. Is your nipples real
          brown?

A pile of stolen COSMETICS falls out of
the girl's jacket and clatters to the
floor.

                    TOUGH GIRL
          Balls!

The three characters in this early scene from *Juno* share the same high-energy, smart-ass dialogue style, but so too do her father ("What did you do, Junebug? Hit someone with the Previa?") and mother ("I was hoping she was expelled or into hard drugs"). The same tone pervades the stage directions:

```
PAUL BLEEKER steps onto the front porch
of his house for early morning track
practice. He wears a cross country
uniform that reads "DANCING ELK CONDORS."
He is eating some kind of microwaved
snack gimmick.
```

The description of what Bleeker's eating communicates attitude more than information. So, although Cody's "voice" in the *Juno* screenplay is distinctive, it does little to distinguish between different characters, or between description and dialogue. Voice can thus, at times, prove detrimental to effective character-isation and description in its efforts to attract attention. Nonetheless, it no doubt contributed to *Juno*'s 2008 Oscar for Original Screenplay and has also raised Cody's profile in the marketplace.

"Screenplays aren't literary because they don't use the figurative rhetoric of literary writing"

In addition to manifesting distinctive voices, screenplays also contain other elements characterising literary writing that are often denied to screenwriting under industrial and blueprint paradigms. Kevin Boon argues in relation to *Fargo* (1996) that verbal constructs within the screenplay aren't necessarily extended by its transition to film:

> The exposition of [a character], its complications
> to the plot, and its revelations about character are
> literary; they are rendered in the text of the
> screenplay. The dialogue and events that shape
> the core thrust of the story exist fully in text. The
> film recasts these elements into visual represent-
> ations, but it does not add complexity or
> complication. Just as Hamlet exists as a textual
> construction outside performance, Jerry Lundegaard
> exists outside the film proper. He is made of
> words, first and foremost, and is merely per-
> formed in the film.

Conceptualising a screenplay character as a "textual construction" contrasts sharply with the rhetoric of screenwriting manuals and practitioners, which tends to emphasise the importance of creating characters who are "real": "How do you make your characters real, multidimensional people?" Field asks. Elsewhere Boon likens the opening of *Fargo* to Imagist poetry and makes the suggestion that "the screenplay represents a conjunction of Imagist poetics and modernist fiction of the 'plain' style." Whether the compressed, imagistic opening of *Fargo* evidences its literary qualities (as Boon proposes) or is merely "a commonplace in this kind of writing" (as Price contends), it remains the case that this and other parts of the same screenplay function in a similar way to literary writing, which as we've seen is generally denied to screenwriting.

If McKee's assertion that the screenwriter "cannot be a poet" and "cannot use metaphor" or other poetic devices (see Chapter 4, section 1) is matched against the cross-section of 88th Academy Award nominees for Original Screenplay, it becomes clear that this drastically undervalues what is going on in screenplays at the level of poetics. Metaphor, for example, constitutes a key element of many screenplays, and one of the writer's tasks at the conceptual stage is to find metaphors that will help her to dramatise both story and characters. Even a screenplay such as *Spotlight*, which takes place within the literal world of journalism, a mode of writing that typically eschews metaphor, employs it. Although this is a very spare screenplay, fast-moving and with minimal narration, metaphor plays a part in its descriptive writing as well as dialogue. Mike, the reporter who will drive the story, is characterised by his desk, described as an "UNHOLY MESS." The mess is literally "unholy," but in the context of this story (newspaper versus Catholic Church) the adjective also predicts that Mike will have no sympathy for religion. Similarly, when Robby refers to himself as "a player-coach" rather than an editor, the baseball metaphor indicates that he conceptualises work relationships in terms of competitive sports and team loyalties. Matt Carroll "shepherds his family" from his front door towards church, a metaphor which invokes Jesus the Good Shepherd in a context where priests are the opposite, abusing children and covering up their crimes.

Straight Outta Compton, too, uses metaphors in its action lines, although most of them are sleeping or conventional and clichéd: "shell-shocked," "infectious vibe," eyes that "light up," a car "filled to the brim," a pastor who "wraps up his eulogy," a crowd (later a "sea of people") that "goes ape-shit," someone who "stares cold daggers," a "[l]ot of water under the bridge," and many more. These are joined by some striking mixed metaphors: "Cube enters -- Lets the SONIC ACROBATICS BOOMING from Dre's turntables marinate on him," and a character's "[i]instinct" is "in overdrive." The characters' street names (in particular Ice Cube and Eazy) are also metaphorical.

The title of *Bridge of Spies* is its first and governing metaphor. An ironic word-play on the "Bridge of Sighs" in Venice, it manages to be both literally true (there's a bridge in

Berlin across which two spies are exchanged) and metaphorical (protagonist Donovan becomes the bridge between the two governments running the spies). *Spotlight*'s title is similarly both the literal name of the investigative department on the *Boston Globe* newspaper and the metaphor for what the characters do – brilliantly illuminate and reveal the scandal. Otherwise, metaphor in *Bridge of Spies* is mostly limited to its dialogue, but here too verbal metaphor survives as words in the film, refuting McKee's claim that screenplays can't employ it. The most striking instance of this in the action lines is one that equates the spy plane's camera with a gun: "[t]he telephoto lens at the front of the U-2 lets fly, rapid-firing as it focuses on the earth below." While the gun/camera metaphor is common enough, here light entering a camera becomes projectiles shot out of it, drawing attention to the Cold War spy plane's double function in surveillance (gathering visual information) and metaphorically shooting the enemy.

By contrast, the *Inside Out* screenplay is entirely metaphorical as a visualisation of the inside of a child's mind. Emotions (Joy, Sadness, Fear, Anger, Disgust) become characters, while each memory is a "GLOWING SPHERE" coloured according to the dominant emotion it contains. The screenplays of animated features are written (and rewritten) in parallel with the production process, itself more likely to be measured in years rather than weeks or months. This means that a metaphorical idea, such as a memory as a glowing ball, might originate graphically as a sketch, and only subsequently be verbalised in the script. Nonetheless, other metaphors clearly have their origins in the screenplay.

In *Ex Machina*, metaphors abound. In this science fiction film, they're often used to blur distinctions between organic life and machines: camera lenses are described as "twitching" like live things, while phone handsets, CCTV cameras and monitors are at points rendered "dead." The "POWER DIES" and "all the screens die." Ava's artificial brain is a "neon jellyfish." *Ex Machina* is even richer in similes than in metaphors, science fiction being the least literal and most figurative of all genres. Sunlight is commodified: "like a jewel in the icy mountains." Later a sunset is technologised when it makes cloud edges "glow like light-bulb filaments," while "the backdrop of mountains and clouds look like an Ansel Adams," a reversal in which life resembles art rather than the other way round. An android brain has "axon-like tendrils." In Nathan's study, fallen Post-it notes "have collected like a miniature yellow snow drift." The *Ex Machina* screenplay is able to sustain the kind of rhetorical reading conventionally applied to literary texts, such as those written by its novelist-screenwriter author, Alex Garland, and exploits as wide a range of stylistic devices as one of Garland's novels. Meiosis (ironic understatement), meanwhile, is a hallmark of original screenplays by the Coen brothers. Much of both the humour and the horror in their screenplay *Fargo* derives from the ironic gap between how the characters describe themselves and their actions, and how the viewer (or reader) perceives the same things. Many more examples could be cited; the point here is that screenplays demonstrably use many of the devices that film scholars, screenwriting manuals, and some screenwriters themselves deny to them and reserve for literary texts.

Even McKee contradicts his own pronouncement a few pages later in *Story*: "'Pity the poor screenwriter, for he cannot be a poet' is not in fact true." He goes on to introduce the idea of the "poetic" screenplay, but in a very particular sense, in which "*poetic* means an *enhanced expressivity*." This, according to McKee, is achieved by creating "an *Image System*," as with the recurrent water motif in *Les Diaboliques* (1955). McKee thus locates the poetic in screenplays at the conceptual level, which is then realised visually in production. Yet as other examples show, the poetic is also present at the verbal level, in screenplays' words.

"Screenplays are distinct from literature because they're produced by a different kind of writer"

[S]creenwriting probably isn't seen as writing in the same way that novel-writing is seen as writing. But I certainly don't see it that way.
Alex Garland

McKee asks rhetorically, "who, after all, invented screen-writing?" and answers "Novelists and playwrights." While this claim isn't wholly accurate (screenwriters in the classical studio period of Hollywood were more likely to be journalists than anything else – see Chapter 3, section 6), many screenplays have been written by those who also write plays and novels. Of the nominees for the 88th Academy Award for Original Screenplay, one (Charman) is a playwright, while another (Garland) was a successful novelist before adapting his own novel, *The Beach*, for film and moving on to author original screenplays. Extending the sample to nominees for Adapted Screenplay adds another six writers, of whom three (Nick Hornby, Emma Donoghue, and Drew Goddard) are novelists and one (Phyllis Nagy) is a playwright. Only two, Charles Randolph and Adam McKay, are primarily screenwriters. Based on this sample, it's clear that a substantial proportion of celebrated screenwriters are literary authors. Unsurprisingly, of the nominees for Original Screenplay, it's the novelist-screenwriter Garland who makes most frequent use of metaphor and simile, two devices common in prose fiction. It seems reasonable to expect some interchange between the different kinds of writing among those who write screenplays and literature.

Nor do most current novelist-screenwriters disparage their own screenplays, as their predecessors did. Garland, for example, publishes his screenplays alongside his novels, and his publisher's covers don't distinguish in design between

Garland's novels (*The Beach, The Coma, The Tesseract*) and his screenplays (*28 Days Later, Sunshine*). Faber would doubtless like readers of bestseller *The Beach* to buy *Sunshine* as well.

Beyond such publication practices, the screenplay and the novel are converging, a fact confirmed even by screenwriting gurus, who once sought to keep them apart. McKee embraces postmodern hybridity and ignores older ideas of medium specificity and the modernist separation of art forms into different spheres: "Screen and prose writers create the same density of world, character, and story." Truby also stresses the continuities between novelists' and screenwriters' work, encouraging writers to undertake both. Since 2015, he has offered a new seminar promising to teach "10 essential techniques for writing the Great American Novel," together with "[k]ey techniques for adapting your screenplay to novel." He maintains that "[t]he biggest differences between novel and film" relate not to the division between the literary and non-literary, but are instead a matter of "structure and point of view." The latest "strategy for success" is for screenwriters "to take your story idea – and maybe you had it originally for a film – to take that story idea and write it as a novel." According to Truby, "[t]he novel, two hundred years ago, was the great story form. It is now once again the great story form… it (ha)s become the most important medium for writers to tell their story in the worldwide entertainment business.... It is absolutely the most important medium for writers today." His claim is supported by the publication in 2020 of screenwriter Kaufman's first novel, *Antkind*. Truby's recently added class, "Story for Novelists," actively promotes novel-writing to screenwriters and, conversely, his film-based structural story steps to novelists. This bi-directional crossover class is geared towards adaptation from one medium to the other, offering advice on both "[k]ey techniques for adapting your screenplay to novel" and "[k]ey techniques for adapting your novel to screenplay." Truby affirms that screenplays and novels are interchangeable and adaptable not on the basis of fine writing versus technical writing, but narratologically. Screenplays share narrative ideas with novels, but not narrative structures or points of view. These are what need to be adapted, but this, according to Truby, can be readily achieved by applying his principles. His contention corresponds to Brian McFarlane's application of narratological theories of deep structure and surface structure to a theory of adaptation in which he divides what can be transferred wholesale from novel to film in adaptation (what is told) from what requires "adaptation proper" (how it is told). Here Truby proposes a reverse direction of adaptation from film to novel: what is shared doesn't need adaptation; what isn't shared does.

"Screenplays differ from literature in their relationship to industry and modes of production"

Finally, screenplays aren't disqualified from sharing attributes with literary texts by their industrial associations. Price contends that "Any commentary on screenwriting is bound to observe that it is tied to a particular industry in a way that the novel, poem or even theatrical play is not." However, similarities between the American film and publishing industries have long been recognised. James L. West III wrote in 1988 that "What has happened to publishing over the last twenty years is similar to what has taken place in two related mass-culture industries – motion pictures and popular music." In both publishing and film industries, there is a wide choice of material available, from which a relatively small fraction is selected for production. "Movie producers gamble in the same way that publishers do" by following educated guesses as to what will prove commercial. Furthermore, "Many of the major studios are now under the wings of conglomerates – often the same ones that control publishing houses." Since publication of West's own book in the 1980s, the two industries have moved ever closer as both market themselves, and each other, to consumers across the globe. Writing in *Value and the Media* (2011), Göran Bolin notes:

> media organisations that had previously concentrated on a single specific medium, say print... have today developed into media houses that are moving into other sectors like the broadcast media, the film industry, etc. These kinds of tie-ins have, of course, long been observed by scholars within the field of political economy of the media (for example, Herman and McChesney 1997), but are increasingly hard to ignore even for those more interested in media aesthetics and media reception, since these relations have effects on the construction of media content.

Moreover, in the twenty-first century, some major publishing concerns are divisions of corporations that also produce films. The tendency for media corporations to operate in both film and book publishing (and also in related industries such as television) is well established. Since 1986, Twentieth Century Fox has been part of Rupert Murdoch's global media empire, which also owns major publishers HarperCollins. Simon & Schuster and Paramount Studios were part of the same media group (Viacom) until 2005; Simon & Schuster is still owned by media giant ViacomCBS. Penguin Random House, one of the world's largest book publishing concerns, is in 2020 wholly owned by German media group Bertelsmann, which also has major television and film interests.

Nor is book publishing a smaller industry than film production. In 2018, the world's largest book publisher, Penguin Random House, had revenues of €3.43 billion ($4.05 billion), greater than those of Viacom ($3.16 billion). Novels, like movies, are part of an industry; the Harry Potter books are as closely aligned with the requirements of the publishing industry as the Harry Potter screenplays and films are with those of the film industry. The received view among scholars from Staiger onwards that the film industry is somehow more industrial than the publishing industry may owe less to fact than to the visibility of filmmaking's physical processes, and to the attention that these have attracted.

The ability of screenplays to travel across media platforms further underlines the continuities between screenplays and other kinds of writing. While in the twenty-first century plays infrequently become films, theatre productions of films (often in the form of musicals) have become increasingly common. In June 2016, Australian playwright-screenwriter-director Simon Stone staged his adaptation in the Netherlands of Woody Allen's film *Husbands and Wives* – which Stone called "a ready-made play" – with Allen's approval. In the summer of 2017, no fewer than twelve stage shows based on films were playing or taking advance bookings in London's West End, undermining further the perceived barriers separating screenplays from theatre plays. As an example of what's becoming familiar practice, the successful film, *Sideways* (2004), began life as an unpublished novel by screenwriter Rex Pickett. Alexander Payne (the director) and Jim Taylor then wrote the screenplay for the film, after which the novel was published, and subsequently adapted by Pickett into a stage play. Pickett thus exploited his property in three branches of the entertainment industry, to which all versions of *Sideways* are tied. It would be difficult to argue convincingly that any one version of *Sideways* is either more industrial or less literary than another.

Like those piled on the desk of the studio production chief in Mamet's 1988 play *Speed-the-Plow*, many screenplays are "not quite 'Art' "and "not quite 'Entertainment'" – yet the very difficulty of drawing a line between the two categories confirms that many screenplays share attributes with art as well as with entertainment. Differences remain between screenplays and literature, but even if one rejects Nannicelli's assertion that "Many, if not most, screenplays can plausibly be identified as literary works," it's possible to conclude that screenplays can't be classified as unliterary or cordoned off in a separate sphere, given the many formal features that they share with literary works such as novels and stage plays. This is underlined by the fact that both are often produced by the same writers, and that their marketing and production are closely interrelated. The next chapter shows that screenplays not only share characteristics with other imaginative fictional forms, but that they also endure, as novels and plays do.

5

ENDURING SCREENPLAYS

I dream of an I.B.M. machine in which I'd insert the screenplay at one end and the film would emerge at the other end, completed, and in color.

Alfred Hitchcock

Screenplays are more than just technical documents. Not only do they do many things that literary texts also do, but they also endure – whether or not films have been made from them.

Scholars and practitioners have frequently asserted that screenplays are consumed by the process of filmmaking and disappear, as in Alfred Hitchcock's dream. In fact screenplays can and do endure in various ways. Screenplay words persist in films, and screenplays aren't merely intermedial texts, lacking a separate existence of their own. Nor is it true that screenplays can be performed only once, and are emptied or consumed by that single performance. Related contentions that screenplays disappear before and during production to be replaced by technical shooting scripts don't stand up, either. Screenplays aren't ephemeral and don't vanish, as has frequently been asserted. They don't become invisible once films are made, despite the way in which concepts such as auteurism and mise-en-scène have removed screenplays from view and have inaccurately located style in finished films when this can sometimes already be found in the screenplays that precede them. Screenplays endure even when unproduced. Claims that screenplays are incomplete and never achieve a fixed state, meanwhile, need to be related to films themselves, where the same conditions apply.

"Screenplay words don't persist in films"

At the most literal level, critics argue that a majority of screenplay words don't persist in films but are turned into something else. However, the words of screenplays remain both visible and audible in the films made from them.

Kamilla Elliott has shown that disappearing words are a common theme in film criticism, which often suggests that "films in general base their creative process on a visual dissolution of their words. The process of filmmaking is one of deverbalizing, deliteralizing, and dewording verbal language to make film 'language.'" As shown in Chapter 3, section 2, similar views can be detected in the distinction that Kathryn Millard makes between the "words on a page" of a screenplay and "images, sounds, gestures, rhythm or... cinematic qualities."

Yet the much admired and highly cinematic opening sequence of *Citizen Kane* (1941) can be traced all the way back to the words of the first draft of its screenplay. Dated 16 April 1940, titled *American,* and written by Herman Mankiewicz and John Houseman, the first *Kane* screenplay is described by scholar Robert Carringer in "The Scripts of Citizen Kane":

> *American* opens in the manner of the German expressionists, with directions for the camera to move through an iron gate and, after a series of dissolve-views of the dilapidated grounds of Kane's estate (called "The Alhambra" at this point), to enter the front door, proceed across the great hall, ascend the staircase, and pass down a long gallery filled with art objects, arriving at last at Kane's bedroom, where a nurse is just entering with a hospital table. From inside we are to hear a voice say, faintly, "Rosebud." We are to see falling snowflakes, then the glass globe held by the

> figure on the bed. He is to say "Rosebud" three
> more times...

Here, before Orson Welles became a co-writer, is substantially the opening scene of the film as it was subsequently directed. Mankiewicz and Houseman effectively set up, as words on a page, exactly those elements that Millard prizes: images, sounds, gestures, rhythm, cinematic qualities. These remain present in the film. The voice of Kane whispering the single word, "Rosebud," is probably the most important and most instantly recognisable moment – and word – in the film. His gesture of releasing the glass ball frames the film's main action, Kane grabbing and holding onto everything he sees. Rhythm established in the screenplay by instructions for shots, camera movements, and transitions also survives into the filmed scene. The many other sets and locations are established verbally in the same way, before they're constructed physically and/or photographically.

Other elements of the *Citizen Kane* screenplays survive into the completed film even more literally. In the "shooting script" written by Mankiewicz and Welles, the dialogue, of course, is present, but so also is much more besides. There are the many headlines from Kane's newspapers, intertitles from old newsreels, and other onscreen texts, including the large sign that "reads 'Colorado Lode Mining Co.,'" the neon-illuminated words "'EL RANCHO' Floor Show Susan Alexander Kane Twice Nightly," "a large sign reading "MRS KANE'S BOARDINGHOUSE," the "THATCHER MANUSCRIPT," a sign reading "EDITORIAL AND EXECUTIVE STAFF OF THE NEW YORK CHRONICLE," packing boxes bearing the words "To Charles Foster Kane, New York – HOLD FOR ARRIVAL," among numerous examples. Welles had learned from his experience in the largely verbal medium of radio drama the power of words to evoke the visual, and the words of the final version of the screenplay that he and Mankiewicz wrote persist visibly in the film of *Citizen Kane*.

Nor is it only in exceptional cases that screenplay words survive into films. *The Neon Demon* (2016) is a glossy film set in the fashion world, and the screenplay establishes this very different world verbally, just as Mankiewicz's and Welles's establishes Xanadu:

```
INT. STUDIO - DAY 1


CLOSE ON JESSE'S face, eyes closed,
angelic, beautiful.


Slowly, the CAMERA PULLS BACK and her
twisted, bleeding body is revealed,
tangled in a tattered dress. It appears a
violent crime has just taken place.


CLOSE ON a man's face. It is DEAN,
handsome, slightly awkward. He stares at
the scene, entranced by Jesse's figure.


He raises a still camera. Jesse's image
is reflected in miniature in the glass
lens. He takes a photo, and the black
shutter closes and opens on Jesse's body,
the mechanical sound a startling contrast
to the eerie quiet of the room.


The CAMERA PULLS BACK again, revealing
that the crime scene is actually a
fashion photo shoot.
```

> The clicks of Dean's camera, uneven at
> first, grow rapid and regular. A
> frenetic, percussive score.

In a few lines of description, Mary Laws's and Nicolas Winding Refn's screenplay sets up not only the highly stylised world of fashion photography and the film's principal character, but also its genre (horror-thriller) and tone, relating visuality to sexuality, and connecting fashion and photography with the expected, sex, but also with death. This emphatically visual and "cinematic" film enacts actual words from the screenplay, which remains present in it, even though there is as yet no dialogue. As well as the highly specific mise-en-scène, the music score is specified, along with camera movement (the instructions to pull back), and even the cuts between shots of Jesse and the reverse shots of Dean. Just as with the canonical *Citizen Kane*, most of the words in this screenplay persist, directly or indirectly, into the film that it brings into being.

"Screenplays are intermedial texts with no separate existence of their own"

The common assertion that screenplays are intermedial texts and therefore don't endure once the film has been made can be traced back to the contested blueprint metaphor (see Chapter 2), and is no more sustainable than that metaphor is. Barbara Korte and Ralf Schneider argue that "the screenplay is an essentially intermedial text type," which they gloss as "a verbal text originally written as a blueprint for a production." Although Korte and Schneider go on to award certain screenplays literary status, it's on the basis that they share their authorship with other texts already acknowledged to be literary (see Chapter 4, section 2). Screenplays remain, in their eyes, "intermedial writing" that may, in specific cases, have a double function as "writing suitable for translation into film, but also worth reading in its own right." Similarly Steven Maras accepts the screenplay's "intermediality," which supports his concern regarding anything that might "take the script out of its production context" or privilege it.

Some practitioners have also endorsed the notion that screenplays are intermedial texts, but have done so to advance their status as writers in various ways. By choosing to write *The Third Man* as a short story first, Graham Greene effectively made his screenplay an intermedial text that stood between story and film. His choice formed part of a strategy for retaining control of his writing, while F. Scott Fitzgerald, Budd Schulberg, and Larry McMurtry have supported the idea that their screenplays don't persist in order to promote their more prestigious (but less remunerative) careers as novelists (see Chapter 3, section 6). Others, such as Pixar's Andrew Stanton, do so to restrict the power of the verbal to dictate the visual. Stanton calls the screenplay "an intermediary form... what I would call 'cinematic dictation'" because Pixar produces animated films, where screenplays typically develop alongside visual storyboards (see Chapter 3, section 1). However, what may be an accurate description within the specialised arena of animation isn't applicable to live-action filmmaking, where words almost invariably pre-exist any visual images.

"Screenplays are performed only once, and are emptied or consumed by that single performance"

The fallacy that screenplays are read and produced a single time, and consumed in the process, sets them against theatre plays, which are read and performed many times. Yet screenplays persist in published formats as theatre plays do, and some screenplays have been produced more than once. Korte and Schneider cite German screenwriter Jochen Brunow's view that "the film scenario is entirely 'burnt up' in the production process." Nonetheless the screenplay of *Fargo* and many other celebrated screenplays have not been entirely burnt up in the production process, but instead have been published or uploaded online, making it possible to read and analyse them alongside or independently of their film texts. The screenplays continue an independent, parallel existence; in Charlie Kaufman's case multiple drafts endure as books (*Adaptation* in the *Newmarket Shooting Script* series), downloaded files (from the fan site *Beingcharliekaufman.com*), and transcripts on screenplay sites such as *Simply Scripts, The Daily Script,* and the *Internet Movie Screenplay Database.*

Nor does the continued existence of such screenplays derive solely from the films made from them. "I am well aware that some collectors keep them, and that sometimes they are even published, but that's only if the film works," Jean-Claude Carrière observes. "Then they live on in its slipstream." However, Samuel Beckett's screenplay *Film* lives on more in the slipstream of its author's literary reputation than of the screenplay's realisation, as do screenplays by Greene and others discussed in previous chapters. Screenplays written by Beckett and Greene continue to exist in print alongside their other writings.

Moreover, things have changed since 1994, when Carrière published those words. Many screenplays underpinning less successful and prestigious films now live on in other forms, and are available to readers on numerous internet sites. Thus screenplays for *Superman IV: The Quest for Peace* (1987), *The Bonfire of the Vanities* (1990), and *Highlander: Endgame* (2000) continue to exist long after the films themselves, which failed at the box office, have slipped out of sight.

Some screenplays have already been made into films more than once. As well as his screenplay for a short film, Beckett wrote several for television, all of them produced. *Eh, Joe* has already received more than one production: the first in 1965 has been followed by another (in Dutch) in 1974, and a third (in English) in 2005, while film schools may give scenes from produced screenplays to their students for production practice.

Screenplays may be performed more than once, and theatre plays have also been subjected to the same challenges as the screenplay, further undermining distinctions between the status of these two kinds of play. "A theatre text is only a blueprint for a theatre event, not a piece of art in and of itself," according to Australian playwright and screenwriter-director Simon Stone, who also directed a theatre production of Woody Allen's screen-play *Husbands and Wives* (see Chapter 4, section 7). This stage production ran for 46 performances in the Netherlands between 19th June 2016 and 4th March 2017. Allen's screenplay has thus been performed multiple times, as both film and stage play.

A single "performance" (if one ignores pre-production actor auditions, cast "table readings," rehearsals off and on set, and multiple takes of each "slate" or set-up) is in no way a necessary condition of the screenplay as a written text. It's rather a consequence of filmmaking production technologies and economics. These have also resulted in the common practice of (especially) studios, producers, and others who commission or acquire screenplays, today as in the past, to purchase blanket rights. Typically these endure in perpetuity and are inclusive of all territories, formats, and media. Thus the current standard short-form Writers Guild of America writers' agreement asserts that the "Producer shall solely and exclusively own throughout the universe in perpetuity all rights of every kind and nature" in the screenplay (see Chapter 3, section 6). Custom and practice have dictated that a producer should acquire all rights in a screenplay in order to be able fully to exploit the resulting film, but rights in theatre plays and novels are usually handled on a principle of licensing rather than outright acquisition. The same principle could in the future be applied to screenplays. There's no intrinsic reason why, if the economics of production and library-building change, outright purchase shouldn't be replaced by licensing in film, as currently happens in television. Then it would be quite plausible that a screenplay by a writer such as Kaufman, enjoying critical and public esteem, should be re-made, just as so many literary and television "properties" are.

Nor is it impossible that more than one production might in the future result from a single screenplay. If a screenplay is more highly regarded than its film, then there could be a pressing commercial incentive to seek another, different realisation. Hollywood is certainly not unfamiliar with the idea of remaking adaptations of novels, comic books, and films themselves; original screenplays could be remade in the same way. Evidently it's possible, and not implausible, that in the future another director, such as Kaufman himself, might choose to make a new film from one of his earlier screenplays. It's possible to contemplate a new film of *Being John Malkovich*, with someone other than Spike Jonze in the director's chair. Nor would this second film exhaust the screenplay any more than a theatre play is exhausted by two productions. The possibility of other such further performances is alone sufficient to refute claims of its inevitable and universal exhaustion by a single performance.

Indeed, although subsequently *Being John Malkovich* went into production, it was in a form different from Kaufman's first draft, which nevertheless continues to exist. The same thing happened with his later screenplay, *Eternal Sunshine of the Spotless Mind*. The first draft of this begins with Clementine as an old woman fifty years after the main action, trying to interest a publisher in her story, while the film *Eternal Sunshine of the Spotless Mind* (2004) opens with Joel, the other principal character, waking up. Old Clementine returns at the end of the screenplay (but not the film), bookending the "present" of the film's action. These versions, not produced, nevertheless continue to exist, and provide another motivation for Kaufman's fans to seek out and read the screenplays long after the films have been released. Fans read his screenplays as screenwriting, rather than for insights into a literary author's writing process (as with some readers), or to explore differences and similarities between literary writing and film writing. Long after the films based on them were made, Kaufman's screenplays not only still exist, but also, far from being consumed, they continue to address new readers. Moreover, while you can view the written text of a theatre play as a template for performances, screenplays are commonly less prescriptive and also allow or even encourage multiple readings.

"Screenplays disappear during the processes of film production"

As well as denying that screenplay words persist in finished films, some commentators have insisted that they disappear during the process of film production. In the case of film scholars this view is often the consequence of working backwards from the completed film, focusing on processes such as cinematography and the work of the director while over-looking other processes that take place during development and pre-production. Just as the shooting is the most visible aspect of filmmaking, so too the director is the person most visibly in control of it. As a result, other crucial film production processes, such as script development, are often overlooked. It's usually critics rather than filmmakers who make screenplays invisible by focusing attention on directors as auteurs and disregarding the screenplays from which they work. Thus in *Me and You and* Memento *and* Fargo, J.J. Murphy ignores his own subtitle, *How Independent Screenplays Work*, and concentrates instead on the films made from them. Each of the twelve films that Murphy chooses to analyse is the work of a writer-director, and few references are made to the actual screenplays of these twelve films or, crucially, to the interaction between the writer-directors' two roles. Those that are made mainly relate to plot and character choices, as though these were the screenplays' only components. Others, such as style, he locates instead in the films that follow. Murphy writes "That *Trust* turns out to be as brilliant on the page as it is on the screen is a tribute to [Hal] Hartley's rare ability to mix the literary and the visual." By reversing chronology in this way – only after the film has been watched and admired does attention turn to the screenplay – Murphy inverts the actual process of filmmaking.

Millard takes a similar approach. Although a filmmaker herself, she obscures screenplays by overlooking, merging, or confusing different elements of the filmmaking process, particularly in her examples of "alternative" screenwriting. Discussing the films of Hong Kong writer-director Kar-wai Wong, she writes that he "allows his stories to evolve as he films them; he simply sketches an outline of the story, finds locations, and begins shooting." Something that Millard doesn't mention, however, is Wong's substantial experience as a screenwriter. IMDb lists 34 screenwriting credits for him, dating back to 1982, first in television and subsequently in film, prior to his first project as director in 1988. It is also his usual practice to base his films on writing in the form of short stories. While Wong may play down the importance of screenplays in interviews, his improvisation as a director is built on his solid experience of writing conventional screenplays (most of his screenwriting credits are for genre, mainly crime, films). Thus Wong's screenplays can only be made to appear invisible because his experience as a writer permits him to minimise his use of a fully developed written screenplay. Despite this, awards for his screenplays draw attention to their presence in Wong's films. *The Grandmaster* (2013) won Wong multiple awards and nominations for Best Original Screenplay, as well as for Best Director, and his earlier screenplays have also earned him several screenplay nominations and awards. Nor is there anything new about this hiding of screenplays by writer-directors. Film scholar Edward Azlant refers to the "[m]yth of D.W. Griffith as a director who didn't use a script – in fact he was a highly experienced writer, often using pseudonyms."

As well as making screenplays invisible, scholars have argued that screenplays have no agency of their own, and require production to activate them. This view is encountered mostly in film studies, particularly in those areas that still entertain versions of auteur theory – which assumes that style isn't located in a screenplay, but only enters a film along with the director and camera. Closely related to this is the concept of mise-en-scène, which foregrounds the director's role and minimises or makes invisible that of the screenplay. As John Gibbs notes in his 2002 book *Mise-en-Scène: Film Style and Interpretation*, "mise-en-scène is intimately connected to arguments about why the director, rather than the scriptwriter, should be considered the artist responsible for a film." Gibbs acknowledges that "mise-en-scène went out of fashion," but sees no reason to abandon it. On the contrary, he insists that "mise-en-scène criticism made possible a more profound sense of how films work,'" despite that fact that, even if true, this is achieved at the cost of understanding how screenplays work. He goes on to endorse what he sees as its central articles of faith: "that style determines meaning, that how an event is portrayed on the screen defines its significance." Gibbs quotes with approval Robin Wood's view that "The tone and atmosphere of the film, visual metaphor, the establishment of relationships between characters, the relation of all parts to the whole: all this is mise-en-scène." Yet tone, atmosphere, visual metaphor, and relationships of all kinds are very much part of any screenplay, as we've already seen with *Citizen Kane*. The opening pages of screenplays create the world of *Fargo*, establish Caden and his family in *Synecdoche, New York* (2008), and set up the main characters and their problem in *Butch Cassidy and the Sundance Kid*. Diablo Cody's screenplay for *Juno* (2007) introduces her "artfully bedraggled burnout kid" gazing at "the most magnificent discarded living room set" she has ever seen; Nancy Meyers's screenplay for *The Intern* (2015) introduces hero Ben doing tai-chi in a Brooklyn park as he mis-quotes Freud: "'Love and work, work and love. That's all there is.' Well, I'm retired and my wife is dead." These and countless other examples indicate that a film's "style" and "meaning" often originate and remain embedded in screenplays.

While for Wood (and, perhaps, Gibbs) "The script… is only one creative element among many at the director's disposal," the reverse is also true. The director is only one of many creative elements involved in the realisation of the screenplay. Director Nicholas Ray's much cited quote, "it was never all in the script. If it were, why make the movie?" can be similarly reversed: all of a screenplay can't remain in a movie, unless its pages are photographed. While between the verbal construct and the audio-visual construct variable areas of overlap exist, there will always be part of any screenplay that remains unfilmed. Thus a screenplay persists in a film, but can't be wholly subsumed by it any more than a film can be created from nothing but a screenplay.

By contrast to many film critics, film practitioners, including directors, reject auteurism and its corollary, the invisible screenplay. In an interview published in the *Paris Review*, Billy Wilder remarks that "Film's thought of as a director's medium because the director creates the end product that appears on the screen. It's that stupid auteur theory again, that the director is the author of the film. But what does the director shoot – the telephone book?" Not even Wilder himself can make a "Billy Wilder film" without a script. Wilder shifted roles from screenwriter to writer-director, he says, in order "to protect the script." His credits on IMDb (79 as writer, 27 as director) underline the priority of Wilder's screenplays in his career as a filmmaker. "I didn't particularly have ambitions to be a director, to be a despot of the soundstage," he has said. "As someone who directed scripts that I myself had cowritten, what I demanded from actors was very simple: learn your lines." Wilder's concern was not to overlay the screenplays with film style, but to realise what already existed in the screenplay's words.

Wilder's respect for screenplays, both his own and those of others, led him to deny that he had any "vision or theory I wanted to express as a director; I had no signature or style." Yet despite Wilder's rejection of auteurist tenets, the films that he wrote and directed do have a style that many critics have identified as his. Films such as *Some Like It Hot* (1959) and *The Apartment* (1960), both co-written with I.A.L. Diamond, appear, along with two others directed by Wilder, in the American Film Institute's list of the "100 Greatest American Movies of All Time," demonstrating that a film's style can be located as much in the screenplay as in the direction. The persistence of Wilder's screenplays in his films contradicts not only the assumptions of auteurism, but also the notion that it is solely the acts performed by the director that produce film style.

Another, even more substantial, example of critics at odds with actual screenplays and films lies in the contradiction between David Bordwell's and Kristin Thompson's definition of film style in their influential and ubiquitous textbook, *Film Art: An Introduction*, and Robert Towne's screenplay for *Chinatown* (1974). Bordwell and Thompson define style as "the way a film uses the techniques of filmmaking" and divide it into four categories: mise-en-scène ("the arrangement of people, places, and objects to be filmed"), cinematography ("the use of cameras and other machines"), editing ("the piecing together of individual shots"), and sound ("voices, effects, and music"). The implication is clear: these are areas under the director's control, and film style is therefore part of the director's function, and can't be attributed to the screenplay. The point is reinforced in *The Way Hollywood Tells It: Story and Style in Modern Movies*. Here Bordwell refers throughout to "filmmakers," but his examples are all directors; it as though film style has nothing to do with screenplays. Of the book's seven references to the film *Chinatown*, six discuss its director, Roman Polanski, but none credits its screenwriter or screenplay, which creates much of the style that they admire in the film. Bordwell and Thompson define their primary component of "Film Style," mise-en-scène, as "the director's control over what appears in the film frame." Yet all of the elements comprising mise-en-scène ("the arrangement of people, places, and objects to be filmed") are present in the first scene of the *Chinatown* screenplay. The screenplay arranges people: Gittes, "cool and brisk in a white linen suit despite the heat," and, standing over him, Curly, who "sweats heavily through his workman's clothes." It describes and furnishes the flashy new office where the scene is set, with its "signed photos of several movie stars" and the Venetian blinds "just... installed on Wednesday." It details objects: the compromising photographs of Curly's unfaithful wife and several whisky bottles (including a cheaper bourbon for those, like Curly, who can't tell the difference) and the fan that establishes the heatwave affecting everyone.

However, the screenplay for *Chinatown* does more than set up the film's mise-en-scène. It also attends to Bordwell and Thompson's other three elements of film style. Editing and cinematography are both clearly indicated: the screenplay makes it clear that the opening shot is a close-up (a photograph filling the frame), cutting to a medium wide shot that will show

how "Curly towers over GITTES," and will keep both in the frame as "Curly bites the blinds" while "Gittes doesn't move from his chair." The fourth element, sound, appears not only in the dialogue of this brief, two-page scene, but also as mysterious moaning, the "plunk" of the sweat drop hitting the desk, and the whir of the fan. Gestures are clearly present in the dispassionate, detached way in which Gittes "notes" and "glances," but doesn't move. The rhythm of repetition that permeates the whole screenplay begins here, as in the surveillance of Curly's wife that will be echoed in Gittes's surveillance of Mulwray, Evelyn, Cross, and others. The film's philosophical and symbolic themes also derive from the screenplay, such as the pervasive drought – meteorological, emotional, and moral – established here in its first scene.

Chinatown's screenplay is by no means unique. Popular, non-canonical screenplays also establish the mise-en-scène. Thus, even as Bordwell and Thompson assert that "many of our most sharply etched memories of the cinema turn out to center on mise-en-scene," one of their filmic examples is present in its screenplay. The memorable scene that they cite of "Michael J. Fox escaping high-school bullies on an improvised skateboard (*Back to the Future*)" may have been photographed and directed, but before that it was written in the screenplay:

```
EXT. CAFE AND STREET

Marty dashes down the street, followed by
Biff and the boys. Most of the kids in
the cafe hurry outside to watch,
including LORRAINE and her friends.

Marty looks behind him - Biff and company
are gaining. Then one of the kids on the
scooters comes by. Thinking quickly,
Marty yanks the scooter out from under
```

```
him, kicks off the orange crate and
creates a homemade SKATEBOARD! Marty hops
on it and sails down the sidewalk!

Biff and the boys have never seen
anything like it - nor has the kid whose
scooter it was! Everyone stares as Marty
whizzes down the sidewalk.

                KID
        Wow! Look at him go!


            ANOTHER KID
        What is that thing?


                BIFF
            (to his boys)
        In the car!

Biff and the gang jump into Biff's
convertible parked nearby. Biff peels out
after Marty.
```

The *Back to the Future* screenplay, cowritten by Bob Gale and director Robert Zemeckis in 1985, already displays crucial elements of the film's style. As with *Chinatown*, the screenplay as much as the director attends to "the arrangement of people, places, and objects," while shots and cuts are implicit in the writing. Sound too is present in the dialogue.

Gibbs, Bordwell, and Thompson also unduly credit directors for mise-en-scène when it's an *unavoidable* component of filmmaking. Directors are obliged to have mise-en-scène of some sort, unless they resort to such extremes as the reduction to a single colour in Derek Jarman's *Blue* (1993). Even a stripped-down Dogme film such as *Dogville* (2003), with chalk lines on a wooden stage replacing sets, and the frame in *Vanya on 42nd Street* (1994), Louis Malle's film of a rehearsal for a theatre production never staged, are filled with elements that may or may not have been chosen by the director. For the director, mise-en-scène is inescapable. The writer, however, can exercise more control over mise-en-scène in a screenplay. The screenplay of *Fargo* includes a minimalist scene, where the two inept kidnappers-for-hire take a break for sex:

```
MOTEL ROOM


Carl Showalter and Gaear Grimsrud are in
the twin beds having sex with two
truck-stop hookers.


              CARL
    Oh, Jesus, yeah.


           HIS HOOKER
    There ya go, sugar.


            GRIMSRUD
    Nnph.


           HIS HOOKER
    Yeah. Yeah. Oh, yeah.
```

Motormouth Carl's inability to satisfy his hooker is sharply juxtaposed with the taciturn Grimsrud and his more responsive partner. Much of the scene's humour derives from the extreme economy of the pared-down writing, which condenses one of the film's themes – talkers talk; doers do – into a tiny but dense miniature. The writing here takes advantage of one of screenplays' greatest strengths: the ability to *exclude* whatever the writers choose. The film is unable to do likewise to anything like the same extent. The motel room, with its unavoidable props and dressing, and the specificity of hookers played by two different actresses (in contrast to the screenplay's shared character designation, "His Hooker"), are in some sense surplus to requirements, while the scene's style is already present in the screenplay and persists into the film.

Fargo's admired opening offers further support that the film's style originates in its screenplay rather than being brought into being by the process of production. After a title over black comes the instruction:

```
FLARE TO WHITE


FADE IN FROM WHITE


Slowly the white becomes a barely
perceptible image: white particles wave
over a white background. A snowfall.


A car bursts through the curtain of snow.
```

As the screenplay repeats: "WHITE... WHITE... white... white... white... snowfall... snow," a cold, snowy world is rhetorically brought into existence. Even the typography reinforces this: the expanse of white on the page, extended by the shortness of the opening lines, initiates the minimalist mise-en-scène in which both the snow and the blank page serve as a canvas on which the narrative is inscribed. "In controlling the mise-en-scene, the director *stages the event* for the camera," write Bordwell and Thompson. However, it would be equally true to say that the screenplay of *Fargo* "stages the event" for its directors. Kevin Boon has argued for the "concrete" nature of screenplay imagery, and Steven Price has responded that the examples

Boon chooses are in fact "rather abstract, indefinite, vague." But a more substantial claim to the screenplay's persistence lies in its ability not only to deploy imagery which can be concretised by sets, props, and characters, but also to choose to deploy no imagery whatsoever. The motel scene demonstrates how screenplays can not only bring a film scene into being, but also deliver a version different from, and coexisting with, that of the film. Long before the director steps onto the set and the camera starts to run, the screenplay has already initiated the style of production, which isn't created purely by the director, cinematographer, and other technical collaborators.

"Screenplays disappear when they're replaced by technical shooting scripts"

Although scholars and practitioners may acknowledge the master-scene screenplay's agency, some then undermine it by asserting that its words disappear before production begins, replaced by a more technical shooting script, without style or verbal distinctiveness. Price contends that "it is undoubtedly the case that the vast majority of screenplays do not circulate within a production context" Strictly speaking this is accurate, but only because the vast majority of screenplays never reach production at all – not because the scripts of films that *are* produced circulate in a different form. Price claims that the master-scene screenplay is merely a "selling script" that precedes the actual shooting script used on set, and so is "a relatively autonomous document, intended for particular kinds of reader, but removed from production." This doesn't describe any actual production context that I've come across in professional practice. The master-scene screenplay, rather than being supplanted by a new, technical document, usually *becomes* the shooting script. Nor is this a recent state of affairs.

As long ago as 1948, Greene's master-scene screenplay for *The Third Man* continued into production, as can be seen from Trevor Howard's copy used during the film shoot (see page 20). Howard's personal copy of the screenplay, with his handwritten annotations, including dialogue and action changes, without camera directions or other technical information, is clearly being used during production. Similarly, Syd Field recounts his experience of watching the shooting of *Coming Home* (1978) three decades later. The actors block the scene, watched by the director and the director of photography, who then discuss how they will film it (size, length, and number of shots). As Field writes, "That's the way it is. Film is a collaborative medium; people work together to create a movie." Price's claim that the master-scene screenplay, "by eliminating technical directions such as shot specification... separates the 'screenplay' from, and places it prior to, the 'shooting script'" isn't evidenced by most actual film productions. The script page that director Jonze holds up to camera in a photograph reproduced in the published screenplay of *Adaptation* is one from a reduced A5 copy of Kaufman's master-scene screenplay, heavily annotated in the margins with production notes. All crew members will have their own copies of the master-scene screenplay, and most will annotate it as the director does his, with information specific to their departments and roles. Revisions, which continue once the script is "locked" (usually several weeks before shooting begins), are issued as single coloured pages for insertion into crew members' existing scripts, since no one wants to replace his or her personal, annotated copy of the screenplay with a pristine one just because a scene has been cut or a line of dialogue altered. The same physical copy of the screenplay will continue through the latter part of pre-production and into the shoot itself, gathering more notes and probably pink, blue, and other coloured pages in the process. The director may well compile his or her own shot list;

but the notion that his or the crew's screenplay copies are replaced by a new technical document known as the "shooting script" once they hit the set doesn't match what actually happens in practice.

This is borne out not only by my own experience and the testimony of scripts from *The Third Man* and *Adaptation*, but also by the evidence of Christopher Riley's screenplay formatting manual, *The Hollywood Standard*. Riley notes that "production drafts are rarely anything other than spec scripts that have been purchased" and emphasises that, "until cameras start rolling, no one knows which draft will be the final, or production, draft" (20). The only difference between a spec screenplay and a typical shooting script is that in the latter the scenes will be numbered, and sometimes specific shots implied (but not stated) in the screenplay will be placed on a separate line. Adding the numbers traditionally happens when the script is budgeted, since the budget depends on a shooting schedule, which in turns depends on a "locked" script – otherwise scene numbers may change and thus confuse many departments' pre-production work, which is organised by scene numbers. In Final Draft, the most common script formatting software, used throughout the Anglo-American film industry, the screenplay is locked by clicking on a menu, and the numbering of scenes switched on (or off) in the same way. During production "individual shots... are hand-written into the script by the script supervisor;" in other words, the script supervisor records the creative choices made on set as part of the shooting process. Crucially, these choices aren't made at an earlier stage and then brought onto set in the form of a separate "shooting script."

You can see that the screenplay persists as the shooting script in the Oscar-nominated screenplays from the 88th Academy Awards. The Academy of Motion Picture Arts and Sciences requires producers to submit the actual shooting script of the film, since it's on the basis of this that credits (and therefore awards) are allocated. *Spotlight, Bridge of Spies, Ex Machina, Straight Outta Compton,* and *Inside Out* all employ master-scene format and don't include technical instructions about shots.

The master-scene screenplay's combination of flexibility and creative agency has ensured that it sustains its position as the script format of choice throughout most of the film industry. In the process it's been adapted to extend its capabilities well beyond those of a generic template, and carries these from the development stage of a project through into production. As a result the master-scene screenplay, inflected or not, can be modified at will by practitioners to fit their individual requirements, and so persists throughout the process of production. Actors and film crew members, like directors, use their master-scene screenplays to understand at a glance what the work of a scene is, its structure and shape. Until they've seen their cast run the action and dialogue of a scene on the film set, experienced directors understand that they can't know all of a scene's possibilities, and therefore are less likely than beginners to plan detailed shots in advance. Asking actors to match a detailed shot-by-shot plan made during pre-production may not maximise the actors' contribution to a scene's realisation, nor that of the director of photography and other heads of departments. The director of a film in which performance is a central consideration will often try to provide his cast with creative opportunities, rather than the restrictions of a rigidly preconceived template.

Detailed shot pre-planning is also often unrealisable, since the coverage of any given scene will depend on how much time remains in the schedule to complete it, and on other unpredictable factors such as weather, budget, and location restrictions. For example, a scene that in ideal circumstances might comprise five set-ups, one of them a time-consuming tracking shot, might for practical reasons have to be accomplished instead in three or two shots, or even in a single one. One of the master-scene screenplay's strengths is its flexibility; it can accommodate equally the five-shot and single-shot versions. Adaptability is a key skill for directors, while inflexible directors will struggle to maintain a career.

Certain directors may work from a shooting script resembling those of the classical studio period, but this is more likely on high-budget studio productions, especially those where computer animation and special effects must be integrated with live action. Studios cover the additional costs when such a production falls behind schedule or goes over budget. For the majority of shoots, however, which take place outside the studios, budget and schedule exert constant pressure on shot choice and coverage.

The notion that screenplays are erased by shooting scripts in production exists primarily among critics who endorse variants of auteur theory and wish to ascribe the screenplay's creative capabilities to the director. This is a fallacy mainly confined to academia, as practitioners are well aware that screenplays survive into and beyond the production process. The fallacy thus calls attention to the gap between theory and practice in another instance of critics reading the filmmaking process backwards from the finished film, in ways that (intentionally or not) make the screenplay disappear. In some instances, however, they read backwards from the post-production script (see Chapter 1, section 1), which records the shot choices made during the shoot and editing, and which is written only at the end of post-production. Post-production scripts (also known as cutting continuities) include descriptions of shots, required for subtitling and dubbing dialogue into foreign languages, although the descriptions aren't written by the director. Some directors may collude in the fallacy that these are "shooting scripts" in order to enhance the status of direction at the expense of the screenplay.

"Screenplays are ephemeral and vanish, or must be destroyed, in the process of filmmaking"

A range of various, contested, and partial occlusions of the screenplay all contribute to the idea that screenplays are ephemeral and vanish. Erwin Panofsky's 1947 assertion that the *"'screen play'... has no aesthetic existence independent of its performance"* is one denial of the screenplay's existence that has persisted in scholarship. Maras and others also cite Carrière, who elaborates the idea of the screenplay as condemned to disappear:

> a good screenplay is one that gives birth to a good
> film. Once the film exists, the screenplay is no
> more. It is probably the least visible component of
> the finished work. It is the first incarnation of a
> film and appears to be a self-contained whole. But
> it is fated to undergo metamorphosis, to disappear,
> to melt into another form, the final form.

Scholars may quote this to underwrite the idea of a "vanishing screenplay," as Maras does, but the language that Carrière employs resists such a narrow conceptualisation. He also invokes transformation ("metamorphosis"), change of physical state ("melting"), and continuing materiality ("incarnation"). Nor does the screenplay become invisible, but rather "the least visible component" of an audio-visual work; the screenplay's lesser visibility is thus set against a very high standard of visuality. Even as it seems to dismiss the screenplay, Carrière's imagery insists on the screenplay's generative power: it "gives birth" to the film, aligned with a fundamental act of creation. Like certain deities, for example the Christian god, it is an "incarnation," and like others, such as Osiris and Dionysus, it dies ("is no more") in order to create. Through "metamorphosis"

Carrière invokes further transformations of ancient gods and heroes, as well as the magical changes of fairy tales (frogs into princes, princes into beasts), and natural ones of biology, as in the metamorphosis from egg through to butterfly. All Carrière's metaphors articulate the screenplay as concerned with process, especially the processes of living things. They don't invoke its replacement *by* the film so much as its transformation *into* the film, which is the screenplay's "final form." Thus Carrière's "vanishing screenplay" comes to subsume the screenplay within the film to which it "gives birth." Nor is the screenplay emptied or consumed by this process, since it continues its existence in a different shape, that of the film. Yet while birth may be cyclical but not reversible, metamorphosis and melting are – so that what has disappeared may reappear once more.

Some accounts of the vanishing screenplay, however, are actively hostile. Not content with asserting its invisibility, they insist that the screenplay must be compelled to vanish and destroyed in order to make the film. Anecdotes about non-writing directors' hostility towards screenplays are common in Hollywood: "The town is full of legends of John Ford mistreating his script," according to Nunnally Johnson.

Writer-directors may also seek to erase screenplays that they have themselves written, for various reasons. In an early interview with Kevin Conroy Scott, Darren Aronofsky (*Pi, Mother!*) insists that "You can read my two screenplays and there's barely *anything* in those screenplays that's in the movies, because to write everything visual that's going on my mind or what we develop as a screenplay just wouldn't make a screenplay." For Aronofsky, screenplays – even those written by himself – appear to threaten his authority as director: "Once we get the screenplay," Aronofsky said, "my team and I just rip it apart." At this point in his career (2004), directing not screenwriting was Aronofsky's goal, and the interview he gave then serves that end.

Less violent, but equally resolute, Andrey Tarkovsky insists, like Carrière, on the death of the screenplay to birth the film: "The scenario dies in the film." Also like Carrière, he employs a metaphor of melting, although here it is melting in an industrial context: the screenplay's "literary element must be *smelted*." Destruction by smelting sounds particularly aggressive in light of Tarkovsky's characterisation of the screenplay as "fragile" and "living."

Screenplays endure even when unproduced

The vast majority of screenplays aren't performed (in the sense of being produced) even once, since most screenplays are never made as films.

As Ted Nannicelli points out, no screenplay can be considered "intermedial" until it first becomes a film – something that the majority of screenplays never do. Ever since the factory writing of the classical studio period (see Chapter 3, sections 3 and 6), the over-commissioning of screenplays has remained a feature of the Hollywood film business and its UK equivalent. The surplus of screenplays has increased substantially with the self-commissioning of aspiring screen-writers encouraged by screenwriting manuals, seminars, online tutorials, and academic courses. While many of these screenplays may never even be submitted to producers, others will continue to circulate and be read for years and even decades. Some may be highly regarded: since 2005, an annual "Black List" of unproduced screenplays doing the Hollywood rounds that have been "most liked" by professional script readers has been published. Several of these scripts eventually find their way into production. Recent examples include 2016 Oscar winner, *Spotlight,* as well as commercial and critical hits *Slumdog Millionaire* (2008), *The King's Speech* (2010), *Argo* (2012),

Manchester by the Sea (2016), and *I, Tonya* (2017). Unproduced screenplays, then, aren't unread, nor are they seen within the film industry as intrinsically valueless; on the contrary, the fact that many screenwriting Oscars have been won by screenplays from the Black List indicates the potential that unproduced screenplays represent.

Nor is it only screenplays on the Black List that continue to exist in the absence of production. William Froug cites Walter Brown Newman's unproduced *Harrow Alley* as a favourite screenplay with industry insiders back in 1972; in 2018, it was once again "in development" by British screenwriter (also actress and producer) Emma Thompson. Written in the early 1960s, bought outright by actor George C. Scott and held by him until his death, *Harrow Alley* remains in existence and in circulation half a century later and is available to read on the Internet. More famous than *Harrow Alley*, Harold Pinter's unproduced screenplay for *À la recherche du temps perdu*, known as *The Proust Screenplay*, has long survived the projected but unmade film that brought it into being. Like some other screenplays rendered autonomous by circumstances that prevented production, usually the collapse of financing, this has continued as a text in its own right that exists alongside the rest of Pinter's critically acclaimed oeuvre. Written from 1972 to 1973 and published in 1978, it has long survived the abortive production that occasioned its writing, and remains in print in 2020. The writer of twenty-two screenplays, "of which seventeen have been made exactly as written," Pinter worked successfully within the Hollywood mainstream, gaining two Oscar nominations as well as many other awards, including the Nobel Prize for Literature. Just as Pinter's theatre plays give the lie to simplistic notions that theatre is all dialogue, so the opening of *The Proust Screenplay* creates a tessellation of sounds, images, and transitions of the kind that many film scholars attribute automatically to directors rather than to writers:

1. Yellow screen. Sound of a garden gate bell.

2. Open countryside, a line of trees, seen from a railway carriage. The train is still. No sound. Quick fade out.

3. Momentary yellow screen.

4. The sea, seen from a high window, a towel hanging on a towel rack in foreground. No sound. Quick fade out.

5. Momentary yellow screen.

6. Venice. A window in a palazzo, seen from a gondola. No sound. Quick fade out.

7. Momentary yellow screen.

8. The dining room at Balbec. No sound. Empty.

For Price, "the readability of Harold Pinter's unfilmed *Proust Screenplay* is a reminder that, at most, the screenplay is a textual invocation of a film; never *the* film." But by framing the screenplay in this way, Price reverses positives into negatives. It is exactly the power of the screenplay that it invokes a plurality, a multiplicity, even an infinity of films, while "the" film (if it should ever come into existence) is highly likely to be only itself, singular. Price's "at most" imposes an artificial ceiling on the screenplay's aspirations and leads him to overlook the fact that, by outliving the planned film by nearly half a century,

Pinter's screenplay has rendered the unmade film, rather than itself, redundant. Like *Harrow Alley*, the Black List favourites, and the multitudes of less favoured, unproduced screenplays, Pinter's *Proust Screenplay* persists – and not as an intermedial text, but as distinctive and independent writing.

"Screenplays are incomplete and never achieve a fixed state"

Views of the screenplay as ephemeral, passive, invisible, unstable, and consumed by performance all contribute to the notion that screenplays are incomplete and never achieve a fixed state. This contradicts assertions that the screenplay achieves completion when the film is made, and does so by dying and vanishing. At the same time, such an incomplete and unstable entity is seen as threatening the film, which is itself only complete, according to Carrière, "when the screenplay has vanished." However, something that's shifted significantly since publication of Carrière's book in 1994 is confidence in the certainty of a film's completeness. The notion of a film as fixed and static has been challenged by reconceptions of it as an "open text," capable of existing simultaneously in multiple versions and on different platforms. No film may be complete, after all; any director may release a new director's cut. And, if a film can never be declared finally, definitively "complete," then the screenplay isn't after all condemned to vanish. Indeed, the screenplay's continued existence, its refusal to be disposed of, calls into question the film's completion and wholeness.

As I've tried to show, the case for screenplays as invisible, disappearing, consumed, or destroyed isn't supported by actual filmmaking practice. Screenplays enjoy continuing existences during production, in finished films, and apart from their films. The films that they've brought into being, highly regarded as many of them are, have not exhausted the screenplays themselves. The resistance from many quarters to acknowledging the screenplay's endurance nevertheless persists because so much is at stake. For those who have controlled the film industry throughout its history, the studios and other powerful producers, the incentive is clear: allowing higher status to the screenplay expands the financial and creative power of writers, to the producers' own cost. Film theorists who read backwards from projected films to screenplays also stand to lose power and cultural authority if they cede territory to the literary in film studies and share expertise with literary theorists. For screenwriters themselves, meanwhile, there's the implicit threat of being branded unprofessional (the greatest sin, according to many manuals): only an amateur with no grasp of the realities of film production, the manuals charge, would make such extravagant and naive claims for their own work.

The next and final chapter examines why screenplays have proved so tenacious and enduring and why, despite continuing hostility, they remain central to filmmaking.

6

GENERATIVE SCREENPLAYS

[A]s you start the process of writing a screenplay – or probably anything – you're dreaming a dream. The job is to make a dream come true. It starts as a daydream, which is to say that you're the one who's actively pushing the fantasy. If you get lucky, at a certain point the conscious part of you goes to sleep and it becomes a night dream. It takes over. You lose conscious control over it. The characters have a life of their own, and you just have to follow the logic of them and say, "Oh, that's what they do."

Robert Towne

[T]hink of the writing in terms of discovery, which is to say that creation must take place between the pen and the paper, not before in a thought or afterwards in a recasting... it will be creation if it came out of the pen and out of you and not out of an architectural drawing of the thing you are doing

Gertrude Stein

The academic, pedagogic, and practitioner discourses about screenplays tend to remain separate from one another, but there's one place where they intersect: all take account, in their different ways, of Aristotle's *Poetics*. However, the familiar debate about three-act structure, a concept frequently mis-attributed to Aristotle, isn't the focus here. Nor are the three aspects of the *Poetics* that have resonated most forcefully with those who write and read screenplays: the primacy of plot, the importance of genre, and the centrality of audience experience. Instead this chapter looks beyond these to Aristotle's theories of writing in relation to performance and his rejection of deductive templates. Another useful Aristotelian insight is his distinction between poiesis and praxis, which offers an escape from the confines of the conception/execution dichotomy. The scholarly focus on a separation between conception and execution has helped to obscure what screenplays are and how they function. Attempts to assign only one, or neither, of these two functions to screenplays misrepresent them

Building on Aristotle's ideas, we can challenge the notion that screenplays' lack of completeness undermines their agency. Instead, their hybridity and mutability align screenplays not with completion but instead with process.

Another key concept from the *Poetics*, visualisation – using the "mind's eye" – has widely informed screenplay practice and pedagogy. Aristotle's writing in this area refutes conventional notions that the visual enters the screenplay (and later, the film) only via the camera or the director.

Finally, this chapter proposes that the generative agency of screenplays stems from their linking of visualisation with the act of writing. Practitioners' accounts of their own writing processes show how this combination can result in works laying claim to conceptual and formal independence – works that remain separate from the films that may follow. This independence explains why screenwriters, despite the hostility directed against screenplays, may nevertheless choose to write them in preference to other kinds of writing, or to other roles within filmmaking.

Screenplay discourse and Aristotle

> *It's 42 pages of simple, irrefutable truths and the best book on screenwriting*
>
> Gary Ross

In the twenty-three centuries since Aristotle wrote The Poetics, *the "secrets" of story have been as public as the library down the street.*

Robert McKee

The global success of Hollywood might be even more patterned on Aristotle's principles than has previously been understood.

Ari Hiltunen

Scholarly theorising in academic monographs, edited collections, and journal articles is conducted in writing – ironically so in light of all the questions that scholars raise about the limitations of writing for film and in general. Its readership, as for screenplays themselves, is a narrow one. The discourse of screenwriting teachers, meanwhile, isn't limited to published manuals (which sell in far greater numbers than academic publications), but extends to live seminars, online tutorials, personal blogs, and beyond into formal education through university and film school screenwriting courses. Robert McKee is known as much for his *Story* seminar as for the book that followed some years later, and since the seminar was dramatised in *Adaptation* (2002) the actor Brian Cox's performance in the role of McKee has provided memorable visual imagery to perpetuate this. Neither McKee nor John Truby has yet published a second book, but both are still busy delivering seminars around the world, not only in person but also, in Truby's case, online via his website *truby.com*. A lot of faith has been placed in writing *about* screenplays, even while writing *within* screenplays is routinely called into question.

There are also differences in style, persona, and the way that scholars and teachers address their readerships and audiences. Whilst academics may write in the third person, screenwriting pedagogues frequently adopt a personal, con-versational diction, as each addresses the reader directly in the various formats, including written manuals: "Welcome to the second edition of *Screenplay: Writing the Picture*. What's new?" begin Robin Russin and William Downs. The books often mimic the style of a motivational talk: "We will not cheerlead or sugarcoat how difficult it will be for you," Russin and Downs promise. Blake Snyder takes pride in presenting himself through "a certain slangy shorthand," as used by "screenwriters and movie executives."

By comparison to both scholarship and screenwriting pedagogy, the discourse of screenwriters about their craft is almost invisible. The main source for information about screenplays as discussed by screenwriters is published interviews, conducted mainly by media journalists. The writers' opinions and accounts of their experience are rarely volunteered apart from promoting films or careers to the press, although some screenwriters do maintain blogs and web pages. Even then, the range of published interviews is narrow, further limited by the fact that the same interviewees (and sometimes interviews) recur across different collections, while numerous other screenwriters choose not to discuss their work in public. Many writers are superstitious about inquiring too closely into a creative process that is understood as instinctive rather than rational, and thereby disrupting it; Scott Frank says that "The best writing is also subconscious where you don't know that you're doing it and you don't realize you've done it."

These three modes of discourse – academic, pedagogical, and practitioner – may overlap but for the most part remain largely separate from one another, conducted in different places and in different voices. There is little, if any, evidence that practitioners read what scholars have theorised about their practice, while screenwriters are often suspicious and dismissive of the manual authors who, while they rarely invoke theoretical concepts, occasionally act as conduits for theoretical concepts. "It's just jargon, really" according to novelist-screenwriter William Boyd (*Stars and Bars, Chaplin*). "I don't know any screenwriter who doesn't regard these courses as laughable." Playwright-screenwriter Martin McDonagh (*In Bruges, Three Billboards*) insists that "I've never subscribed to that... Robert McKee bullshit," while Darren Aronofsky claims that "those Syd Field books were evil."

Indeed, practitioners are wary of most interventions in or commentaries on their practice from other parties. Often they reject the notion that outsiders understand their work, including those in the industry who don't themselves write. Patrick McGrath (*Spider, Asylum*), who came to filmmaking as an established novelist and has subsequently written screenplays based on his own novels, said "What surprised me in Hollywood was that people who are in the business of making movies are so astonishingly naive about the process through which scripts are actually created." McGrath isn't the only writer to voice this opinion. Bruce Robinson told an interviewer that development executives

> get hold of the script, and it's like a blacksmith opening up the back of a wristwatch. A brief look inside and he says, "This wheel is going like crazy, but these two big guys with the teeth aren't even moving. Fuck them, then, they can come out." Watch stops. That's how screenplays are treated all the time.

Screenwriters may also reject instructional seminars and manuals for their association with development personnel. Boyd suggests that "these screenwriting courses are designed so executives can come back from them and say knowing things to writers about 'character arcs' and 'three-act structure.'"

The separate discourses intersect only at certain points, one of which is in citing Aristotle as an authority on screenplay writing. The *Poetics* is one of the very few written texts to enjoy currency within all three discourses of practice, of theory, and of pedagogy. As such it offers the possibility of bridging the gaps between them. Aristotle's ideas, and received but inaccurate versions of them, permeate all three discourses. He's cited by most theorists and manual authors, and also by many screenwriters. Kevin Boon devotes a chapter of *Script Culture and the American Screenplay* to "Aristotle, Aesthetics, and Critical Approaches," while the *Poetics* is referenced by Steven Maras, J.J. Murphy, and Steven Price. Kathryn Millard complains that "we hear more about the principles of Aristotelian drama rather than other forms of ancient drama," and Aristotle makes regular appearances in Ian Macdonald's *Screenwriting Poetics and the Screen Idea,* usually as the perceived source of "current orthodoxy."

In screenwriting manuals, Aristotle is equally, if not more, visible. Two books make him their focus: Michael Tierno's *Aristotle's Poetics for Screenwriters* and Ari Hiltunen's *Aristotle in Hollywood.* Hiltunen, as an acquisitions executive, is more attuned to the commercial appeal of the "Aristotelian" screenplay, while Tierno is another "story analyst" promising his readers "Storytelling Secrets from the Greatest Mind in Western Civilization" (his book's subtitle). Tierno uses a quotation from *Entertainment Weekly* to set up his subject's importance: "Aristotle's *Poetics* has become to Hollywood screenwriters what Sun-tzu's *The Art of War* is to Mike Ovitz. So what if it's more than 2,000 years old?"

Ovitz, a turn-of-the-century "über-agent," may have receded into Hollywood history since 1999, along with the fashion for Sun-tzu, but Aristotle remains the entertainment capital's most popular philosopher. He's cited also in many other manuals, from Irwin Blacker's 1986 textbook *The Elements of Screenwriting: A Guide for Film and Television Writers* ("the basic theory of Aristotelian dramaturgy has not been superseded by any basic reforms") to Josh Golding's less mainstream *Maverick Screenwriting* from 2012. Not all early how-to books invoke Aristotle; he's absent from both Epes Winthrop Sargent's *Technique of the Photoplay* (1916) and Jeanie Macpherson's "Development of Photodramatic Writing" (1917). Others, however, do. Eustace Hale Ball in *Photoplay Scenarios* (1915) notes that "The Greek unities, so-called, of 'time, place and action' give a solidarity to the photoplay which makes for artistic completeness." It isn't clear whether Ball is referring (inaccurately) to Aristotle (who insists only on unity of action, not of time or place), or merely to the tradition of dramatic unities that was developed from the sixteenth century by Lodovico Castelvetro and others. Other early references are less ambiguous. J. Arthur Nelson, in *The Photo-play: How to Write and Sell Them* (1913), lifts a number of terms directly from a translation of the *Poetics*. Invoking the "Law of dramatic construction," Nelson instructs his reader that "The photo-play must have a beginning, a middle and an end," echoing Aristotle's description of a satisfactory plot ("with beginning, middle and end." "A dramatic action should be ONE. That is, it must possess unity" in turn reproduces Aristotle's "the plot, since it is mimesis of an action, should be of a unitary and indeed whole action." Nelson continues "A drama, then, is an action complete in itself," and also picks up Aristotle's insistence on probability. Some of these early references may have reached screenwriting manuals via popular theatre play writing guides by authors such as August von Kotzebue, René Pixérécourt, and Eugène Scribe. Later manuals citing Aristotle include those by Field, Robin Russin and William Downs, McKee, Lew Hunter, Truby, and Joseph McBride.

While early screenwriters show little or no interest in Aristotle and the *Poetics*, Aristotelian ideas were subsequently transmitted through pedagogy to later generations who went on to write screenplays. David Bordwell suggests that "In the

1970s screenwriting became an academic enterprise" – although screenwriting has been studied in colleges since the early twentieth century. "Schools" offered correspondence courses in screenwriting as early as 1910, while the first university in America to teach film, the University of Southern California, opened its Department of Cinema in 1929. Christopher Vogler remembers being taught there several decades later by Blacker:

> One of the great screenwriting teachers at the University of Southern California was the late Irwin Blacker, a formidable person who left his strong imprint on generations of film students, including John Milius and George Lucas... he expected us to read *The Poetics* in its entirety, make some sense of it, and put it to work in our stories... His emphasis on *The Poetics* had a far-reaching effect, and is carried on by his students, now making films and teaching at all the major film schools.

Vogler went on to become not a screenwriter but the author of another ubiquitous screenwriting manual, *The Writer's Journey*, celebrating its 25th anniversary in 2020 with a new edition. He describes himself as "one of Hollywood's premier story consultants and a popular speaker on screenwriting, movies and myth." Vogler cites only two theorists in *The Writer's Journey*: Aristotle, and Vogler's own predecessor in mythology, Joseph Campbell.

Meanwhile, at the California Institute of the Arts, Alexander Mackendrick also used Aristotle's text as a teaching aid from the 1960s. Paul Cronin's introduction to Mackendrick's *On Film-making* notes that Mackendrick created his own "lengthy handout on Aristotle's *Poetics* – primarily made up of excerpts from the Greek classic with short commentary interspersed."

Screenwriter Nicholas Meyer remembers being "trained by Howard Stein at the University of Iowa Writers' Workshop. He said that everybody had to read Aristotle's *Poetics*, which we did." Lewis John Carlino told William Froug that he applied his knowledge of Aristotle to screenwriting. Back in 1941 Leo Rosten noted that 48.6% of Hollywood screenwriters had college degrees (see Chapter 3, section 6). In 2005, of the twenty screenwriters interviewed by Kevin Conroy Scott, all attended university or film school, the great majority studying arts subjects (often English literature or drama) at university. Thus the transmission of Aristotelian concepts from the academy to professional practice is likely to have increased. Screenwriters may or may not choose to apply Aristotle's teaching to their screenwriting practice, but the *Poetics* still forms part of the intellectual context within which screenplays are written, taught, and theorised.

So much is Aristotle a familiar element of this field that it's easy to overlook the strangeness of the fact that an ancient text, incomplete and lacking an authoritative final form, and describing highly specific Athenian artworks (epic poems and tragedies), should become a commonplace of Hollywood script meetings. The role of institutions of higher education in screenwriting theory can't alone explain the *Poetics*' persistence. To remain current in the aggressively commercial arena of the entertainment business, the *Poetics* must have something more than a place on the curricula of humanities degree courses. One explanation is that Aristotle lends authority to all three screenplay discourses – scholarly, pedagogical, practitioner – and thus supports screenplays' appeal for serious consideration by association with one of the most respected figures in the Western intellectual tradition.

But there are more pragmatic reasons for his ongoing presence in screenplay discourses, most of which further enhance the prestige and authority of screenwriters, screenwriting, and screenplays. In the *Poetics*, as elsewhere, Aristotle is concerned with definition and classification, a methodology valuable to scholars seeking to define and classify screenplays (see Chapter 1, section 1). Just as the *Poetics* demarcates poetry as an area of independent study, thereby inaugurating literary criticism as distinct from other kinds of writing, so too screenwriting discourses engage Aristotle to demarcate screenplays as a separate genre. In terms of the film industry, Aristotle attends to three topics that are as current in mainstream narrative filmmaking today as they were in Athens in the fourth century BCE: the primacy of plot, the importance of genre, and the centrality of the audience's emotional response. All of these are frequently referenced by a majority of manual authors, as well as some screenwriters.

For the authors of screenwriting manuals, Aristotle models a pedagogical approach and presents a comprehensive conception of what his subject is and how it functions, along with a clear set of rules that can be followed by practitioners. Screenwriting tutors are drawn to his emphasis on structure, and this more than any other single aspect of the *Poetics* has shaped both practitioner and pedagogical discourse. However, Aristotle's conception of structure isn't a purely mechanistic one, like the building and architecture metaphors so frequently employed in screenwriting manuals. On the contrary, Aristotle's translator and editor Stephen Halliwell points out that Aristotle offers "a conception of artistic form which relates it to the organic forms crucial to his understanding of nature," and connects this to Aristotle's "central emphasis on form and structure as fundamental to the understanding of poems as 'objects' in their own right." Screenplays can be seen as sharing the same intimate relationship with structure – the structure of living organisms, such as plants and animals, as much as that of buildings – and also like them having an independent existence, as "'object[s]' in their own right."

Beyond rules that screenwriters may or may not respect or follow, Aristotle offers them practical advice. He backs this up with the kind of aesthetic value judgments and advice about how to make "good" plays that abound in professional practice, media reviews, and some areas of academia (although aesthetic pronouncements remain taboo in others).

Aristotle's preference for induction over deduction, moving in his discussion of tragedy from the particular (individual elements of single plays) to the universal (such as the most effective kinds of plot), also appeals to many screenwriters. Screenwriting templates and formulas do the opposite, attempting to impose a universal conception onto an individual screenplay. Aristotle can thus be seen to oppose industrial or blueprint notions of screenwriting as uniform or formulaic. Furthermore, against the anonymity and collective writing practices of the film industry, the *Poetics* unequivocally identifies writers as the authors of their works, frequently referencing them by name. While the physical staging of the plays is often mentioned, such considerations are secondary to writing, a point that Aristotle makes unambiguously: "[T]ragedy's capacity is independent of performance and actors."

Not only does the *Poetics* grant respect to writers and independent status to writing independent of performance, it further insists on distinguishing the *process* of writing (poiesis, making) from the *end* of writing (praxis, acting or performance). In the same way the writing of a screenplay is separate from its end, the completed screenplay – which looks forward in turn to another end, the film. Poiesis is also the term that Aristotle applies to distinguish the writing, or "making," of poems and plays, which similarly looks forward to separate ends in reading and performance. By emphasising process, Aristotle thus offers an alternative conception of the relationship between screenplays and filmmaking to that of conception/ execution (see Chapter 2 section 3) – a process that continues beyond both conception and execution to the audience's emotional response, their pity and fear, through which tragedy accomplishes katharsis. A play made by Sophocles no more contains its end in itself than a screenplay does, and thus can be described as incomplete; yet there's no sense in the *Poetics* that Aristotle considers *Oedipus* in any way diminished by being part of a larger creative process. Indeed, Aristotle locates the essence of tragedy within its conception and reception rather than its execution. He states explicitly that "the plot should be so structured that, even without seeing it performed, the person who hears the events that occur experiences horror and pity at what comes about (as one would feel when hearing the plot of the *Oedipus*)." The essence of tragedy is thus specifically separated from performance, and in particular from the visuality of performance, "seeing it performed." For writers, this endorses the independent character of the play, and – by extension – the screenplay.

Aristotle further appeals to those who think and write about screenplays because of his emphasis on the visual in writing. According to Aristotle,

> One should construct plots, and work them out in diction, with the material as much as possible in the mind's eye. In this way, by seeing things most vividly, as if present at the actual events, one will discover what is apposite and not miss contra- dictions.

Similar advice is found even in those earliest manual authors who don't invoke the authority of Aristotle, such as Sargent:

> To write in action you must first acquire the ability to think in action and to visualize that action. You think, for example, that Paul kisses

Mary. You must, at the same time, with your mental vision, see Paul kissing Mary. You must see this so distinctly that you can write the action as you see it and not merely write an action.

Phil Lang, of the Kalem Company, has happily called this the "Picture Eye." That is precisely what it is, but the eye is the eye of the mind...

This conception of the "mind's eye" (or "Picture Eye") places visuality at the centre of conception, writing, and the screenplay. Aristotle and Sargent both articulate this in similar terms, and in so doing demonstrate that the visual doesn't enter with the camera, or even with the director, but, on the contrary, is a central element of play and screenplay writing. Some later manual-writers make similar recommendations. Viki King tells her reader to "[i]magine you're in a theater and your movie comes up on the screen. Run it in your head right now," while according to Dwight and Joye Swain:

The first step in writing any master scene script is to visualize the action, no matter how clumsily... Close your eyes, now. Envision that opening scene, the way your imagination would like to see it on the screen.

Visualisation allows a writer to preview not only her screenplay, but also an imaginary production of it, playing in a cinema. It expresses clearly how the writing comprehends both conception (the idea) and execution (what allows it to be seen), as well as the larger process that extends beyond these terms. Crucially, visualisation calls on the screenwriter not just to write a screenplay but also to direct it. Accounts by practitioners bear this out, although they may move visualisation to a later stage in the process, during rather than before writing. "Of course I do" is Towne's response to the question, "Don't you see the movie in your mind's eye while you're creating it?" He continues, "When I write a screenplay I describe a movie that's already been shot." Ernest Lehman remembers in similar terms his work with Alfred Hitchcock: "With Hitch, it's like the picture is all finished before it's filmed. It is all on paper. We sat together and figured out every shot." Bruce Joel Rubin talks of "images that your mind conjures for itself."

Scholarly discourse often addresses visualisation as a part of reading, rather than writing, screenplays. Acknowledging that "The idea of a reader seeing and hearing a film 'on the screen of the mind's eye,' in a kind of immersive experience, is an important aspect of the screenplay," Maras nonetheless remains sceptical, wondering "if the claims made about this aspect of the screenplay can be overstated." Nannicelli challenges this, rejecting the idea that screenplays can produce in their readers a specifically "cinematic" visualisation. Instead, he makes this part of his case that screenplays belong to literature, arguing that "there is no compelling reason to think that our screenplay-cued mental imagery is different in kind from mental imagery fostered by more familiar sorts of literary works, such as poems or novels." Scholars rarely if ever address visualisation as a creative act embedded in writing itself. Maras cites Truby asserting this, but then goes on to discuss, and dismiss, visualisation in terms of reading screenplays, rather than of writing them.

Visualisation remains an area where argument is impeded by the absence of data; we can only compare subjective experiences. The scepticism of Maras's negation may be further instances of the gap between writers' readings of screenplays and those of others, such as studio executives. It's also possible that an individual may share with the former president of Pixar,

Ed Catmull, the condition known as aphantasia, an inability to create mental imagery. My own experience of writing and reading screenplays matches those described by Aristotle, Sargent, King, the Swains, Towne, Lehman, and Rubin. While it's easy to accept that not everyone reads (or writes) screenplays in this way, there's sufficient evidence that many writers and readers do. If the experience of some scholars is different, that may not disprove visualisation so much as illustrate the gulf between actual screenplay practice and attempts by scholars to understand it. As screenwriter William Bowers said of "most studio people," they "do not know how to read a screenplay. That's all there is to it. They can't see the film in their heads as they read the words on the paper." Bowers goes on to make an obvious, but often overlooked, point: "It takes some training to do that, some ability." Scholars, like "studio people," may lack the necessary training or ability – but that's an insufficient basis on which to argue that visualisation doesn't or can't occur. In practitioner discourse, visualisation remains a key component not simply of how screenplays are read, nor only of the ways by which they become cinema, but also of screenplays' generative processes.

Screenplays as process

I think the least interesting part of the work is the end product.

Robert Towne

We should view the absence of a definitive published text for a screenplay in the context of other, related forms, rather than employ it to deny screenplays the status of written texts in their own right. As Macdonald notes, "Script drafts are not incomplete at the time they are written, and may even (on occasion) prove more satisfying expressions of the screen idea than the film itself – one more reason why we should not always accept the film as the final, 'correct version.'" Price too emphasises the "provisional and unstable nature of all screenplays." This is a conception that literary scholar Stephen Greenblatt's essay, "The Dream of the Master Text," applies to the most canonical of all English dramatists:

> there is no sign that Shakespeare sought through such revision to bring each of his plays to its "perfect," "final" form. On the contrary, many of the revisions seem to indicate that the scripts remained open texts, that the playwright and his company expected to add, cut, and rewrite as the occasion demanded.

The various exigencies of production and performance are, after all, not new. Textual variants, such as different screenplay drafts, have been part of literary performance writing for centuries.

Nor is the absence of a definitive text any obstacle to valuing writing highly or studying it in its own right:

> Neither the Folio nor the quarto texts of Shakespeare's plays bear the seal of final authorial intention, the mark of decisive closure that has served, at least ideally, as the guarantee of textual authenticity. We want to believe, as we read the text, "This is the play as Shakespeare himself wanted it read," but there is no license for such a reassuring sentiment. To be "not of an age, but for all time" means in Shakespeare's case not that the plays have achieved a static perfection, but that they're creatively, inexhaustibly unfinished.

However much scholars might long for the closure of willed and achieved completeness, it may prove unavailable. Yet this lack of "static perfection" doesn't prevent our acceptance of Shakespeare's plays, regardless of their instability or openness as texts and their close relationship with performance. If we put to one side the question of literary status and look instead at how they function, screenplays by Harold Pinter, Charlie Kaufman, Robert Towne, Ethan and Joel Coen, and others also continue to exist as written texts, and they too can be viewed as "creatively, inexhaustibly unfinished."

Sally Bushell's argument against the New Critical privileging of a "final work" over process can be brought to bear on screenplays and films, as well as literature. Tracing this back to Martin Heidegger's phenomenology, she writes that, under New Critical theories, "Process is acknowledged for the literary work of art but no value can be given to it since all the emphasis is placed on the self-sufficiency of the final thing." Where this "final thing" is a film rather than a poem, and part of the "process" takes the form of screenplay drafts, the same New Critical conception can be seen to operate with even more force within film studies, which often disposes of the screenplay altogether and does not even allow final versions of it to remain. Bushell cites critic Klaus Hurlebusch: "His aim is to bring together the two aspects of writing that exist in a dialectical tension between 'the mainly reproductive, work-genetic writing process ('poiesis') and the mainly constructive, psycho-genetic writing ('praxis').'" The attempt to bring together poiesis and praxis in a single concept of process which Bushell relates to literature is also applicable to screenplays, and the following section develops this further.

Skull cinema: screenplays as generative writing

*[W]ords do not come after a psychic reality which they verbalize,
but... are its very origin: In the beginning was the word... Words
create things instead of being a pale reflection of them.*

Tzvetan Todorov

Writing is a concentrated form of thinking.

Don DeLillo

Visualisation is only part of the generative, creative work going into screenplays. If visualisation took place wholly prior to writing, then Macdonald's proposition that a screenplay "is the record of an idea for a screenwork" would hold. However, this definition is problematic since it pushes conception away from the screenplay as writing to relocate it in a pre-writing mind. Although Macdonald conceptualises the two as a connected, ongoing process, by making the screenplay nothing more than a "record" of a pre-existing "idea," he denies creativity to the writing of the screenplay. Generative conception has already taken place; all that is left for the screenplay to do is write down the ideas. Like Macdonald's "pre-existing idea," other attempts by scholars to relocate the generative function of screenplays, for example in activities such as improvisation (Millard) and digital pre-visualisation (Maras), similarly obscure the agency of screenplay writing. By contrast, Aristotle's statement that "One should construct plots, and work them out in diction" places conception or construction *in* the writing, the working out of ideas through writing – so that ideas are still actively being negotiated within the process of writing, and don't simply pre-exist it.

Screenwriters themselves understand that the act of writing generates ideas, as well as screenplays and films. The generative aspect of screenwriting is a common theme within practitioner discourse, a process that's characterised as active and organic. Many describe the writing of screenplays as an act that's in some way autonomous, one that creates the plot rather than pre-existing it: "I never know what's going to happen," says Horton Foote (*To Kill a Mockingbird*, *Tender Mercies*); "when you're creating, you want this thing to take you over – to take *you* over." Caroline Thompson (*Edward Scissorhands*, *Black Beauty*) explains that "The best things are like that for me, where I'm rushing to keep up with the story; not that I'm inventing the story, but that it's inventing itself." Towne agrees: "The best that I feel is when I feel I have nothing to do with it... when the characters assume a life of their own." Richard LaGravenese (*The Fisher King*, *Water for Elephants*) says of a screenplay that it "kind of wrote itself... I do have a direction. I just let the story tell me how to get there," while Anthony Minghella writes that he's "often taken by surprise." McDonagh, a highly successful playwright as well as screenwriter, says, "I never really plot it out beforehand, in either the plays or the films. I let the plot or story tell itself and let the characters take me to the place where they're going to." For Andrew Bergman (*Blazing Saddles*, *The In-Laws*), "the way I write is by jumping out of a plane without knowing if the parachute will open. It's dangerous." Beyond being generative, screenwriting is unpredictable, involving risk, and writers embrace the idea that it assumes a dynamic of its own. Some kind of preparatory work, whether written or not, has established a direction, or a theme, or a setting, or a character; for many, though, it's the act of writing, of placing one word after another, that creates the story, what will become the screenplay. An element of unpredictability is built into this process, while a record, if it is to have any value as a record, must be definite and definitive.

Indeed, ceding control is an essential part of the writing process as screenwriters describe it. According to Kaufman, "It's a step into the abyss. It necessarily starts somewhere, anywhere; there is a starting point but the rest is undetermined. It is a secret, even from you." Much of writing (and most of rewriting) involves a high degree of conscious control, the practice of a craft (praxis). Yet that remains dependent on a generative process, one of making (poiesis). Screenwriters characterise this as an unconscious, rather than conscious, process. Towne goes so far as to attribute it to another identity contained within himself:

> As I've gotten older, I've been able to be more accepting of the fact that there's some little gnome at work inside of me; sort of like I'm the maiden who's been ordered to spin flax into gold in 'Rumpelstiltskin.' I can't do that. But, contained somewhere inside of me, I've concluded, is this little dwarf, this vicious little prick, who, if I go to sleep and let him go to work, he'll do it...

The mixture of delight and abhorrence in Towne's sustained metaphorical explanation articulates the screenwriter's mixed feelings about this abnegation of control. He wants the "flax" of story ideas to be spun into the "gold" of the screenplay, but acknowledges that he needs help from a contaminated source, stunted and "vicious." Towne's invocation of a fairytale bogy seems so remote from scholarly accounts of screenplays that the wide gap once again calls into question how much the two discourses are able to connect with one another, when the focus shifts from the formal qualities or materiality of screenplays to the invisible, intangible processes beneath their surfaces.

The visualisation employed by writers during the early stages of creating their screenplays, when it may draw on material from their unconscious and dreams, is mobilised again once the first draft is complete, this time by readers. It is at this point that the screenplay's agency is least disputed, and most distinct from the film (or films) that it may (or may not) bring into being in the future. Before script readers and development executives get to see it, the movie of the screenplay runs in what can be characterised as the skull cinema, inside the writer's own head. "The single greatest joy you'll ever have is when you're sitting there writing," according to Scott Frank, "because the movie will never be what you thought it would be." This film, playing in the skull cinema, remains unmediated by others, as well as unrealisable, and that holds great appeal for many screenwriters. It's why Marc Norman's studio executives told screenwriters how much they envied them, because they perceived that "screenwriters had the purest experience with their product. They got to see the movie first, entire, in their minds." The writing of screenplays not only generates movies, but it also offers their authors an ideal, abstract cinema – a film totally free from the compromises that come with the materiality of filmmaking. As Lee and Janet Scott Batchler have said of their screenplay, *Smoke and Mirrors*, mired in "development hell," "the fact that the movie hasn't been made means that no one has ruined a frame of it yet." Although existing solely in the form of writing, the screenplay is here conceptualised as a physical film print composed of many individual frames, each of them retaining the ideality of the screenplay, and ready to be projected, whenever desired, within the skull cinema. If there is such a thing as pure cinema, this – before directors and cameras enter the picture – may be it.

Conclusion

The different screenplay discourses rarely come together, and when they do it's often in support of myths and fallacies about screenwriting. Many factors contribute to this: the difficulties of definition, historical obfuscation, distortions caused by conceptions of screenplays in industrial terms and employing outdated industrial language and metaphors, disavowals both of words and of the visuality of screenplays, the denial to them of individuality or style, insistence on their invisibility and ephemerality, and refusal to acknowledge their creative agency. If academic approaches to screenplays are to engage with them more effectively, then practice – how screenplays are written, as well as read – may prove the most helpful corrective to some of the misconceptions that have arisen and continue to be propagated. Meanwhile any approach that downplays or marginalises these aspects of what is an essentially a creative and generative process will struggle to capture what screenplays do.

Screenwriter Steve Tesich provides one of few sustained descriptions detailing the process of screenplay writing, in *Karoo*, his only novel. In this fictional account of a script doctor's transformation into a screenwriter, Tesich offers a rare account of how a screenplay is generated. Choosing as his protagonist someone who cuts screenplay words for a living instead of writing them, Tesich organises his tragicomic climax around the protagonist's recovery of his agency as a writer. This happens as he's dying, through a restored ability to visualise the story he had begun and abandoned decades before. However, Karoo is a writer so alienated from his craft that he no longer carries the basic materials required to practise it. Trapped in a toilet by a haemorrhage, "He wished he had one of those little portable Olivetti typewriters and some paper... [e]ven one of those stupid laptop things... [b]ut he didn't even have a ballpoint pen." Like screenwriting manuals that look back to classical times for inspiration and practical advice, Karoo, "As a last resort... hit[s] upon an old device, used by men in ancient times. He would remember. He would remember it all." The story that the dying Karoo visualises is the *Odyssey*, relocated in the future and in space. Over the final thirteen pages of the novel, Karoo visualises the entire screenplay; the process of visualisation allows him to leave rewriting behind and become instead a maker in his final moments. However, as he writes nothing down, his film will never be made or visualised by another. Karoo is his own audience, but he dies happy and redeemed as a creative being.

This book has drawn on my own experience of different practices and discourses as it seeks to redeem the creative and generative aspects of screenplays. It endeavours to achieve a better understanding of how these practices and discourses interact, and to identify their capabilities for illuminating one another. If the separate discourses that discuss screenplays cannot meet on the same page, they can perhaps at least be induced to share the same space. My underlying motivation has been throughout to arrive at a clearer perception of how screenplays work, as writing, which I and perhaps others can bring to bear upon our own practice. Practice, after all, is where screenplays began, and where they continue to flourish.

NOTES

INTRODUCTION

page
1   *"Un peu de polémique"* – Truffaut, *Plaisir* 211
1   "'The greatest joy'" – Engel 286
6   "McKee's dictum" – McKee 394

DEFINING AND HISTORICISING SCREENPLAYS

7   *"the dream of a film"* – Carrière 154

Defining Screenplays

7   *"A screenplay is an exploration"* – Kaufman, *BAFTA*
8   "the Oxford English Dictionary offers" – OED online
8   "characterised as pre-text and text" – E.g. Price, *History* 2, 162, 174. Ian Macdonald refers to "screen idea documents" that constitute "an avant-texte to the screenwork" (*Poetics* 162), while Barbara Korte and Ralf Schneider categorise the screenplay as an "intermedial text type" (22).
9   "an 'Object Problem'" – Maras 11
9   "an 'intermediate work'" – Maras 48
9   "'helped to solidify the screenplay'" – Price, *History* 201
9   "'but removed from production'" – Price, *History* 211
10   "'x is a screenplay'" – Nannicelli 31
10   "'as an 'artifact'" – Nannicelli 34
10   "be or become obsolescent" – See Price, *History* 219, 238; Maras 186; and Millard 157.
10   "'tends towards metaphor'" – Price, *Screenplay* 44
11   "'38 times in 22 languages'" – *SydField.com*
11   "'TOLD WITH PICTURES'" – Field, *Screenplay* 7; capitalisation in original
11   "Marc Norman refers to Sargent" – Norman 65
11   "author of 144 screenplays" – IMDb
11   "'told in pictured action'" – Sargent 363
12   "to 'spotlight specific instructions'" – Cole & Haag 55
12   "'SCREENPLAYS ARE STRUCTURE'" – Goldman, *Adventures* 195
12   "'And every second, the action freezes'" – Goldman, *Four Screenplays* 114-5
13   "'what the Great American Novel was'" – Hauge xvii

16   "released by Mosfilm in 1976" – WorldCat

16   "contents page specifically identified it" – Eisenstein, *Potemkin* 3. A note on the copyright page of the 1968 Lorrimer edition states "Original Russian language edition entitled *The Battleship Potemkin* published in a book of scenarios in Russia. 1926." This note was not included in the Faber and Faber reissue in 1988, which does however provide the following: "British Library Cataloguing in Publication Data . . . . *Russian cinema films – Scripts.*"

16   "no extant full version" – In 1974 Lorrimer published another version of *Battleship Potemkin* along with *October* and *Alexander Nevsky* in their Classic Film Scripts series, noting that the "texts and notes are based on various published and manuscript sources" (6). Its editor Jay Leyda refers to *Battleship Potemkin* as both a "scenario" and a "script," and identifies its source: "this script was found among Eisenstein's papers and published (for the first time in 1956) to show that this masterpiece also required paper work" (8-9). However, this version is an intermediate draft ("[t]he script published here is the director's shooting script, which was produced by Eisenstein late in 1925 on the basis of what was originally a single episode in the *1905* scenario" (15). It is in fact little more than a shot list, no more than 15 pages long, in contrast to the 55 pages of text in the 1968 Lorrimer edition subsequently reissued by Faber and Faber. Price refers to this shot list as the director's "shooting script" (*History* 115) and notes that his "Subsequent quotations from Eisenstein's scripts are from this edition" (250)

16   "Bordwell explains the difference" – Bordwell et al. 60

17   "located within the screenplay itself" – Of course, a planned découpage sequence still has to be not only shot as scripted but also edited in post-production, to the same accuracy of a single frame, and so in the cutting room will become subject to the same editing requirements as a montage sequence.

17   "from 'the script of *The Player*'" – Rush and Baughman 28

18   "the published screenplay" – See Tolkin, The Player, The Rapture, The New Age – *Three Screenplays.*

18   "their list of works cited" – Rush and Baughman 37

18   "'no such beast as an original version'" – Tolkin 1

18   "'kept changing who said what'" – Tarantino, Faber xiii

19   "managed to retain publishing rights" – Greene, *Third Man* [Faber] 6

19   "published screenplay gives" – Greene, *Third Man* [Faber] 110

21   "'Oklahoma Kid' I think it was" – *The Third Man* (1949) 01:25:12-15
22   "'the warts'n'all version'" – Walker xxii
22   "'the scripts in this book'" – Walker xxii
22   "'*Princess Bride* is pretty close'" – Goldman, *Four Screenplays* x
23   "'pragmatic production tool'" – Macdonald, *Poetics* 162
23   "'story worlds'" – Maras 70
24   "*always the dream of a film*" – Carrière 154

Historicising Screenplays

25   "digital cinematography" – *Collateral* used the Sony CineAlta HDW-F900 and Thomson VIPER FilmStream, two early high definition digital cameras in addition to 35mm film cameras (IMDb)
25   "'fake correspondence schools'" – Sargent 351
25   "'frankly fraudulent'" – Sargent 352
25   "his character Pat Hobby" – Fitzgerald includes this description of Pat Hobby in a note accompanying one of the stories; see the introduction to *The Pat Hobby Stories* 9.
25   "'*Secrets of Film Writing*'" – Fitzgerald, *Pat Hobby* 52
26   "including Columbia" – Boon, *Script Culture* 43
26   "University of Southern California" – Maras 143
26   "'text book, to be studied'" – Sargent vii
26   "It is now a profession" – Sargent 5
26   "vast majority of manual-writers" – For example, Field, *Screenplay*; King; Swaine and Swaine; Hauge; Hunter; Tierno; Snyder; Golding; Russin and Downs; McBride. Seger's book is unusual in addressing itself equally to someone "writing your first script" and to the "veteran screenwriter," xii.
26   "a 'student'" – Sargent 1
26   "a 'novice writer'" – Sargent 2
26   "an 'artist-author'" – Sargent 2
26   "six decades later" – Field, *Screenplay* 232
26   "Millard and Price both identify" – Millard 41; Price, *History* 203
26   "acquire a 'typewriting machine'" – Sargent 319
26   "with a 'twelve point type'" – Sargent 320
27   "'a box of paper clips'" – Sargent 323
27   "'to see his name in type'" – Fitzgerald, *Pat Hobby* 58-9; non-Courier typeface in original
28   "'industry standard is brass brads'" – Russin and Downs 19
28   "'How to Get a Plot'" – Sargent 73
28   "how to train his memory" – Sargent 22

28   "read books about railroads" – Sargent 23

28   "the best kind of notebook" – Sargent 24

28   "they should 'read prodigiously'" – McBride 56

28   "'take notes'" – McBride 59

28   "'[k]eep scenes short'" – McBride 69

28   "'Read Chekhov'" – McBride 248

28   "'Get a job'" – McBride 297

28   "'Make your own breaks'" – McBride 304

28   "but by story analysts" – Bordwell, *Way* 28

29   "'I feel particularly qualified'" – Snyder xiii; italics in original

29   "'the three-act paradigm'" – Murphy 16

30   "Maras references McKee" – Maras 10, 63, 65, 67, 70, 104, 175-76

30   "Field's 'structuralist tendencies'" – Maras 10

30   "'the how-to books'" – Bordwell, *Way* 35

30   "'[t]heory is embedded'" – Maras 10

30   "'profound story analyst'" – Price, *Screenplay* 61

30   "more than a 'textual construct'" – Price, *Screenplay* 130

30   "'Too many story templates'" – Millard 40

30   "'water down the distinctiveness'" – Millard 28-29

30   "'to schematize all of cinema'" – McKee 80

31   "'like the Tower of Babel'" – McKee 80

32   "'Artists master the form'" – McKee 3

32   "'No amount of talk or theory'" – Swain and Swain ix

32   "as do McBride..." – McBride 180

32   "... and Riley" – Riley xx

32   "'qualified to follow your profession'" – Epps 5

32   "strive for '[p]rofessional success'" – Field, *Screenplay* 240

32   "'professional writer' and 'the amateur'" – Friedmann 29

33   "'occasionally rises to the level of art'" – Field, *Workbook* 7

32   "the value of persistence" – Field, *Screenplay* 240

33   "'in control of the craft'" – McKee 410

33   "'generally easier than selling it'" – Sargent 324

33   "'a gold-rush mentality developed'" – Maras 141

34   "'not intended as literature'" – Russin and Downs 3

35   "'get behind the camera and dream'" – Fitzgerald, *Pat Hobby* 55

35   "'a good man for structure'" – Fitzgerald, *Pat Hobby* 51

35   "'and doing what you do'" – Norman 481

35   "'see the movie first, entire'" – Norman 484

35   "'they unspooled in my head'" – Epps 265

SCREENPLAYS AS BLUEPRINTS

The blueprint metaphor and practitioners

37   "'must tell the director how'" – Lescaboura 4

37   "in many of the earliest manuals" – Although he doesn't employ the term "blueprint," James Slevin in his manual of 1912 suggests a similar idea when he notes that a screenwriter's "outline" is as necessary "as a set of plans is to an architect" 35.

37   "'There is this difference" – Lescaboura 4

38   "'At its best, a shooting script'" – Kozlenko and Golden 666

38   "'lies a blueprint – the script'" – Greene, Robert S. 10

39   "Field poses the question" – Field, *Screenplay* 7

39   "he nominates the sequence" – Field, *Screenplay* 93

39   "a 'blueprint' for teaching purposes" – Field, *Screenplay* 4

39   "'functions as a blueprint'" – Van Nostran 53

39   "'part stage play and part blueprint'" – Epps x

39   "'A blueprint is a program of action'" – Gillis 13

39   "'Takes are assembled from dailies'" – Clark and Spohr 135

39   "screenwriters are identified" – Grierson 8

40   "'not complete works in themselves'" – Gassner and Nichols xxxv

40   "'a blueprint with no life of its own'" – Aurthur 12

40   "'blueprint for something – for a building'" – Engel 82

40   "'come off the assembly line'" – Gassner and Nichols xxxi

40   "'not really a writer'" – Schrader 141

41   "'Any film is a community effort'" – Goldman, *Butch* Author's Note

41   "'hate them, always will'" – Goldman, *Four Screenplays* 3

41   "'approach them as a blueprint'" – Field, *Four Screenplays* 256

41   "'nobody goes around saying'" – Froug 166

41   "'Frank Lloyd Wright also supervised'" – Froug 278

41   "'the screenplay's really a blueprint'" – Scott 130

42   "'exists as a blueprint of the film'" – Minghella 29

42   "'only the foundations'" – Pomeranz

42   "'Try to take them as the blueprints'" – Gibbs 60

42   "'make it into a novel'" – Pomeranz

42   "'The first job of a writer'" – Engel 23

42   "'blueprint for a motion picture'" – Engel 168

The blueprint metaphor and scholars

43   "'I will be emphasizing'" – Bordwell et al. 94

43   "'the manufacturers transformed'" – Bordwell et al. 126

44	"'the shot-by-shot breakdown'" – Bordwell et al. 135
44	"'physical capacities and labor force'" – Bordwell et al. 146
44	"'cogs of the big Ince machine'" – Bordwell et al. 136
45	"'classic metaphor used to characterize'" – Sternberg 50
45	"'blueprint-readers' who use the screenplay" – Sternberg 107
45	"'everything derives from the screenplay'" – Sternberg 1; Sternberg identifies the source of Chandler's remark as "Writers in Hollywood," *Atlantic Monthly*, 176, No.5 (November 1945): 50-54
46	"'performance blueprint'" – Sternberg 232
46	"'overidentification of the writer'" – Maras 124
46	"'minimise the creative input'" – Maras 124
46	"'*On the one hand the blueprint*'" – Maras 117; italics in original
47	"'I have suggested'" – Maras 186
47	"'serve as a counterbalance'" – Maras 121
47	"'goes against the visual bias'" – Maras 121
47	"'highlights the industrial scale'" – Maras 121
47	"'industrial planning documents'" – Macdonald, *Poetics* 17
47	"'the need to consider'" – Maras 179
48	"'drawer-up of recondite documents'" – Price, *Screenplay* 46
48	"'narrator of Wordsworth's ballad'" – Price, *Screenplay* 46
48	"'in the trenches digging away'" – Epps 17
48	"'interested in other potentialities'" – Price, *History* 10
48	"'we know better than to read" – Macdonald, *Poetics* 225
48	"'the script is often the cornerstone'" – Murphy 6

Further objections to the blueprint metaphor

49	"'the silent continuity from 1914 to 1929'" – Price, *History* 235
50	"University of Iowa's BA in Screenwriting Arts" – Iowa
50	"the Golden Gate Bridge" – http://aradersf.blogspot.com/2012/11/blueprints-of-landmark.html
51	"'drawn and researched by Herb Kelley'" – http://www.joelshorwitz.com/data-science/design/
51	"available to buy on eBay" – See https://www.ebay.co.uk/itm/Star-Trek-Enterprise-Blueprints-Poster-A1-A2-A3-A4-sizes-/321442577925
51	"as Irwin Blacker does" – Blacker xii
51	"to repeat that claim" – Russin and Downs 3
52	"'the manufacturers transformed'" – Bordwell et al. 126
52	"'electricians and stage carpenters'" – Norman 133
52	"Anecdotal evidence" – See Norman 141-2
52	"'write what I was asked to write'" – Norman 132

53   "'not money, it's credits'" – Clarke 18:28

53   "at the whim of management" – See Norman 141

54   "'foundation of your screenplay'" – Field, *Screenplay* 22

54   "explain the process of 'building' it" – Field, *Screenplay* 30

54   "'The Gap in Progression'" – McKee 151

54   "'cast design' is presented" – McKee 379-80

55   "'try *withholding* a lot of information'" – Truby, *Anatomy* 273;
        italics in original

55   "'Mystery, Suspense, and Dramatic Irony'" – McKee 349

56   "'simply a blueprint for making a film'" – Blacker xii

56   "'not intended as literature'" – Russin and Downs 3

56   "the auteurist variant" – See, for example, Sarris 215

56   "originally by François Truffaut" – Truffaut, *Plaisir* 211-29

56   "'everything goes to pieces'" – Truffaut, *Hitchcock* 330

57   "'it's ridiculous to regard the script'" – Sennett 14

57   "'even the best-written script'" – Ray 25

57   "in his study of *The Birds*" – Price, *Screenplay* 74-93

58   "'A-11 INT. NEFF'S OFFICE'" – Chandler and Wilder 9-10

59   "Clifford C. Paine's blueprint" – http://aradersf.blogspot.com/
        2012/11/blueprints-of-landmark.html

60   "'FULL SCREEN PHOTOGRAPH'" – Towne 1

62   "Roland Barthes's distinction"– This is articulated in *Image,
        Music, Text*: "we may say immediately that the literal image is
        denoted and the symbolic image *connoted*" 37; italics in original

63   "'EXT. ROCKY TERRAIN.'" – Kaufman, *Adaptation* 2nd draft 1

65   "'At its heart'" – Moreno and Tuxford

WRITING AND READING SCREENPLAYS

67   *"the less can it claim literary status"* – Tarkovsky 126

"Films aren't based on writing"

67   *"I write cinema"* – Engel 168

67   "Vachel Lindsay characterises films" – Lindsay 4

67   "modes of '[d]igital [s]criptings'" – Maras 179

68   "involved only a single person" – See Bordwell et al. 116-17

68   "'Rossellini was opposed to scripts'" – Millard 115

68   "'leading a team of writers'" – Millard 106

68   "Steven Price identifies Zavattini" – Price, *Screenplay* 51

68   "115 writing credits" – IMDb

68   "'carefully shaped stories'" – Price, *Screenplay* 51

68   "'fluid rather than fixed documents'" – Millard 106

69   "made without a screenplay" – Murphy 162-3

69   "'sticking to the script'" – Froug xiii
69   "'There's lots of misconceptions'" – Scott 289
70   "'distilled from improvisations'" – Leigh xv-xvi
70   "'no reason to deviate'" – Leigh xvi
70   "'rather than scripted'" – Murphy 255
71   "'a roughly fifteen-page treatment'" – Murphy 243
71   "'created after the fact'" – Murphy 243
71   "'very specific 50-page outline'" – *Prospero*
71   "'most actors aren't writers'" – Lumet 41
72   "'screenwriting is not writing'" – Stanton

"Film is visual not verbal and words are uncinematic"
73   "'the most enduring and pernicious'" – Leitch 153
73   "'radio aesthetics'" – Leitch 153
73   "'visual iconicity'" – Leitch 154
73   "'constant streams of dialogue'" – Lumet 36
73   "'I told Hitch'" – Engel 52; brackets in original
74   "'virtually unfilmable'" – Price, *History* 46
74   "the commonly held notion" – For example, theorist Siegfried
         Kracauer categorises "uncinematic films" as "those with verbal
         statements in the lead" (239).   See also Kamilla Elliott's
         discussion of "uncinematic words" in *Rethinking the Novel/Film
         Debate* 79-83 and Noël Carroll, *Engaging the Moving Image* 153.
         The fallacy is common in professional practice, as evidenced by
         industry website *Studiodaily* ("the leading source of news,
         opinions and best practices for the digital content creation
         market"): "Nothing can kill the cinematic experience of a film
         faster than the use of excessive dialogue over imagery. This is
         because dialogue is inherently uncinematic. It originated in
         Greek drama and then developed through the plays of
         Shakespeare right up to modern-day TV" (Bloom).
74   "'a more satisfying balance'" – Price, *History* 47
74   "'Rather than simply adapting'" – Sternberg 65
74   "'remarkably lean and cinematic'" – Price, *History* 89
75   "'Chatman, for instance, dismisses'" – Leitch 151
75   "'a celebration of the talk'" – Price, *Screenplay* 169
75   "'leave here right now'" – Kaufman, *Adaptation* 2nd draft 87
76   "'[c]ounterpoint narration'" – McKee 344
76   "'looked down on'" – Russin and Downs 279; italics in original
77   "'effective cinematic device'" – Field, *Screenplay* 84
77   "'can easily make a story talky'" – Seger 126
77   "'your writing shouldn't show'" – King 47

77   "'reality or truth of appearances'" – Golding 51

77   "'should be approached with caution'" – Golding 270

77   "'Bernard F. Dick put it this way'" – Elliott 83

77   "'does not accord with aesthetic practice'" – Elliott 83

78   "'as literary, uncinematic other'" – Elliott 85

78   "'primarily a visual arts context' – Murphy 238

78   "'always invariably words on a page'" – Millard 29

78   "'screenwriter is a cine-composer" – Millard 157

79   "'no more emblematic moment" – Martin 285

79   "'now being seen on television'" – Martin 285

79   "'TV is the most powerful writing medium'" – Clarke 21:50

79   "'the writing is great'" – Romano

80   "'and never the directors'" – Norman 299

80   "'two people in a room'" – Martin 276

80   "'most visually stylized show'" – Martin 276

80   "'the director means *nothing*'" – Martin 257; italics in original

81   "'rather like plumbing'" – Froug 202

81   "'How Things Work'" – Martin 276

81   "'Midway through season three'" – Martin 276

82   "'I write visually'" – Cohen 43

82   "'I put them on paper'"– Cohen 43

83   "the cinema of multiple attractions" – Price refers to "the two dominant readings of Hollywood film – as a narrative medium or as a cinema of multiple attractions" (*History* 126).

84   "ELVISH SINGING....A WOMAN'S VOICE" – Boyens et al. 1; italics in original

"Screenplays should be read as industrial documents"

85   "Macdonald, who rejects the blueprint metaphor" – Macdonald, *Poetics* 75, 176, 225

85   "'a pragmatic production tool'" – Macdonald, *Poetics* 162

85   "'plot of action'" – Sargent 378-85

86   "'a hundred and four!'" – Wilder

86   "'studio was going to go broke'" – Wilder

87   "'at work on the same script'" – Stempel 71

87   "'couldn't really tell who had written what'" – Froug 131-32

87   "'the writing just gathered dust'" – Wilder

88   "'Hollywood's writers are employees'" – Rosten 313

88   "sound of continuous typing" – Norman 136

88   "'tied to a particular industry'" – Price, *History* 5

88   "'take account of Staiger's work'" – Price, *History* 6

88   "'costed and produced'" – Macdonald, *Poetics* 162

89   "'The main titles and the following'" – Gassner and Nichols 996
90   "'the white man's will'" – Gassner and Nichols 996
90   "'good business for the banks'" – Gassner and Nichols 999
90   "exposed as a liar and a thief" – Gassner and Nichols 1034
90   "'over the Border'" – Gassner and Nichols 1038

"The camera does the writing, not the screenplay"

91   "'without intertitles... without a script'" – *"The Man with a Movie Camera* constitutes an experiment in the cinematic transmission of visual phenomena without the aid of intertitles (a film with no intertitles), script (a film with no script), theater (a film with neither actors nor sets)" Vertov 283

91   "nominated this 'pure cinema'" – For example, Jonathan Romney's 2015 *Guardian* review of the film refers to it as "pure cinema, still unparalleled" (Romney)

91   "'directly in sequences and shots'" – Hicks 63
92   "'the age of *caméra-stylo*'" – Astruc 32
92   "'the overwhelming temptation'" – Mackendrick 69
92   "'writes with his camera'" – Astruc 35
92   "'the scriptwriter directs his own scripts'" – Astruc 35
93   "'to write ideas directly on film'" – Astruc 33
93   "'writing his philosophy on film'" – Astruc 33
94   "'enfin, on peut dire'" – Bazin, 80; my trans.; italics in original
94   "'subtle as written language'" – Astruc 32
95   "Elliott, however, has argued" – Elliott 77-112

"The authorship of auteur directors is more important "

95   "'cinéastes français'" – Truffaut, *Plaisir* 226; my trans.; italics in original

96   "'gentleman who lines up'" – Truffaut, *Plaisir* 224; my trans.
95   "'screenwriters' films'" – Truffaut, *Plaisir* 212; my trans.
97   "the basis of improvisations" – Belmondo
97   "much of a conventional screenplay" – Brody 62
97   "pre-eminence of the director" – "Directors, not writers, are the ultimate auteurs of the cinema, at least of cinema that has any visual meaning and merit" (Sarris 215)
97   "'Sarris and others established'" – Stempel 192
98   "'don't dig English dialogue'" – Froug 167
99   "'What have you got now'" – Welles 142

Industry reasons for the devaluation of screenplays as writing

99   *"extremely expensive commodity"* – Rosten 306; italics in original

100   "'the studio, hereinafter referred to'" – Norman 132

100   "'the Gene Gauntier days'" – Norman 132

100   "'angry and humiliated'" – Froug 345

100   "'Writer acknowledges that'" – WGA

102   "'Most directors think'" – Rosten 301

102   "'Will it make money?'" – Rosten 307

102   "'rewrote the screenplay himself'" – Norman 119-20

102   "'a sentimental girl from Brooklyn'" – Norman 120

102   "'arises a hundred times a week'" – Rosten 308

102   "'the basic motivation of writers'" – Rosten 307

103   "the production norm after 1955" – Bordwell et al. 330

103   "postwar currency controls" – Drazin 4-5

104   "'immoral purposes'" – Greene, *Mornings* 449

104   "'wisely retained all literary rights'" – Greene, *Third Man* [Faber] 6

105   "'the dull shorthand of a script'" – Greene, *TMFI* 3

105   "in the form of a 'story'" – Greene, *TMFI* 3

105   "'I had paid my last farewell'" – Greene, *TMFI* 1

105   "'an opening paragraph'" – Greene, *TMFI* 3

105   "'I've got a *book* coming'" – Drazin 2; italics in original

105   "Reed and I worked closely together'" – Greene, *TMFI* 4

106   "'suggested by the author'" – Greene, *TMFI* 3

106   "'ANNA moves from the bed'" – Greene, *Third Man* [Faber] 42

107   "'Anne Crowder walked up and down'" – Greene, *Three Ents* 20

107   "'Greeneland'" – According to Greene's biographer Michael Shelden, Arthur Calder-Marshall "was the first critic to use the convenient term 'Greeneland' to describe the world portrayed in the novels" (285).

107   "Greene demonstrates" – Greene's own account of the development process isn't completely reliable. He writes that "Carol Reed and I worked closely together" and that "[n]o third ever joined our conferences" (*TMFI* 4), despite the fact that the pair suffered gruelling script meetings with Selznick (*Mornings* 453). In addition Drazin claims that Korda hired an American screenwriter, Jerome Chodorov, to work with Reed on the screenplay. Chodorov told Drazin that he met Greene only once. "We just said hello and he looked at me suspiciously. Nobody likes another writer to come in on his stuff" (Drazin 43-5).

108   "'worked on *Blue Streak*'" – August

108   "3.5 credited writers" – Follows

108   "31 on *Mulan...*" – IMDb

109   "'through the rewriting mill'" – Hunter 333

109   "'to protect your work'" – Seger 190

110   "'I never expected it to be'" – Cohen 183

110   "'unfortunately, not an alternative'" – Seger xiv

110   "'any and all such requests'" – Hunter 333; italics in original

111   "'belongs to the writer'" – Goldman, *Four Screenplays* x

111   "'a script usually gets worse'" – Mamet, *Whore's Profession* 312

111   "'use it to get work'" – *Beingcharliekaufman.com*

111   "'I wasn't really expecting it'" – Kaufman, "Why I Wrote"

112   "'because of who'd written the movie'" – Norman 466

112   "Irving Thalberg is credited" – Norman 137

113   "'36.1 percent of Hollywood's producers'" – Rosten 322

113   "'[t]he percentage of movie writers'" – Rosten 321

113   "'the dialogue don't add up'" – Rosten 310

113   "'contemptuous of the producer's vocabulary'" – Rosten 310

114   "'can work together amicably'" – Rosten 301

114   "'given too much praise for the screenplay'" – Rosten 302

115   "'the men who hammered it together'" – Norman 133

115   "just not enough writers in the movie colony'" – Rosten 312

115   "'put under suspicion'" – Gassner and Nichols xiii

115   "'I never knew when I was writing'" – Hecht, *Mike Wallace*

116   "referred to his own screenplays" – Norman 84

116   "'make me write like that'" – Norman 131

116   "'who find it easiest to adjust'" – Rosten 310

117   "'dull, unoriginal work, esp. to order'" – OED

117   "'I think it was jealousy'" – Froug 241

117   "'closer to 150 screenplays'" – Froug 239

118   "'not easy to get a good script'" – Froug 242

118   "pursued a successful parallel career" – British author Glyn published 22 popular novels between 1902 and 1934 and wrote at least six screenplays. She also directed two films from her own screenplays, *Knowing Men* (1930) and *The Price of Things* (1930), and produced three.

118   "Hecht was similarly active" – *IMDb* lists 165 screenwriting credits for Ben Hecht, whose *Underworld* (1927) won the Oscar for Best Writing (Original Story) at the first ever Academy Awards in 1929. He also wrote eleven novels. The reputation of these has declined as that of his most highly regarded screenplays, such as those for *Notorious* (1946), and *Scarface* (1932) has grown. Books that cover Hecht's career in detail include *The Five Lives of Ben Hecht* by Doug Fetherling (1977) and Hecht's own autobiography, *A Child of the Century* (1954).

118   "Aldous Huxley" – Huxley wrote the screenplays for *Pride and Prejudice* (1940) and *Jane Eyre* (1943), among others.

118   "screenplay for the 1919 film *Battling Jane*" – Higham 75-6

118   "'MILLIONS ARE TO BE GRABBED'" – Norman 84

118   "'months of work'" – Norman 120

119   "appeared anxious to succeed" – Norman 113-23

119   "'prentice scripts'" – Greene, *Ways* 64

119   "'a terrible affair'" – Greene, *Mornings* 446

119   "'very short of money'" – Greene, *Mornings* 540

119   "'worst and least successful'" – Greene, *Mornings* 452; In fact, *The Green Cockatoo* was produced not by Korda, but by William K. Howard. Korda and London Films did, however, produce *21 Days Together.*

119   "'positively bad films'" – Greene, *Mornings* 401

119   "'ready to defend'" – Greene, *Mornings* 447

119   "'dialogue inserted during production'" – Greene, *Mornings* 447

119   "'If you are using words in one craft'" – Greene, *Mornings* 444

120   "'the dull shorthand of a script'" – Greene, *TMFI* 3

120   "'the shortest number of letters'" – Shelden 131

120   "'many reasons why I prefer it'" – Greene, *Mornings* 434-5

120   "'more a director's film'" – Greene, *Mornings* 558

121   "'the small house in Anacapri'" – Greene, *Mornings* 434

121   "'It was aesthetically slumming'" – Engel 200

121   "'it made his head bang'" – Fitzgerald, *Pat Hobby* 36

121   "'this was an industry'" – Fitzgerald, *Pat Hobby* 43

122   "'ditch-digging work'" – Schulberg 50

122   "'who don't have any talent either'" – Tesich 32

122   "'I could have written them myself'" – Tesich 34

122   "'doesn't need any fixing'" – Tesich 33

122   "'very rarely, of course'" – Tesich 33

122   "'my adult life'" – McMurtry 7; ellipses in original

122   "'quickly forget what I may have just written'" – McMurtry 7

123   "'We're not talking great literature'" – Engel 28

123   "'it helps to be illiterate'" – Engel 98

123   "'the idea of being third-class citizens'" – Dunne, *Monster* 7

123   "'The movie writer does not need'" – Rosten 313

123   "'Story talent is primary'" – McKee 28

124   "'There are just great movies'" – Dunne, "Art"; this is a view of screenwriting and Hollywood informed by Dunne's broader interest in the Hollywood system, something that's clear from his non-fiction publications: *The Studio*, a portrait of Fox under the Zanucks in 1967, and *Monster*, the saga of his work (with

wife and cowriter Joan Didion) on *Up Close & Personal* (1996), for which he claims to have written twenty-seven drafts.

124   "'not in control of the finished product'" – Dunne, *Monster* 7
124   "'studio people do not know how to read'" – Froug 81
124   "'most people can't read'" – Stempel 237
124   "Diamond, quoting Wilder" – Froug 158
124   "'I hate reading a screenplay'" – Froug 52
125   "'Now the production guy looking at this'" – Froug 302-3
125   "'doomed to the the smallest readership'" – Carrière 151
126   "'a bastard art'" – Froug 221
126   "'Will it make money?'" – Rosten 307
126   "'only concerned with the appearance'" – Greene, *Mornings* 447
127   "'whether it's a movie or anything else'" – Engel 88

4 SCREENPLAY STYLE AND VOICE

129   "'If it's not quite art'" – Mamet, *Plays: 3* 123
129   "'highly inflected screenplay'" – Rush and Baughman

"Screenplays aren't distinctive in ways that resemble literature"

130   "may be the first publication" – There are earlier anthologies of screenplays (or their variant forms), such as *Motion Picture Continuities* (1929). However, Frances Taylor Patterson's introduction makes clear that her intention in publishing them is educational, as "working models" from which "[t]he style and form of continuity may be learned" (v), and distinguishes these "technical" works from "original photoplays" (viii).
130   "'spare modern kind of poetry'" – Gassner and Nichols xv
130   "'it is not and never can be'" – Gassner and Nichols xxxiii
130   "'a series of creations'" – Gassner and Nichols xxxii
131   "'contemporary textual theory'" – Maras 62
131   "'an idea of the 'text''" – Price, *Screenplay* 37
131   "'not intended as literature'" – Russin and Downs 3
131   "'not read as literary material'" – Epps x
131   "'a good source of material'" – Hauge 13
131   "another blueprint enthusiast"– "A film script is... a blueprint for the actual filming" McBride 31
132   "'it's not writing'" – McBride 31
132   "'story talent'" – McKee 26-7
132   "'not writing prose'" – Rosten 308
132   "'rarely and unintentionally'" – Scott 70
132   "'the theatre is literary'" – Ray 192
132   "'Pity the poor screenwriter'" – McKee 394

Screenplays share the characteristics of literary writing

133   "'Today, as in the past'" – Sargent 5
133   "'texture of the story world'" – Truby, *Anatomy* 146
134   "'like any other kind of writing'" – Froug 221
134   "'leather-bound volumes'" – Froug 231
134   "'honorable to write'" – Froug 339
134   "'the first job of a writer'" – Engel 23
134   "'may not be 'great literature''" – Engel 28
134   "'used as working scripts'" – Sternberg 58
134   "'discuss historical practices'" – Korte and Schneider 89-105
135   "'the Screenplay as Literature'" – Nannicelli 191-218
135   "'screenplays as literary works'" – Nannicelli 148
136   "'tightly knit work of fiction'" – Burroughs

"Screenplays are unliterary because they're bound by normative format rules"

136   "According to Janet Staiger" – Bordwell et al. 322
137   "'INT. OFFICES'" – Meyers 27-8
138   "'written in the late 1970s'" – Price, *History* 16; Price also refers to the "emergence of the 'master-scene' script as the default screenplay form" in the 1960s (*History* 21), but the formal similarities of Froug's examples extend beyond the sharing of master-scene format with its omission of camera directions.
138   "'include shots and angles'" – Froug 52
138   "'in arbitration proceedings'" – Froug 76
139   "'out of date'" – Froug 77
139   "'ONLY WRITE IN MASTER SCENES'" – Hunter 120; capitals in original
139   "'proper, contemporary'" – Field, *Screenplay* 170-1; italics in original
139   "Russin and Downs" – Russin and Downs 16
139   "Hauge" – Hauge 112
139   "'standard format exists today'" – Riley xx-xxi
139   "'also essentially correct'" – Price, *History* 210
139   "'Don't use bold or italics'" – Riley 86; bold in original
140   "'1. INT. POLICE STATION'" – Singer and McCarthy 1
140   "SUPERIMPOSE:" – Riley 73
140   "'capitalize that character's name'" – Riley 7
140   "'tabbed far to the right'" – Riley 2
140   "'opening scene of *Ex Machina*'" – Garland, *Ex Machina* 1
141   "'rule against capitalising props'" – Riley 74

Distinctive screenplay style, voice and authorial self-reflexivity

141   "'Description, description'" – McKee 410-11; McKee isn't arguing here against the master-scene format, but against reading and writing it solely on the surface level.

142   "'pure story form itself is limited'" – Rush and Baughman 31

142   "'evocative language functions'" – Rush and Baughman 28

142   "'character and narrator'" – Rush and Baughman 32

142   "'become polyvocal'" – Rush and Baughman 34

143   "'focus is on the tension'" – Rush and Baughman 30

143   "'like a professional'" – Greene, *Third Man* [Faber],12; italics in original

143   "'Lime, Harry Lime'" – Greene, *Third Man* [Faber],12-13

144   "'simply to *tell* the story'" – Mamet, *Whore's Profession* 347; italics in original

144   "'juxtaposition of uninflected images'" – Mamet, *Whore's Profession* 349

144   "'you have narration'" – Mamet, *Whore's Profession* 347

144   "'images that are basically uninflected'" – Mamet, *Whore's Profession* 347

144   "'Look: okay. Okay. Look:'" – Mamet, *State and Main* 90

144   "'You need money?'" – Mamet, *Glengarry Glen Ross* 35-6

145   "'evocative language'" – Rush and Baughman 36

145   "'EAZY vibes with it'" – Herman and Berloff 26

145   "'A hustler is always hustlin''" – Herman and Berloff 28

146   "'experiential rather than dramatic'" – Rush and Baughman 36

146   "Reading a screenplay is like" – Rush and Baughman 30

146   "'savagery and desperation'" – Gassner and Nichols 1008

146   "'CAMERA CONTINUES TO MOVE IN'" – Black 1

147   "'Riggs, completely heedless'" – Black 4-5

148   "'And then Punk #1 springs'" – Black 5

148   "'Riggs, meanwhile, looking around'" – Black 26

148   "'wearing his purple sweater'" – Kaufman, *Adaptation* 2nd draft 3-4

149   "'Sans teeth, eyes,'" – Shakespeare, *As You Like It* 2.vii.165

149   "'get out of the way of the story'" – McKee 's Story Structure Seminar, London, 20-22 October 1989 [personal note]

150   "'destroy that individuality'" – Gassner and Nichols xxxi

150   "taught themselves to write" – Harris 12-13

150   "'The camera pulls back'" – Benton and Newman 8

150   "'repressed excitement'" – Benton and Newman 6

151   "'almost Mack Sennett stuff'" – Benton and Newman 8; Mack Sennett was a prolific producer of fast-paced slapstick comedies between 1911 and 1935.

151   "French New Wave" – Benton and Newman sent their screenplay to both Truffaut and Jean-Luc Godard in the hope they would direct it; see Harris for a detailed account of these relationships.

152   "'What unites *Billy Elliott*'" – NAWE

152   "total output of 274" – IMDb

153   "'looking for a new and distinctive voice'" – Film4

153   "old industry wisdom" – "'The script is everything.' 'It all begins with the script.' 'There is no film without the script.' This has become a litany of the Writers Guild newsletter" (Dunne, *Crooning* 170-1).

153   "'describe seeking an original voice'" – Macdonald, *Poetics* 112

153   "'a personal storytelling style'" – McKee 9

153   "'If you show a brilliant, original script'" – McKee 6

155   "'Agent Felicity Blunt'" – Curtis Brown

154   "'It is essential that'" – Clarke 18:38

154   "relatively recent in film practitioner discourse" – British television writer Dennis Potter, whose scripts are frequently cited as exemplars of an original voice, wrote in 1984: "What you are waiting for is your own voice" 22.

154   "'a mistake writers make'" – Engel 283

154   "'your voice and his voice'" – Froug 190

154   "'That was what I wanted'" – Owen, *Smoking* 16

154   "'If the script is a comedy'" – Owen, *Smoking* 241

154   "'Most films in Hollywood'" – Engel 5

155   "'I think the last one was defective'" – Cody 2

156   "'What did you do, Junebug?'" – Cody 21

156   "'hoping she was expelled'" – Cody 25

156   "'Paul Bleeker steps onto'" – Cody 6

"Screenplays don't use the figurative rhetoric of literary writing"

157   "'The exposition of [a character]'" – Boon, *Script Culture* 53

157   "'make your characters real'" – Field, *Screenplay* 25

157   "'conjunction of Imagist poetics'" – Boon, "Screenplay" 35

157   "'commonplace in this kind'" – Price, *Screenplay* 36

158   "find metaphors that will help" – See, for example, King 89-90

158   "'UNHOLY MESS'" – Singer and McCarthy 4

158   "'a player-coach'" – Singer and McCarthy 8

158   "'shepherds his family'" – Singer and McCarthy 38

158   "'shell-shocked'" – Herman and Berloff 10

158   "'infectious vibe'" – Herman and Berloff 17

158   "'light up'" – Herman and Berloff 20

158	"'filled to the brim'" – Herman and Berloff 41
158	"'wraps up his eulogy'" – Herman and Berloff 57
158	"'goes ape-shit'" – Herman and Berloff 63
158	"'stares cold daggers'" – Herman and Berloff 141
158	"'water under the bridge'" – Herman and Berloff 138
158	"'marinate on him'" – Herman and Berloff 12
158	"'in overdrive'" – Herman and Berloff 55
159	"McKee's claim that screenplays can't employ" – McKee 394
159	"'[t]he telephoto lens'" – Charman et al. 48
159	"'GLOWING SPHERE'" – Docter et al. 1
159	"'twitching' like live things" – Garland, *Ex Machina* 20
159	"phone handsets" –Garland, *Ex Machina* 30
159	"CCTV cameras" – Garland, *Ex Machina* 39
159	"monitors" – Garland, *Ex Machina* 86
159	"'POWER DIES'" – Garland, *Ex Machina* 95
159	"'all the screens die'" – Garland, *Ex Machina* 113
160	"'neon jellyfish'" – Garland, *Ex Machina* 86
160	"'jewel in the icy mountains'" – Garland, *Ex Machina* 6
160	"'light-bulb filaments'" – Garland, *Ex Machina* 24
160	"'backdrop of mountains'" – Garland, *Ex Machina* 49
160	"'axon-like tendrils'" – Garland, *Ex Machina* 63
160	"'yellow snow drift'" – Garland, *Ex Machina* 66
160	"'not in fact true'" – McKee 400
160	"'*Image System*'" – McKee 401; italics in original

"Screenplays are produced by a different kind of writer"

161	"*I certainly don't see it that way*" – Garland, *Guardian* interview
161	"'Novelists and playwrights'" – McKee 407
162	"'Screen and prose writers'" – McKee 5
162	"'10 essential techniques'" – Truby, "Screenplay vs. Novel"
162	"'write it as a novel'" – Clarke 23:03
162	"most important medium for writers today'" – Clarke 23:24
162	"'techniques for adapting your novel'" – Truby.com

"Screenplays differ in their relationship to industry and modes of production"

163	"'tied to a particular industry'" – Price, *History* 5
163	"'What has happened to publishing'" – West 146-7
164	"'media organisations that had previously'" – Bolin 14
164	"revenues of €3.43 billion ($4.05 billion) – *Publishers Weekly*
165	"with Allen's approval" – Stone
165	"twelve stage shows based on films" – The musicals were *Kinky Boots, School of Rock, Nativity, An American in Paris, Disney's*

Aladdin, Disney's *The Lion King*, *42nd Street*, Mel Brooks' *Young Frankenstein*, *The Toxic Avenger*, *Big Fish*, *Footloose*, and *Wicked*, a spin-off from *The Wizard of Oz* (1939).

165   "adapted by Pickett into a stage play" – Honeycutt
166   "'Many, if not most screenplays'" – Nannicelli 148

5 ENDURING SCREENPLAYS

167   *"I dream of an I.B.M. machine"* – Truffaut, *Hitchcock* 330-31

"Screenplay words don't persist in films"

168   "'films in general base their creative process'" – Elliott 83
168   "'words on a page'" – Millard 29
168   "*American* opens in the manner" – Carringer 29
169   "'intertitles from old newsreels'" – Kael 107
169   "'Colorado Lode Mining Co.'" – Kael 105
169   "'EL RANCHO'" – Kael 127
169   "'a large sign reading MRS KANE'S'" – Kael 137
169   "'THATCHER MANUSCRIPT'" – Kael 136, 148, 152
169   "'NEW YORK CHRONICLE'" – Kael 174
169   "'HOLD FOR ARRIVAL'" – Kael 187
170   "that he and Mankiewicz wrote" – This draft of the screenplay is identified as "The Shooting Script Dated July 16, 1940" (87), and credited to Mankiewicz and Welles.
170   "'INT. STUDIO - DAY 1'" – Laws and Refn 1

"Screenplays are intermedial texts with no separate existence of their own"

171   "'essentially intermedial text type'" – Korte and Schneider 97
172   "'worth reading in its own right'" – Korte and Schneider 101
172   "Steven Maras accepts" – Maras 48
172   "'out of its production context'" – Maras 48
172   "'an intermediary form'" – Stanton

"Screenplays are emptied or consumed by a single performance"

173   "'the film scenario is entirely'" – Korte and Schneider 90
173   "'live on in its slipstream'" – Carrière 151
174   "film schools may give scenes" – As at Westminster University
174   "'A theatre text is only a blueprint'" – Stone
174   "ran for 46 performances" – TGA
174   "'Producer shall solely and exclusively'" – WGA
175   "Kaufman's first draft" – The first draft begins with Craig's dream, in which he reads a book at first titled *Sit*, then titled

Die; this scene appears nowhere in the film, which starts instead with a puppet theatre performance.

"Screenplays disappear during the processes of film production"

177   "'as brilliant on the page'" – Murphy 104
178   "multiple awards and nominations" – IMDb
178   "'often using pseudonyms'" – Griffith's pseudonyms included "Granville Warwick," "Gaston de Tolignac," "Roy Sinclair," and "Irene Sinclair"; Azlant 245
178   "'the artist responsible for a film'" – Gibbs 55
178   "'mise-en-scène went out of fashion'" – Gibbs 99
178   "'how films work'" – Gibbs 66
178   "'defines its significance'" – Gibbs 100
178   "'all this is mise-en-scène'" – Gibbs 57
179   "'discarded living room set'" – Cody 1
179   "'and my wife is dead'" – Meyers 1
179   "'only one creative element'" – Gibbs 58
179   "'why make the movie?'" – Ray 191
180   "'the telephone book?'" – Wilder
180   "American Film Institute's list" – AFI
180   "'the way a film uses the techniques'" – Bordwell and Thompson 4; Gibbs prefers the spelling "mise-en-scène," which I've also used except when quoting Bordwell and Thompson.
181   "'appears in the film frame'" – Bordwell and Thompson 118
181   "'installed on Wednesday'" – Towne 1
182   "'EXT. CAFE AND STREET'" – Zemeckis and Gale 58
184   "'MOTEL ROOM'" – Ethan and Joel Coen 13-14
185   "'FLARE TO WHITE'" – Ethan and Joel Coen 1
185   "'the director *stages the event*'" – Bordwell and Thompson 118; italics in original
186   "'abstract, indefinite, vague'" – Price *Screenplay* 37

"Screenplays disappear when they're replaced by technical shooting scripts"

186   "'screenplays do not circulate'" – Price, *History* 216
186   "merely a 'selling script'" – Price, *History* 216
186   "'relatively autonomous document'" – Price, *History* 211
187   "'people work together'" – Field, *Screenplay* 169
187   "'by eliminating technical directions'" – Price, *History* 211
187   "Jonze holds up to camera" – Kaufman, *Adaptation: The Shooting Script* 114; The display of physical screenplays such as this one, that of *The Third Man* in the Third Man Museum in Vienna, and another of *The Godfather: Part II* (1974) in Italy's National Film

Museum in Turin, demonstrates that the archive is another form of valorisation that challenges notions of screenplays as ephemeral. There are also extensive collections of screenplays in a number of American university libraries, such as those of Wisconsin-Madison, UCLA, and USC.

188   "'hand-written into the script'" – Riley 20

"Screenplays are ephemeral and vanish, or must be destroyed"

191   "*has no aesthetic existence*'" – Maras 58; italics in original
191   "Maras and others also cite" – Citations include those by Price (*History* 19-20), Millard (7), Macdonald (*Poetics* 14, 20), Norman (390), and Maras (44, 48, 50, 55, 70).
191   "'one that gives birth'" – Carrière 148
191   "as Maras does" – Maras 70
192   "'mistreating his script'" – Froug 240
192   "'just wouldn't make a screenplay'" – Scott 130; italics in original
192   "'just rip it apart'" – Scott 130
193   "'the scenario dies in the film'" – Tarkovsky 134
193   "'must be *smelted*'" – Tarkovsky 134; italics in original
193   "Tarkovsky's characterisation" – Tarkovsky 131

Screenplays endure even when unproduced

193   "As Ted Nannicelli points out" – Nannicelli 200-1
194   "screenplays from the Black List" – Black List
194   "once again 'in development'" – Deadline
194   "'made exactly as written'" – Billington 324
195   "'1. *Yellow screen*'" – Pinter 3; italics in original
195   "'never *the* film'" – Price, *Screenplay* 48; italics in original

"Screenplays are incomplete and never achieve a fixed state"

196   "'when the screenplay has vanished'" – Carrière 170

GENERATIVE SCREENPLAYS

199   "*[A]s you start the process*" – Engel 203
199   "*in terms of discovery*" – Stein

Screenplay discourse and Aristotle

200   "*42 pages of simple, irrefutable truths*" – Ross
201   "*the library down the street*" – McKee 5
201   "*the global success of Hollywood*" – Hiltunen 129
201   "'Welcome to the second edition'" – Russin and Downs xiii
202   "'We will not cheerlead'" – Russin and Downs xiii

202   "'a certain slangy shorthand'" – Snyder xii
202   "'The best writing is also subconscious'" – Scott 222
202   "'It's just jargon, really'" – Owen, *Story* 233
203   "'that... Robert McKee bullshit'" – McDonagh
203   "'those Syd Field books were evil'" – Scott 133; some screenwriters do admit to attending a McKee seminar or reading Field's books, but usually at the start of a screenwriting career; for example, Shawn Slovo (Owen, *Story* 186) and Patrick McGrath (Scott 148).
203   "'so astonishingly naive about the process'" – Scott 153
203   "'get hold of the script, and it's like'" – Owen, *Smoking* 252
203   "so executives can come back" – Owen, *Story* 233
204   "referenced by Steven Maras" – See Maras 171, 177
204   "J.J. Murphy" – See Murphy 8, 16, 203
204   "Steven Price" – See Price, *Screenplay* 122
204   "Kathryn Millard complains" – See Millard 122
204   "'current orthodoxy'" – Macdonald, *Poetics* 10; Ted Nannicelli, the only screenplay scholar to concentrate on philosophy in his book *A Philosophy of the Screenplay*, is unusual in not citing Aristotle.
204   "'more than 2,000 years old'" – Tierno vii
204   "'basic theory of Aristotelian dramaturgy'" – Blacker xi
205   *"Maverick Screenwriting"* – See Golding 246
205   "'artistic completeness'" – Eustace Hale Ball 47
205   "Nelson instructs his reader" – Nelson 76
205   "'a beginning, middle and end'" – Aristotle, *Poetics* 115-117
205   "'it must possess unity'" – Nelson 77
205   "'mimesis of an action'" – Aristotle *Poetics* 59
205   "'action complete in itself'" – Nelson 79
205   "Aristotle's insistence on probability" – See Nelson 80
205   "those by Field" – See Field, *Screenwriter's Workbook* 55, 151
205   "Robin Russin and William Downs" – See Russin and Downs 41, 60, 76, 94-6, 109, 138, 150, 195),
205   "McKee" – See McKee 5, 11, 13, 79, 100, 109, 110, 186, 217, 338, 357-8, 376-7
205   "Lew Hunter" – See Hunter 19-20, 44-7, 59, 60, 65, 79, 81-2, 87, 88, 91, 104, 105, 115, 125-6, 266, 333
205   "Truby" – See Truby, *Anatomy* 3, 4, 262
205   "Joseph McBride" – See McBride 42-4, 108, 150, 151
205   "'In the 1970s'" – Bordwell, *Way* 34
206   "as early as 1910" – See Sargent 352
206   "great screenwriting teachers" – Hiltunen ix

206   "'one of Hollywood's premier story consultants'" – Vogler 407

206   "'lengthy handout'" – Mackendrick xxvi

207   "'trained by Howard Stein'" – Engel 89

207   "applied his knowledge of Aristotle" – Froug 8

207   "lacking an authoritative final form" – The *Poetics*, like the plays of Shakespeare, exists in several versions, none of which has unequivocal authority. Some are translations, from Greek to Latin and Arabic, and others are copies made in Greek and discovered more than a millennium after the lost original manuscript. The composite Greek version reconstructed from these sources has then been translated into numerous versions in English and other languages (Harvard).

207   "Hollywood script meetings" – "[A]nyone in a Hollywood story meeting today would be assumed to have at least a passing understanding of what Aristotle had to say," according to screenwriting website *4Filmmaking*.

208   "the primacy of plot" – "Plot, then, is the first principle and, as it were, soul of tragedy, while character is secondary" (*Poetics* 53), according to Aristotle. Truby makes plot the principle of his *Anatomy of Story*, and many other manual authors agree, whether explicitly citing Aristotle or not.

208   "the importance of genre" – Aristotle translator Stephen Halliwell writes that "The establishment and deployment of a concept of genre lies at the basis of Aristotle's enquiry" (*Poetics* 9), while Truby's "first rule of genre" is that "studios don't buy writers, directors or stars; they buy genres" ("Film Genres").

208   "audience's emotional response" – Aristotle's concept of tragedy places the audience's experience of "pity and fear" at its centre and identifies their *katharsis* (purgation) as its purpose (*Poetics* 47-9). According to Michael Hauge, for example, the screenwriter's "primary goal" is to *elicit emotion in the person who reads the screenplay* (3; italics in original).

208   "his emphasis on structure" – See Aristotle: "the plot should be so structured that..." *Poetics* 73

208   "'relates it to the organic forms'" – Aristotle, *Poetics* 10

208   "'central emphasis on form'" – Aristotle, *Poetics* 9

209   "'independent of performance'" – Aristotle, *Poetics* 53-5

209   "distinguishing the *process*" – See Aristotle, *Nicomachean Ethics* 119-20

209   "reading and performance" – See Aristotle, *Poetics* 139

210   "accomplishes katharsis" – See Aristotle, *Poetics* 47

210   "'the plot of the *Oedipus*'" – Aristotle, *Poetics* 73-5

210   "'One should construct plots'" – Aristotle, *Poetics* 87-9
210   "'To write in action you must first'" – Sargent 137
211   "'Run it in your head right now'" – King 16
211   "'The first step in writing'" – Swain and Swain 182-3
212   "'a movie that's already been shot'" – Engel 200
212   "'figured out every shot'" – Engel 41
212   "'conjures for itself'" – Engel 23
212   "'claims made about this aspect'" – Maras 71
212   "'such as poems or novels'" – Nannicelli 215
212   "Maras cites Truby" – See Maras 70
213   "condition known as aphantasia" – BBC
213   "'It takes some training'" – Froug 81

Screenplays as process

213   *"the least interesting part"* – Engel 208
213   "Script drafts are not incomplete" – Macdonald, *Poetics* 213
214   "'provisional and unstable'" – Price, *Screenplay* 111
214   "there is no sign that Shakespeare'" – Greenblatt 67
214   "'Neither the Folio'" – Greenblatt 67
215   "'Process is acknowledged'" – Bushell 217
215   "'His aim is to bring together'" – Bushell 82

Skull cinema: screenplays as generative writing

216   "Skull cinema" – I have borrowed this term from travel writer
        John Hillaby, who uses it in his book *Journey Through Britain*
        (63), and who claims that he took it from J.B. Priestley.
216   *"a pale reflection of them"* – Todorov 96
216   *"a concentrated form of thinking"* – DeLillo
216   "'the record of an idea'" – Macdonald, "Disentangling" 89
216   "improvisation" – Millard 2, 12, 92, 96, 116, 223
216   "digital pre-visualisation'" – Maras 22, 179-81, 183-4
216   "'work them out in diction'" – Aristotle, *Poetics* 87
217   "'to take *you* over'" – Engel 142, 134; italics in original
217   "'it's inventing itself'" – Engel 152
217   "'assume a life of their own'" – Engel 206, 204
217   "'kind of wrote itself'" – Engel 229, 241
217   "'taken by surprise'" – Minghella *Breaking* xiii
217   "'never really plot it out'" – McDonagh
217   "'It's dangerous'" – Engel 256
217   "'It's a step into the abyss'" – Kaufman, BAFTA
218   "'some little gnome at work'" – Engel 205
219   "The single greatest joy" – Engel 286

BIBLIOGRAPHY

Adams, Harrington. *The Photo Play Plot*. United Play Brokerage, 1912.

American Film Institute (AFI). Web page, www.afi.com/100Years/movies.aspx.

Aristotle. *Aristotle's Nicomachean Ethics*. Translated by Robert C. Bartlett and Susan D. Collins, U of Chicago P, 2012.

---. *Poetics*. Translated by Stephen Halliwell, Loeb, 1999.

Astruc, Alexandre. "The Birth of a New Avant-Garde: La Caméra-Stylo." *The French New Wave: Critical Landmarks*, edited by Peter Graham and Ginette Vincendeau, Palgrave Macmillan, 2009.

August, John. "The Problem of Multiple Screenwriters, www.johnaugust.com/2003/the-problem-of-multiple-screenwriters-2.

Aurthur, Robert Alan. "Hanging Out." *Esquire* vol. 83, Feb. 1975, pp.12-6.

AwesomeFilm. Website, www.awesomefilm.com.

Azlant, Edward. "Screenwriting for the Early Silent Film: Forgotten Pioneers, 1897-1911." *Film History* 9.3, 1997, pp. 228-56.

Ball, Alan. *American Beauty*. Newmarket Press, 1999.

Ball, Eustace Hale. *Photoplay Scenarios: How to Write and Sell Them*. 1915. *Film History* 9.3, 1997.

Ballon, Rachel. *Blueprint for Screenwriting*. Lawrence Erlbaum Assocs, 2005.

Barthes, Roland. *Image, Music, Text*. Translated by Stephen Heath, Fontana, 1977.

Bazin, André. *Qu'est-ce que le Cinéma?* Éditions du Cerf, 2011.

BBC. Web page, www.bbc.co.uk/news/health-47830256.

Beingcharliekaufman.com. Website.

Belmondo, Jean-Paul. Web page, www.criterion.com/current/posts/3091-belmondo-on-breathless.

Benton, Robert and David Newman. *Bonnie and Clyde*. Screenplay draft, undated.

BFI. See *British Film Institute*.

Billington, Michael. *The Life and Work of Harold Pinter*. Faber and Faber, 1996.

Black, Shane. *Lethal Weapon*. Screenplay draft, undated.

Blacker, Irwin R. *The Elements of Screenwriting: A Guide for Film and Television Writers*. Macmillan, 1986.

Black List, The. Web page, www.blcklst.com.

Bloom, Alex. "Script Tips: Bring Scenes to Life By Making Them More Cinematic." StudioDaily, June 13 2016, www.studio daily.com/2016/06/script-tips-bring-scenes-to-life-by-maki ng-them-more-cinematic/.

Bolin, Göran. *Value and the Media: Cultural Production and Consumption in Digital Markets*. Ashgate, 2011.

Booker, Christopher. *The Seven Basic Plots: Why We Tell Stories*. Continuum, 2004.

Boon, Kevin Alexander. *Script Culture and the American Screenplay*. Wayne State UP, 2008.

---. "The Screenplay, Imagism, and Modern Aesthetics." *Literature/Film Quarterly* 36, 2008, pp. 259-71.

Bordwell, David. *The Way Hollywood Tells It: Story and Style in Modern Movies*. U of California P, 2006.

Bordwell, David, and Kristin Thompson. *Film Art: An Introduction*. 9th ed., McGraw-Hill, 2010.

Bordwell, David, et al. *The Classical Hollywood Cinema: Film Style and Mode of Production to 1960*. Routledge, 1985.

Boyens, Philippa, et al. *The Lord of the Rings: The Fellowship of the Ring*. Screenplay draft, 2001.

British Film Institute (BFI). Web page, www.bfi.org.uk/sites/ bfi.org.uk/files/downloads/bfi-film-fund-first-feature-pro duction-funding-application-guidelines-2016.pdf.

Brody, Richard. *Everything is Cinema: The Working Life of Jean-Luc Godard*. Holt, 2008.

Buder, Emily. "I, Daniel Blake Writer Paul Laverty on Climbing the 'Enormous Mountain' of a Screenplay." No Film School, www.nofilmschool.com/2017/01/paul-laverty-interview-i-daniel-blake.

Burgess, Anthony. *Mozart and the Wolf Gang*. Hutchinson, 1991.

Burroughs, William. *The Last Words of Dutch Schultz: A Fiction in the Form of a Film Script*. Viking Press, 1975.

Bushell, Sally. *Text as Process: Creative Composition in Wordsworth, Tennyson, and Dickinson*. U of Virginia P, 2009.

Carrière, Jean-Claude. *The Secret Language of Film*. Translated by Jeremy Leggatt, Pantheon, 1994.

Carringer, Robert L. "The Scripts of Citizen Kane." *Critical Enquiry* Vol.5. No. 2 (Winter) 1978, 369-400.

Carroll, Noël. *Engaging the Moving Image*. Yale U P, 2003.

Chandler, Raymond and Billy Wilder. *Double Indemnity*. Edited by Jeffrey Meyers, U of California P, 2000.

Charman, Matt, and Ethan and Joel Coen. *Bridge of Spies*. Screenplay draft, dated 17 Dec. 2014.

Clark, Barbara and Susan Spohr. *Guide to Postproduction for TV and Film: Managing the Process*. Taylor & Francis, 2013.

Clarke, Laura Leigh. Online interview with John Truby, www.lauraleighclarke. leadpages.co/ johntruby-video/.

Cody, Diablo. *Juno*. Screenplay draft, dated 6 Feb. 2007.

Coen, Ethan and Joel Coen. *Fargo*. Screenplay draft, undated.

Cohen, David S. Screen Plays: *How 25 Screenplays Made It to a Theater near You – for Better or Worse*. HarperCollins, 2008.

Cole, Hillis and Judith Haag. *The Complete Guide to Standard Script Formats: Part I – Screenplays*. CMC, 1989.

Collier, *John. Milton's* Paradise Lost: *Screenplay for Cinema of the Mind*. Alfred A. Knopf, 1973.

Curtis Brown. Website, http://submissions.curtisbrown.co.uk/agents/.

Deadline.com. Web page, deadline.com/2018/03/emma-thompson-sets-up-long-lost-hollywood-script-harrow-alley-with-bad-wolf-1202311559/.

DeLillo, Don. "The Art of Fiction No. 135." *The Paris Review* 28, 1993.

Docter, Pete, and Meg LeFauve and Josh Cooley. *Inside Out.* Screenplay draft, undated.

Drazin, Charles. *In Search of the Third Man.* Methuen, 1999.

Dunne, John Gregory. "The Art of Screenwriting No.2." *The Paris Review* 138, 1996.

---. *Crooning: a Collection.* Simon and Schuster, 1991.

---. *Monster: Living off the Big Screen.* Random House, 1997.

---. *The Studio.* Vintage, 1998.

Eisenstein, Sergei. *The Battleship Potemkin.* Lorrimer, 1968.

---. *The Battleship Potemkin.* Faber and Faber, 1988.

---. *Three Films:* Battleship Potemkin, October, Alexander Nevsky. Lorrimer, 1974.

Elliott, Kamilla. *Rethinking the Novel/Film Debate.* Cambridge UP, 2009.

Engel, Joe, editor. *Screenwriters on Screenwriting: the Best in the Business Discuss their Craft.* Hyperion, 1995.

Entertainment Weekly. Cover story. 29 Jun. 1999.

Epps, Jack, Jr. *Screenwriting is Rewriting: The Art and Craft of Professional Revision.* Bloomsbury, 2016.

Fetherling, Doug. *The Five Lives of Ben Hecht.* New York Zoetrope, 1977.

Field, Syd. *Four Screenplays: Studies in the American Screenplay.* Dell, 1998.

---. *Screenplay: The Foundations of Screenwriting.* Expanded ed., Dell,1982.

---. *The Screenwriter's Workbook.* Dell, 1984.

Film4. Website, https://www.film4productions.com/faqs.

Final Draft. Website, www.finaldraft.com.

Fitzgerald, F. Scott. *The Bodley Head Scott Fitzgerald, Vol.1.* The Bodley Head, 1958.

---. *The Pat Hobby Stories.* Penguin, 1967.

Follows, Stephen. "How Many People Work on a Hollywood Film?" Web page, www.stephenfollows.com/ how-many-people-work-on-a-hollywood-film/.

4Filmmaking. Web page, www.screenwriting.4filmmaking.com/script-structure1.html.

Friedmann, Julian. *How to Make Money Scriptwriting*. Boxtree, 1995.

Froug, William, editor. *The Screenwriter Looks at the Screenwriter*. Macmillan, 1972.

Gale, Bob and Robert Zemeckis. *Back to the Future*. Screenplay, Fourth Draft Revised 12 Oct. 1984 with pink revisions of 21 Oct. 1984, www.dailyscript.com/scripts/bttf4th.pdf.

Gallagher, Tad. *John Ford: The Man and His Films*. U of California P, 1988.

Garland, Alex. *The Beach*. Faber and Faber, 2007.

---. *Ex Machina*. Screenplay, final draft, 2015.

---. *The Guardian* interview, www.theguardian.com/culture/2015/jan/11/alex-garland-ex-machina-interview-the-beach-28-days-later.

Gassner, William and Dudley Nichols. *Twenty Best Film Plays*. Crown, 1943.

Gates, Richard. *Production Management for Film and Video*. Routledge, 1999.

Gibbs, John. *Mise-en-Scène: Film Style and Interpretation*. Wallflower, 2002.

Gillis, Joseph. *The Screen Writer's Guide*. Zoetrope, 1987.

Golding, Josh. *Maverick Screenwriting: A Manual for the Adventurous Screenwriter*. Methuen, 2012.

Goldman, William. *Adventures in the Screen Trade*. Futura,1985.

---. *Butch Cassidy and the Sundance Kid*. Corgi, 1969.

---. *Four Screenplays with Essays*. Applause, 1997.

Greenblatt, Stephen, editor. *The Norton Shakespeare*. Norton, 1997.

Greene, Graham. *Mornings in the Dark: The Graham Greene Film Reader*. Edited by David Parkinson, Carcanet, 1993.

---. *The Third Man*. Faber and Faber, 1988.

---. *The Third Man*. Trevor Howard's personal copy of unpublished shooting script, dated 20 Sep. 1948, hand annotated. The Third Man Museum, Vienna.

---. *The Third Man and The Fallen Idol*. Vintage, 2005.

---. *Three Entertainments*. Penguin, 1992.

---. *Ways of Escape*. Bodley Head, 1980.

Greene, Robert S. *Television Writing: Theory and Technique*. Harper, 1952.

Grierson, Tim. *FilmCraft: Screenwriting*. Ilex Press, 2013.

Harris, Mark. *Pictures at a Revolution: Five Movies and the Birth of the New Hollywood*. Penguin, 2008.

Harrison, Tony. *Collected Film Poetry*. Faber and Faber, 2007.

Harvard Centre for Hellenic Studies, The. Web page, www.classical-inquiries.chs.harvard.edu/textual-comment-on-aristotle-poetics-1447b7-9-part-2/.

Hauge, Michael. *Writing Screenplays that Sell*. Elm Tree, 1989.

Hecht, Ben. "*Child of the Century, A*. Simon and Schuster, 1954.

---. "The Mike Wallace Interview" 15 Feb. 1958. U of Texas, Austin,www.hrc.utexas.edu/multimedia/video/2008/wallace/hecht_ben_t.html.

Herman, Jonathan and Andrea Berloff. *Straight Outta Compton*. Screenplay draft, undated.

Hicks, Jeremy. *Dziga Vertov: Defining Documentary Film*. I.B. Tauris, 2007.

Higham, Charles. *Murder in Hollywood: Solving a Silent Screen Mystery*. U of Wisconsin P, 2006.

Hiltunen, Ari. *Aristotle in Hollywood: The Anatomy of Successful Storytelling*. Intellect, 2002.

Hitchcock, Alfred. *Hitchcock on Hitchcock*. Edited by Sidney Gottlieb, Faber and Faber, 1995.

Honeycutt, Kirk. "Sideways the Play." Web page, www.honeycuttshollywood.com/sideways-the-play/.

Hughes, David. *Tales from Development Hell*. Titan Books, 2004.

Hunter, Lew. *Lew Hunter's Screenwriting 434*. Putnam, 1993.

Internet Movie Database (IMDb). Website, www.imdb.com.

Iowa. Web page, https://clas.uiowa.edu/cinematic-arts/undergraduate -program/ba-screenwriting-arts.

Kael, Pauline, editor. *The Citizen Kane Book*. Secker & Warburg, 1971.

Kaufman, Charlie. *Adaptation*. Screenplay 2nd draft, dated 24 Sep. 1999, www.beingcharlie kaufman.com.

---. *Adaptation: The Shooting Script*. Newmarket Press, 2002.

---. screenwriter. *Adaptation*. Columbia Pictures, 2002.

---. BAFTA speech, 30 Sep. 2011. BAFTA, www.bafta. org/media-centre/transcripts/screenwriters-lecture-charlie-kaufman.

---. *Being John Malkovich*. Screenplay first draft, undated, www. beingcharliekaufman.com.

---. *Eternal Sunshine of the Spotless Mind*. Screenplay first draft, undated, www.being charliekaufman.com.

---. "Why I Wrote Being John Malkovich." *The Guardian*, www. theguardian.com/film/2011/oct/03/charlie-kaufman-how-to-write.

Kieslowski, Krzysztof and Krzysztof Piesiewicz. *Decalogue*. Faber and Faber, 1991.

King, Viki. *How to Write a Move in 21 Days*. Harper and Row, 1988.

Korte, Barbara and Ralf Schneider. "The Published Screenplay – A New 'Literary' Genre?" *AAA: Arbeiten aus Anglistik und Amerikanistik*, Vol. 25, No.1 (2000), 89-105, www.jstor.org/stable/43023768.

Kozlenko, William and S. Emerson Golden. *One Act Play Magazine and Radio-drama Review*, vol. 2. One Act Play Magazine, 1938.

Kracauer, Siegfried. *Theory of Film*. Oxford UP, 1965.

Laws, Mary and Nicolas Winding Refn. *The Neon Demon*. Screenplay draft, dated 11 Jan. 2014.

Leigh, Mike. Naked *and other Screenplays*. Faber and Faber, 1995.

Leitch, Thomas. "Twelve Fallacies in Contemporary Adaptation Theory." *Criticism* 45.2, 2003, pp. 149-171, Wayne State UP.

Lescarboura, Austin Celestin. *Behind the Motion-picture Screen*. Scientific American Publishing Company, 1919.

Lindsay, Vachel. *The Art of the Moving Picture*. Macmillan, 1915.

Lumet, Sidney. *Making Movies.* Vintage, 1996.

Macdonald, Ian W. *Screenwriting Poetics and the Screen Idea.* Palgrave Macmillan, 2013.

---. "Disentangling the Screen Idea." *Journal of Media Practice* 5.2, 2004, pp. 89-99.

Mackendrick, Alexander. *On Filmmaking.* Faber and Faber, 2006.

Macpherson, Jeanie. "Development of Photodramatic Writing." *Moving Picture World,* 21 July 1917, reprinted *Film History* 9.3, 1997.

Mamet, David. *Glengarry Glen Ross.* Screenplay draft, undated, www.imsdb.com/scripts/Glengarry-Glen-Gross.html.

---. *Plays: Three.* Methuen, 1968.

---. *State and Main.* Screenplay draft, dated Sep. 1999, www.imsdb.com/scripts/State-and-Main.html.

---. *A Whore's Profession.* Faber and Faber, 1994.

Maras, Steven. *Screenwriting: History, Theory and Practice.* Wallflower, 2009.

Martin, Brett. *Difficult Men.* Faber and Faber, 2013.

McBride, Joseph. *Writing in Pictures: Screenwriting Made (Mostly) Painless.* Faber and Faber, 2012.

McDonagh, Martin. Interview, www.scriptmag.com/features/interviews-features/interview-with-screenwriter-of-seven-psychopaths-martin-mcdonagh.

McFarlane, Brian. *Novel to Film: An Introduction to the Theory of Adaptation.* Oxford U P, 1996.

McKee, Robert. *Story: Substance, Structure Style, and the Principles of Screenwriting.* HarperCollins, 1999.

McMurtry, Larry. *Hollywood: A Third Memoir.* Simon and Schuster, 2010.

McQuarrie, Christopher. *The Usual Suspects.* Faber and Faber, 1996.

Meyers, Nancy. *The Intern.* Screenplay draft, dated Jan. 2014, www.ivanachubbuck.com/wp-content/uploads/2012/02/The-Intern-Ben-Patty-Entire-Screenplay.pdf draft.

Millard, Kathryn. *Screenwriting in a Digital Age.* Palgrave Macmillan, 2014.

Minghella, Anthony. *Breaking and Entering.* Faber and Faber, 2006.

---. *Minghella on Minghella.* Edited by Timothy Bricknell, Faber and Faber, 2005.

Moreno, Mario O. and Kay Tuxford. "How to Write a Screenplay: Script Writing Example & Screenwriting Tips." Writers Store, www.writersstore.com/how-to-write-a-screenplay-a-guide-to-scriptwriting/.

Murphy, J.J. *Me and You and* Memento *and* Fargo*: How Independent Screenplays Work.* Continuum, 2007.

Nannicelli, Ted. *A Philosophy of the Screenplay.* Routledge, 2013.

National Association of Writers in Education (NAWE) "Screenplay First Award." Web page, www. nawe.co.uk /DB/jobs-and-opportunities/screenplay- first-award.html.

NAWE. See National Association of Writers in Education.

Nelson, J. Arthur. *The Photo-play: How to Write and Sell Them.* Photoplay Publishing, 1913.

Newman, Walter Brown. *Harrow Alley.* Screenplay draft, undated, www.scribd.com/document/246034441/ Harrow-Alley-Original-pdf.

New York Times. Obituary for Irwin R. Blacker, 25 Feb. 1985.

Norman, Marc. *What Happens Next: A History of American Screenwriting.* Aurum, 2008.

Owen, Alastair, editor. *Smoking in Bed: Conversations with Bruce Robinson.* Bloomsbury, 2000.

---, editor. *Story and Character: Interviews with British Screenwriters.* Bloomsbury, 2003.

Patterson, Frances Taylor. *Cinema Craftsmanship: A Book for Photoplaywrights.* 1920. BiblioLife, 2009.

---. *Motion Picture Continuities.* 1929. Garland Publishing, 1977.

Payne, Alexander and Jim Taylor. *Sideways.* Newmarket Press, 2004.

Pinter, Harold. *The Proust Screenplay.* Eyre Methuen, 1978.

Player, The. Fine Line Features, 1992.

Pomeranz, Margaret. "At the Movies with Margaret and David." Interview with Kar-wai Wong, www.abc.net.au/atthemovies/txt/s1397057.htm.

Potter, Dennis. *Waiting for the Boat: On Television*. Faber and Faber, 1984.

Price, Steven. *A History of the Screenplay*. Palgrave Macmillan, 2013.

---. *The Screenplay: Authorship, Theory and Criticism*. Palgrave Macmillan, 2010.

Prospero. "The Q&A: Drake Doremus – Film-making without a Script." www.economist.com/blogs/prospero/2012/01/ qa-drake-doremus.

Publishers Weekly. Web page, www.publishersweekly.com/pw/by-topic/industry-news/publisher-news/article/71304-glo bal-publishing-leaders-2016-penguin-random-house.html.

Ray, Nicholas. *I Was Interrupted: Nicholas Ray on Making Movies*. Berkeley: U of California P, 1993.

Riley, Christopher. *The Hollywood Standard: the Complete and Authoritative Guide to Script Format and Style*. 2nd ed., Michael Wiese, 2009.

Romano, Andrew. "The Director Isn't Finished Yet: an Interview with Steven Soderbergh." The Daily Beast, www. thedailybeast.com/the-director-isnt-finished-yet-an-intervie w-with-steven-soderbergh.

Romney, Jonathan. "Man with a Movie Camera." *The Guardian*, www.theguardian.com/film/2015/aug/02/man-with-a-movie-camera-review-pure-cinema-unparalleled.

Ross, Gary. *Entertainment Weekly* cover story, 19 Jun. 1999.

Ross, Lillian. *Picture: John Huston, MGM, and the Making of The Red Badge of Courage*. 1953. André Deutsch, 1986.

Rosten, Leo C. *Hollywood: The Movie Colony, the Movie Makers*. Harcourt, Brace and Co., 1941.

Rush, Jeff and Cynthia Baughman. "Language as Narrative Voice: The Poetics of the Highly Inflected Screenplay." *Journal of Film and Video* 49.3, 1997, pp. 28-37.

Russin, Robin and William Missouri Downs. *Screenplay: Writing the Picture.* 2nd ed., revised and updated, Silman-James, 2012.

Sargent, Epes Winthrop. *Technique of the Photoplay.* 3rd ed., Chalmers, 1916.

Sarris, Andrew. *The American Cinema: Directors and Directions 1929–1968.* U of Chicago P, 1985.

Schrader, Paul. *Schrader on Schrader.* Edited by Kevin Jackson, Faber and Faber, 1990.

Schulberg, Budd. *What Makes Sammy Run?* 1941. Vintage, 1990.

Scott, Kevin Conroy, editor. *Screenwriters' Masterclass.* Bloomsbury, 2005.

Seger, Linda. *Making a Good Script Great.* Samuel French, 1987.

Sennett, Ted. *Great Movie Directors.* Abrams, 1986.

Shelden, Michael. *Graham Greene: The Man Within.* Minerva, 1995.

Shields, Carol. *Mary Swann.* Flamingo, 1993.

Singer, Josh and Tom McCarthy. *Spotlight.* Screenplay draft, undated.

Slevin, James. *Picture-Play Writing.* Farmer Smith, 1912.

Snyder, Blake. *Save the Cat!* Michael Wiese Productions, 2005.

Staiger, Janet. "Dividing Labor for Production Control: Thomas Ince and the Rise of the Studio System." *Cinema Journal* 18.2, 1979, pp.16-25.

Stanton, Andrew. "Understanding Story: or My Journey of Pain." Keynote speech, Expo 5 (2006), www.rageagainstthe page. blogspot.co.uk/2008/12/andrew-stanton-pixar-transcript-keynote.html.

Stein, Gertrude. "A Conversation." *Atlantic Monthly*, CLVI (1935), pp.187-94.

Stempel, Tom. *FrameWork: A History of Screenwriting in the American Film.* Continuum, 1988.

Sternberg, Claudia. *Written for the Screen: The American Motion-Picture Screenplay as Text.* Stauffenberg-Verlag, 1997.

Stone, Simon. *The Guardian*, www.theguardian.com/stage/2016/jun/03/simon-stone-theatre-film-the-daughter-yerma.

Swain, Dwight and Joye Swain. *Scriptwriting: A Practical Manual.* Focal Press, 1988.

SydField.com. Website, www.sydfield.com.

Tarantino, Quentin. *Reservoir Dogs*. Faber and Faber, 2000.

---. *Reservoir Dogs*. Screenplay draft, dated 22 Oct. 1990, Hollywood Scripts.

Tarkovsky, Andrey. *Sculpting in Time: Reflections on the Cinema.* Translated by Kitty Hunter-Blair, U of Texas P, 2003.

Tesich, Steve. *Karoo.* Vintage, 2006.

TGA. See *Toneel Groep Amsterdam.*

Thorpe, Adam. *Ulverton.* Secker & Warburg, 1992.

Tierno, Michael. *Aristotle's Poetics for Screenwriters.* Hyperion, 2002.

Todorov, Tzvetan. *The Poetics of Prose.* Translated by Richard Howard, Cornell U P, 1977.

Tolkin, Michael. The Player, the Rapture, The New Age: *Three Screenplays*. Grove Press, 1995.

Toneel Groep Amsterdam (TGA). Website, www.tga.nl/en/ productions/husbands-and-wives.

Towne, Robert. *Chinatown.* Screenplay 3rd draft, dated 9 Oct. 1973, Hollywood Scripts.

Truby.com. Website, www.trubycom.

Truby, John. *The Anatomy of Story.* Faber and Faber, 2007.

---. "Film Genres." Seminar. University College London. 14/3/05.

---. "Truby on Screenplay vs. Novel Writing." Bulk email received from Truby's Writers Studio, trubystudio@truby. com, 28 Aug. 2015.

Truffaut, François. *Hitchcock.* Simon & Schuster, 1983.

---. *Le plaisir des yeux.* Champs Arts, 2008.

Van Nostran, William. *The Scriptwriter's Handbook.* Focal Press, 1996.

Vertov, Dziga. *The Writings of Dziga Vertov.* U of California P, 1984.

Vogler, Christopher. *The Writer's Journey.* 3rd ed., Michael Wiese Productions, 2007.

Walker, Andrew Kevin. Seven *and* 8MM. Faber and Faber, 1999.

Welles, Orson. *This Is Orson Welles*. Edited by Jonathan Rosenbaum, HarperCollins, 1993.

West, James L. W. III. *American Authors and the Literary Marketplace since 1900*. U of Pennsylvania P, 1988.

WGA. See *Writers Guild of America*.

Wilder, Billy. "The Art of Screenwriting No.1." *The Paris Review* 138, 1996.

WorldCat. Website, worldcat.org.

Writers Guild of America (WGA). Web page. "Writer's Theatrical Short-Form Contract," www.wga.org/contracts/contracts/other-contracts/standard-theatrical.

Zemeckis, Robert and Bob Gale. *Back to the Future*. Screenplay 4th Draft, revised 12 Oct. 1984 with pink revisions of 21 Oct. 1984.

INDEX

www.ingramcontent.com/pod-product-compliance
Lightning Source LLC
Chambersburg PA
CBHW051554030726
47592CB00001B/278